Financial Regulation

WITH
3307430500
from
VERSIT
D0419747

The problem of financial regulation has returned to centre stage in the wake of the turbulence caused by global financial volatility. This volume, published in association with the Bank of England, responds to contemporary developments by presenting an important restatement of the purposes and objectives of financial regulation.

Regulators in the advanced economies are finding that the complexity of banking and the rise of financial intermediation are making external regulation via common ratios increasingly inappropriate. The authors argue that while there must always remain a role for external regulation, there can be no alternative to placing greater reliance on internal risk management. Thus, regulation is essentially about changing the behaviour of financial intermediaries through the creation of the appropriate incentive structure. This analysis is then applied to the nature and costs of regulatory problems in both the advanced and emerging economies, and appropriate techniques to recast the form of regulation are prescribed.

Published with a stimulating foreword by Eddie George, Governor of the Bank of England, this volume will be a vital resource for students of finance, banking and development, as well as for those involved in the formulation of policy.

Charles Goodhart is Deputy Director of the Financial Markets Group and Norman Sosnow Professor of Banking and Finance at the London School of Economics and was recently appointed a member of the Bank of England Monetary Policy Committee. **Philipp Hartmann** was Research Fellow for Financial Regulation at the LSE's Financial Markets Group at the time of this book's preparation and is now an economist at the European Monetary Institute in Frankfurt. **David Llewellyn** is Professor of Money and Banking at Loughborough University and a director of the Personal Investment Authority. **Liliana Rojas-Suárez** is Principal Adviser at the Inter-American Development Bank, Washington, DC. **Steven Weisbrod** is an independent consultant who specialises in analysing financial institutions and markets for government and international agencies and private corporations.

Financial Regulation

Why, how and where now?

WITHDRAWN

from

STIRLING UNIVERSITY LIBRARY

G
30.2
Goo

Charles Goodhart, Philipp Hartmann,
David Llewellyn, Liliana Rojas-Suárez,
Steven Weisbrod

Foreword by Eddie George
Governor of the Bank of England

Published in association with the Bank of England

London and New York

91667

First published 1998
by Routledge
11 New Fetter Lane, London EC4P 4EE

Simultaneously published in the USA and Canada
by Routledge
29 West 35th Street, New York, NY 10001

Reprinted 1999

Routledge is an imprint of the Taylor & Francis Group

© 1998 Bank of England

Typeset in Times by M Rules, London
Printed and bound in Great Britain by
TJ International Ltd, Padstow, Cornwall

All rights reserved. No part of this book may be reprinted or
reproduced or utilised in any form or by any electronic,
mechanical, or other means, now known or hereafter
invented, including photocopying and recording, or in any
information storage or retrieval system, without permission in
writing from the publishers.

British Library Cataloguing in Publication Data
A catalogue record for this book is available from the
British Library

Library of Congress Cataloging in Publication Data
Financial regulation: why, how, and where now?/Charles
    Goodhart . . . [et al.]; with a foreword by Eddie George.
        p.   cm.
    Includes bibliographical references.
    1. Financial services industry – Law and legislation.
    2. Banking law.   I. Goodhart, C. A. E. (Charles Albert
    Eric)
K1066.F565   1998
346′.082–dc21   97–50002

ISBN 0-415-18504-1 (hbk)
ISBN 0-415-18505-X (pbk)

Contents

    (iv) Issues in developing countries
    (v) Management of financial crises
    (vi) The international dimension to regulation
C. Concluding note

Figures

Tables

Notes on authors

Charles Goodhart is the Norman Sosnow Professor of Banking and Finance at the London School of Economics. Before joining the LSE in 1985, he worked at the Bank of England for seventeen years as a monetary adviser, becoming a Chief Adviser in 1980. In 1997 he was appointed one of the outside independent members of the Bank of England's new Monetary Policy Committee. Earlier he had taught at Cambridge and the LSE. Besides numerous articles, he has written a couple of books on monetary history and a graduate monetary textbook, *Money, Information and Uncertainty* (2nd edn 1989). He has also published two collections of papers on monetary policy, *Monetary Theory and Practice* (1984) and *The Central Bank and the Financial System* (1995), and an institutional study, *The Evolution of Central Banks*, revised and republished (MIT Press) in 1988.

Philipp Hartmann is an economist in the Stage-III Division of the European Monetary Institute in Frankfurt. His main work is in the areas of banking regulation, in particular capital adequacy requirements and value-at-risk models, and international monetary economics, including foreign exchange market microstructure analysis and international currency competition. He is a Research Affiliate of the Centre for Economic Policy Research (CEPR, London) and has been an academic expert for the Centre for European Policy Studies (CEPS) working party 'The Transition to the Euro' in Brussels. Dr Hartmann also organised (together with Charles Goodhart) the LSE conference 'Internal Risk Models and Financial Regulation' in the City of London in 1996. He is the author of 'Capital Adequacy and Foreign Exchange Risk Regulation – Theoretical Considerations and Recent Developments in Industrial Countries' (*Kredit und Kapital*, 1997) and 'The Future of the Euro as an International Currency: A Transactions Perspective' (CEPS Research Report, 1996). His current research interests include the consequences of financial innovations for regulation and incentive-oriented financial regulation as well as the external consequences and financial market impact of European Monetary Union. He holds a PhD in economics from the Ecole des Hautes Etudes en Sciences Sociales in Paris, an MA in monetary and macroeconomics from the Université Catholique de

Louvain in Belgium and a Diplom in Volkswirtschaftslehre from Mannheim University in Germany.

David Llewellyn is Professor of Money and Banking at Loughborough University, Chairman of the Loughborough University Banking Centre, and Visiting Professor of Finance at the London Business School. Outside the university he is a Public Interest Director of the Personal Investment Authority and Chairman of its Effectiveness Committee. He is a member of the Financial Services Panel of the DTI's Technology Foresight Programme, and serves on the International Advisory Boards of the Italian Bankers Association and the Financial Systems Group of the NCR Corporation. He has served as a consultant to banks, building societies and regulatory authorities in several countries. In 1992 he was the Bertil Danielsson Foundation Visiting Scholar at the Stockholm and Gothenburg Schools of Economics, and has been a Visiting Scholar at the central banks of Sweden and Finland. He has previously worked as an economist at HM Treasury in London and the International Monetary Fund in Washington.

Liliana Rojas-Suárez is Principal Adviser in the Office of the Chief Economist at the Inter-American Development Bank. Previously she worked as Deputy Chief in the Capital Markets Division of the International Monetary Fund. She was also a professor and Director of the Research Center in Economics at Anahuac University in Mexico and an economic adviser for PEMEX, Mexico's National Petroleum Company. Dr Rojas-Suárez has published widely in leading journals in the areas of financial markets, macroeconomic policy and international economics. She holds a PhD in economics from the University of Western Ontario and an MA in economics from the University of Ottawa.

Steven Weisbrod received a PhD in economics from the University of Chicago in 1978. From 1976 to 1981, he was an economist in the Banking Studies Department at the Federal Reserve Bank of New York, becoming Chief of the Department in 1979. From 1981 to 1989, he worked in the Corporate Planning Department of Chemical Bank, becoming head of the Department in 1986. From 1990 to the present, Dr Weisbrod has been a private consultant on banking and financial issues, focusing on problems in emerging markets. In 1992, he co-authored a money and banking textbook with Professor Peter M. Garber entitled *The Economics of Banking Liquidity and Money*.

Foreword

In June 1997 the Bank of England hosted its fourth Central Bank Governors' Symposium. The monograph presented at this symposium and the discussion which followed form the basis for this book.

Our first symposium was held in 1994, one of the events marking the Bank of England's tercentenary. The papers, and subsequent published books, from this and the two subsequent symposia, in 1995 and 1996, have concentrated primarily on the central bank's main role and responsibility in maintaining price stability. The first of these, *The Future of Central Banking* (by Capie *et al.*, 1994), focused primarily on the history and circumstances of central banking in developed countries. This was complemented by a study for the second symposium (1995) on the problems facing central banks in emerging countries, which was published as *Central Banking in Developing Countries* (Fry *et al.*, 1996). The main problem, of course, is how to finance government borrowing in a non-inflationary manner, in particular to avoid direct central bank finance. The best way to do so is by debt sales to the private sector in free and well-functioning government debt markets. This was the theme of the third paper, at the 1996 symposium, which was prepared by Professor Maxwell Fry, and subsequently published under the title *Emancipating the Banking System and Developing Markets for Government Debt* (Fry, 1997).

On this occasion, for the June 1997 symposium, I decided that I wanted a paper to cover issues relating to the second main concern of central banks, that is the maintenance of financial stability. The maintenance of financial stability is complementary with the pursuit of monetary and price stability. It will be difficult, or impossible, to achieve the latter if the banking system is in a state of collapse, and, similarly, extreme price instability, either high inflation or deflation, will place severe strains on the financial system.

For such reasons the maintenance of financial stability has always been an objective of central banks, but this has led them to take quite differing degrees of direct responsibility for the supervision of banks, of financial markets and even a wider range, in some countries, of financial intermediaries. This differentiation has depended, in part, on the particular histories and circumstances of the countries involved.

Meanwhile, the evolution of financial intermediation, notably the global-isation of the largest players and the blurring of institutional dividing lines between banks and non-bank financial intermediaries, has been clearly lead-ing to pressures to reconsider the questions of what were the basic purposes of financial regulation and how such purposes could best be achieved, includ-ing the question of what the best structure might be. In this respect the title of this book is apt: having considered *why* financial regulation is necessary in the first place (Chapter 1), it concentrates in the next four chapters on *how* this might best be done, and ends in Chapter 8 with a discussion of the appropriate institutional structure. Throughout, the focus is on how financial regulation and supervision might evolve to match the rapid development of financial intermediation in the private sector. Such evolution, the 'Where now?' in the title of the monograph, of financial regulation is likely to take us quite far from our present status quo.

I was aware, when I initiated this study, that there would be a great deal of attention paid to such issues during 1997, including studies by the G-10, Group of Thirty, and OECD, the Wallis Report in Australia, as well as dis-cussions at the G-7 summit in Denver. But I had not expected that the symposium would be held, on 9 June 1997, in the immediate aftermath of the Chancellor of the Exchequer's announcement on 20 May of a complete rearrangement of the UK's supervisory structure, concentrating this in a single 'mega' regulator, the enlarged Securities and Investments Board, now renamed the Financial Services Authority.

This undoubtedly gave an edge, a focus, to the discussion of the paper which we had asked David Llewellyn, Professor of Money and Banking in the Department of Economics of Loughborough University, and Charles Goodhart, the Norman Sosnow Professor of Banking and Finance at the London School of Economics, together with his colleague, Dr Philipp Hartmann of the Financial Markets Group at LSE, to prepare. They, in turn, invited Liliana Rojas-Suárez and Steven Weisbrod, experts in problems of dealing with financial collapses in emerging countries, to contribute with that more specialised subject (Chapter 7 and part of Chapter 6).

We are grateful to Ian MacFarlane, Governor of the Reserve Bank of Australia, Jacob Mwanza, Governor of the Central Bank of Zambia, and Dato-Ahmad Mohd Don, Governor of the Central Bank of Malaysia, for acting as discussants. The subject matter of financial regulation covers a huge span, and the focus and interest of the main authors was, inevitably, on the current developments in developed countries with large established finan-cial markets and institutions. Most of the critical comments from our expert audience were on the coverage of the regulatory problems in emerging coun-tries. While Chapter 6 has been considerably revised and enlarged to take account of these comments, there may nevertheless be some value in revisit-ing this subject at some future stage.

As I have already noted, the monograph was prepared at an opportune moment to influence both thought and actions at a time when the future conduct of financial regulation and supervision is in a state of change. Not only the symposium, but also the academic conference held by the authors at the London School of Economics on the following Monday, 12 June – itself a new initiative – and now the publication of the book should help to inform and guide the continuing debate.

Eddie George
Governor of the
Bank of England

Acknowledgements

We wish to thank the Governor of the Bank of England, Eddie George, and the former and present Directors of the Centre for Central Banking Studies, Lionel Price and Maxwell Fry, for having given us the opportunity to present our views on 'Financial Regulation' in the form of this monograph to the fourth Central Bank Governors' Symposium, hosted by the Bank. In particular, we are indebted to our three official discussants at the Symposium, Governors Ian MacFarlane (Australia), Jacob Mwanza (Zambia) and Dato-Ahmad Mohd Don (Malaysia), for sharp discussions and to the other participants who – by their interventions – greatly enriched our views on regulatory issues all over the world.

We are also most grateful to Peter Andrews (Securities and Investments Board), Rosa-Maria Lastra (Queen Mary and Westfield College), Ian Michael (Bank of England), Kathleen Tyson-Quah (KTQ Consultants), Barry Schachter (Chase Manhattan), Tim Shepheard-Walwyn (Swiss Bank Corporation), Clifford Smout and Liz Willson, who all have commented in private correspondence on an earlier draft of the book. Moreover, the remarks of our discussants at a public conference at the London School of Economics – Franco Bruni (Bocconi University), Vicki Fitt (Securities and Futures Authority), Maxwell Fry (Birmingham University) and Michael Taylor (London Guildhall University) – together with subsequent correspondence have been extremely helpful. The same applies to the discussions we had after the presentation of excerpts from Chapters 2 and 5 at the 33rd Federal Reserve Bank of Chicago Conference on 'Bank Structure and Competition'. In particular, we would like to thank the Chairman of the session on 'Incentive-compatible Regulation', Jim Moser (Chicago Mercantile Exchange), as well as Martyn Kendrick, Brian Tew and Tom Weyman-Jones (all Loughborough University).

We are most grateful to the International Monetary Fund for granting permission to reproduce the material in the appendices to chapters 1 and 6, originally published in *Bank Soundness and Macroeconomic Policy*, by C.-J. Lindgren, G. Garcia and M.I. Saal (1996; Washington, DC: International Monetary Fund).

Introduction

Our starting point is that many countries have experienced significant banking sector problems at some stage during the past fifteen years. The outcome has been worse than in any similar period since the Great Depression of the 1930s. The main causes have been those that have traditionally attended commercial banking problems since its historical beginnings, i.e. poor credit control, connected lending, insufficient liquidity and capital, and in general poor internal governance. In most countries, especially perhaps the emerging and transitional countries, there is a need for enhanced and improved external supervision to reinforce internal controls.

Having shown the scale, nature and costs of the regulatory problems around much of the world, we consider in Chapter 1 a restatement of the purposes and objectives of financial regulation. Within the financial sector such regulation is less about the control of monopoly power and more about maintaining systemic stability and consumer protection. We further divide customer protection into two aspects: prudential regulation and conduct of business regulation, with the latter primarily in the retail, rather than the wholesale, sector. We also distinguish between *regulation* (the establishment of specific rules of behaviour), *monitoring* (observing whether the rules are obeyed), and *supervision* (the more general oversight of financial firms' behaviour).

The systemic dimension enters because the social costs of financial distress, notably in the form of contagious effects, can easily exceed the private costs to shareholders, managers, etc., of failing institutions. We note that the main concerns lie in the banking sector, and we outline why banks are 'special' and query whether securities houses and insurance companies pose significant systemic dangers. External regulation and supervision has traditionally taken the guise of establishing certain required standards, often in the form of ratios, for such factors as cash reserves, capital, liquidity, large or connected loans, etc.

We find that something of a dichotomy is emerging. In Chapter 2 we note that regulators in emerging and transitional countries are still struggling to apply such traditional supervisory techniques successfully, often against a backdrop of insufficient and inadequately trained staff and of political interference with their better judgement. On the other hand, regulators in more developed areas are finding that the complexity of banking, the blurring of functional dividing lines, globalisation, and the speed of portfolio adjustment are making such external regulation via common ratios increasingly inappropriate. While there must always remain a role for *external* regulation, there can be no alternative to placing greater reliance on internal risk management. However, we also note that it is not a question of internal *versus* external regulation as both must be involved; in our view, it is wrong to polarise the issue. It is about the balance between internal and external mechanisms, and our judgement is that there needs to be a shift along the spectrum towards internal risk management systems within a general framework set by external regulation.

Regulators' actions provide incentives for all those involved to change their own behaviour. There are several interacting groups (or stakeholders) in the field of financial regulation, e.g. the public and their parliamentary representatives, the regulators, and the regulated firms within the financial system. We need to consider how each may respond to the regulatory framework and their (differential) information. In Chapter 3 we consider in particular the *principal–agent* relations between the regulators and the regulated, notably whether the regulators can reinforce the *incentives* of the regulated to control their own risks internally. We propose a reinterpretation of financial regulation as a *contract* which is designed so as to make it in institutions' own self-interest to maintain a 'socially desirable' (low) level of risk.

Next, we describe the incentives facing the regulators. In particular, we look at the pressures placed on the regulators to exercise forbearance in the face of failures by the regulated to meet the required (external) capital ratio. One common shortcoming has been that the application of sanctions (the regulator's response to failure to meet these required ratios) has been considered less carefully, and applied in an even more discretionary fashion than is the case with the choice of the ratios themselves. This has led to the further common problems of forbearance and 'too big to fail'.

In Chapter 4 we then consider the question of whether the application of regulatory services through administrative fiat, rather than through an explicit market price, affects the demands by the public, and their representatives, for its provision. Is regulation treated as a free good, with a consequential tendency to excess provision? Is 'regulatory arbitrage' a salutary counterbalance, or a damaging nuisance? A common complaint of regulated firms is that the regulatory and compliance burden placed on them is out of 'proportion' to the likely benefits. Chapter 4, therefore, is about 'proportionality'. The usual academic solution in such cases is to apply cost–benefit analysis, but are either the costs or the benefits sufficiently quantifiable to make this remotely feasible? Alternatively, can regulation be so designed as to provide choices for the regulated, or for their customers, that can signal their preferences within a quasi-market context?

A major theme throughout the monograph is that the main responsibility for risk control has to be shifted back towards *internal* management and away from *external* regulators. The external regulators cannot satisfactorily meet the excessive expectations of the public about ensuring safety and the prevention of loss, at least without an unacceptable extent of intrusion, distortion and cost. But what kind of techniques can be used to effect this shift? In Chapter 5, we discuss some of the new techniques that can be adopted by internal management for the control of risk. We describe value-at-risk (VaR) models as tools for management to assess, analyse and control market and credit risk. Banks' internal VaR models have recently been accepted by G-10 regulators as a means to determine minimum capital against market risk. Can they be applied equally successfully to credit risk? Another important innovation is the emergence of credit derivatives, which may allow banks to hedge their counterparty exposures much more effectively than has been previously the case. If this does develop, then the traditional regulatory distinction between banks' trading book and their banking book will have to be questioned, should counterparty risk become easily tradable through credit derivatives.

But how can the shift of responsibility to these and other internal control mechanisms be realised without an increase in the likelihood of financial distress? The pre-commitment approach, also discussed in Chapter 5, gives an example of how external regulation may be reformed so that excessive risk taking is sufficiently discouraged without constraining too much the internal risk management process and the evolution of financial institutions. This new approach applies the idea of incentive contracts, outlined in Chapter 3, to the area of market risk capital requirements and VaR models.

The conditions of greater geographical and functional diversity that lie behind the need to place more reliance on internal risk management are more advanced in developed than in emerging countries. And some of the current techniques discussed in Chapter 5 may seem somewhat arcane to regulators in developing countries. Nevertheless, we argue that several of the problems caused for regulators, e.g. the use by banks of complex derivatives to get around regulations, either are, or soon will be, extant in many developing countries. So we feel that our analysis is quite generally applicable. It is more a question of timing than relevance.

Nevertheless, conditions are more difficult for regulators in emerging countries, with more fragile banking systems, less liquid and more volatile financial markets, etc. We spell this out in Chapter 6, and discuss the implications for the role of the regulators of banks in such countries. One common problem has been that the liberalisation of previously state-controlled banking systems – as part of a wider programme of liberalisation – welcome though it was, has often led to banking problems and crises.

This leads us naturally, in Chapter 7, on to a consideration of how to handle banking crises. We bring together some examples of practical experiences and develop guidelines on how to handle such a crisis if it should strike. Three basic principles of crisis management apply rather uniformly to developing and industrialised countries: ensure that the parties responsible for the crisis bear most of the costs of restructuring; prevent problem banks from expanding credit to delinquent borrowers; and avoid financing the programme with inflation by making the restructuring programme a high priority. However, since the severity of constraints (funding limits, absence of liquid financial markets, etc.) also shapes a restructuring programme, the attributes of successful programmes in developing countries necessarily differ from those in industrial countries.

Chapter 8 considers issues related to the institutional structure of regulatory agencies, and has been revised in the light of the British Chancellor of the Exchequer's announcement, in May 1997, of the decision to concentrate responsibility for the supervision of all financial institutions in the hands of a single 'mega' regulator, the reformed and enlarged Securities and Investments Board (SIB). Regulation is, almost by definition, based on the rule of law; and supervision generally, though not always, has statutory backing and is bureaucratic by nature. Such laws, and the resultant structures of bureaucratic organisations, are difficult to change. In the meantime, the technology and structure of financial intermediation move on, leaving the regulatory structure out of date. We consider in this chapter some general principles that should guide the creation of an optimal institutional structure of regulatory agencies. Not only have the forces of technology, greater competition and both de- and re-regulation ended functional separation within countries, they have also done so between countries. The growth of the global financial intermediary implies that the failure of an intermediary headquartered, or a market situated, in one country can have ramifications in many others. This means that *autarky* is no longer a viable approach to regulation.

Such globalisation has to date been most marked in wholesale business, and so the main concern of regulators has been about its implications for systemic risk. But technology, notably in the form of the Internet, may soon allow retail products to be advertised and sold from anywhere in the world and paid for electronically by anyone in any other country. This means that: (1) global competition may well become yet more pronounced; and (2) some suppliers of financial services in weakly regulated countries might escape regulation altogether. Finance is rapidly becoming global, but laws and regulation are national. Can international declarations plug the gap? Can the financial industry, supported by the authorities, do so by means of setting standards? But how can standards be given effective teeth, via sanctions, without an (international?) legal basis? These are some of the structural issues that we have selected for a deeper analysis in Chapter 8. This chapter also considers more general questions related to the institutional structure of regulatory agencies and, in particular, on what basis an optimum structure of regulatory institutions might be constructed.

At various points in the discussion, policy implications emerge from the analysis. These are brought together in summary form in the concluding chapter, both for ease of reference and in order to present an overall policy approach to financial regulation.

1   The rationale for regulation

A. The scale of the problem

Financial systems in most countries of the world have been shown to have had a fragile structure in recent decades. It is in that context that we aim to reassess the rationale, mechanisms and modalities of financial regulation.

> A review of the experiences since 1980 of the 181 current Fund [IMF] member countries reveals that 133 have experienced significant banking sector problems at some stage during the past fifteen years [1980 – Spring 1996]. . . . Two general classes [of problem] are identified: 'crisis' (41 instances in 36 countries) and 'significant' problems (108 instances).

Thus begins a recent study by IMF economists entitled *Bank Soundness and Macroeconomic Policy*[1] (see Figure A1.1 and Table A1.1 in the Appendix to this chapter). This outcome is worse than in any other similar period since the Great Depression in the 1930s. The macroeconomic effect of such banking crises has in many cases been so severe as to amount to a sizeable reduction in GDP (see Table 1.2 in the Appendix).

Are these problems more severe in industrial or in developing countries? How do emerging and transitional banking markets perform? We have adjusted and further broken down the IMF data to get a more differentiated picture of banking problems (see Table 1.3 in the Appendix), and it turns out that only a slightly larger share of all developing countries have faced a 'crisis' (20 per cent) or 'significant' problems (53 per cent) when compared with industrial countries (crisis: 17 per cent, significant problems: 52 per cent). However, the greater riskiness of banking systems in developing countries becomes more pronounced (crisis: 23 per cent, significant problems: 59 per cent) when twenty-two small island states are removed from the sample.

We also defined three subgroups for the developing world: emerging countries, economies in transition, and oil-exporting countries.[2] In fact, ten out of sixteen emerging economies, almost two-thirds of the total, have experienced a crisis over the sample period, and not a single one escaped without any banking problems. Similarly, four-fifths of twenty-four transition economies experienced significant problems, although real crises seem to be less frequent in this group than in emerging markets. From this perspective, oil-exporting developing countries seem to have faced fewer problems: ten out of thirteen did not receive any negative entry by the IMF economists.

The main causes of these problems have been those that have traditionally attended commercial banking since its historical beginnings – poor credit control, connected lending, insufficient liquidity and capital – in short, poor internal governance (see Table A1.4 in the Appendix). This record suggests that most countries, especially the emerging and transitional countries, may need enhanced and improved external supervision to reinforce internal controls. Goldstein (1997) has recently put forward a set of proposals for such supervision in emerging countries. We discuss them further in Chapter 6.

B. The case for external regulation, and the need to make such a case

Bank failures around the world in recent years have been common, large and expensive. While they were, perhaps, larger than generally appreciated, their existence does not, of itself, *necessarily* justify the attention currently being given to the reinforcement of financial regulation and supervision. Indeed, many 'liberal' academic economists, e.g. supporters of free banking such as Dowd[3] and Benston and Kaufman[4], would attribute many of these crises and problems to the (indirectly malign) effects of regulatory efforts – perhaps the most extreme example of iatrogenesis (medically induced illness) ever known.

Interposing regulation and supervision into an otherwise free-market context weakens the incentives for the owners and managers to monitor and control themselves, and for their clients to exercise due diligence. Expectations are fostered among both clients and owners/managers about the standards of safety and propriety that supervisors *should* ensure in controlled institutions, but these expectations cannot be satisfied without such an expensive, intrusive and inflexible system that it would be wrong to try to install. In part because one rule can never fit all, regulations inevitably distort the economic outcome, possibly so much that the end result is worse than the unregulated starting point.

Indeed, the numerous additional problems with a highly prescriptive regulatory regime are outlined by Llewellyn (1996: 23–4):

- An excessive degree of prescription may bring the regulatory regime into disrepute because it is perceived by the industry as being excessive, with many redundant rules.
- Risks are often too complex to be covered by simple rules.
- Balance sheet rules reflect the position of an institution only at a particular point in time, although its position can change substantially within a short period.
- An inflexible approach based on a detailed rule book has the effect of impeding firms from choosing their own least-cost way of meeting regulatory objectives, and also thereby stifles financial innovation.

- A prescriptive regime tends in practice to focus upon firms' processes, rather than outcomes, and the ultimate objectives of regulation. Thus, the rules may become the focus, rather than the objectives. It can give rise to a perverse culture of 'box ticking' by firms. The letter of the law may be obeyed at the cost of the spirit.
- A prescriptive approach is inclined towards rules escalation (whereby more rules are added over time, but few are withdrawn).
- Regulation may create a confrontational relationship between the regulator and the regulated firms, or alternatively cause firms to overreact, engaging in excessive efforts at internal compliance out of fear of being challenged by the regulator.
- Forcing a high degree of conformity on regulated firms causes an information loss. If firms are given leeway in satisfying the regulator's objectives and principles, more is learned about consumer preferences in regulation, about how different behaviour affects the objectives, and about the properties of different rules, etc.
- In the interest of 'competitive neutrality' rules may be applied equally to all firms, although firms may be sufficiently heterogeneous to warrant a different approach. Treating as equal firms that in practice are not equal is not competitive neutrality, and it reduces the scope for legitimate differentiations.
- A highly prescriptive rules approach may prove to be inflexible and not sufficiently responsive to market conditions.
- There is a potential moral hazard, because firms may assume that, if something is not explicitly covered in the regulations, there is no regulatory dimension to it.

These concerns are not so much about regulation itself, but about *externally imposed* regulation, as opposed to self-regulation. As Coase (1988) has emphasised, free markets require considerable internal infrastructure and self-regulation to function efficiently with minimal transaction costs. Issues such as the provision of information, the identification and establishment of the roles of the various market agents and dealers, how a deal is to be made, registered, settled and paid, and the resolution of market discrepancies and failures, all have to be agreed upon and codified. While the majority of such market regulations are, indeed, the outcome of private agreement among those involved, private regulations do need the underlying support of commercial and contract law to provide sanctions and to prevent opportunistic behaviour. This is discussed further in Chapter 3.

Given, then, the common failings of externally imposed regulation, why do we not rely on private self-regulation, reinforced by common, commercial and contract law? One reason is that public pressure may not allow that to happen. Whatever the social costs and benefits of an externally imposed system of regulation may be, public revulsion at the effects and outcome of failures in unregulated financial systems can force the establishment of systems of deposit insurance and external regulation, no matter what the reservations of the authorities may be. Those who are invested with the responsibility for supervision are often aware of the poison within the chalice.

But the case for external regulation (in addition to, and partly in place of, private self-regulation) does not rest just on surrender to public pressure; and, if it did, such pressure should be resisted. Instead, the case depends on circumstances in which the private sector, left to itself, produces market failure, or at least suboptimal results, which are arguably worse than public sector regulation, even with all the biases and failings that such regulation may entail.[5]

The three main reasons for public sector regulation are:

1 To protect the customer against monopolistic exploitation.
2 To provide smaller, retail (less informed) clients with protection.
3 To ensure systemic stability.

(i) Protection against monopolies

The first case for intervention arises when there is a private sector monopoly, or a collusive and antisocial oligopoly. Such conditions are much more commonly found among utilities than in the financial sector, and they provide the basis for the greater part of regulation and regulatory bodies in many countries (in the UK, the OFs – e.g. Oftel, Ofgas, etc. – are examples).

Although most of the financial industry is ferociously competitive, several of the supporting systems and markets incorporate network economies and/or economies of scale. For example, it may be most efficient to have a single clearing, or payment, system. The more widely an (electronic) card is used, the more widely it will be accepted as a medium of exchange (this is an example of network economies). Those who command access to the use of such systems (markets), or to the information that they generate, are in a position to generate (monopoly) rents and to exert unfair and undue influence on outsiders. Yet those who have established a system, or a market, must be allowed *some* control over who uses it, and the information that such systems and markets generate is, in a sense, private property. The circumstances under which the public have a right of access to otherwise private systems, markets and information is a difficult area,[6] but one that covers a much broader and more general field than the financial sector. So, beyond noting that ensuring fair and open competition, and reasonable access to systems and information, is an appropriate function for regulators in the financial area, we have little else to say about this aspect of regulation.[7]

(ii) Client protection

The second condition, client protection, arises for two main reasons: (1) because the institution where clients hold their funds fails; or (2) because of the adverse behaviour (unsatisfactory conduct of business) of a firm with its customers. The failure of an individual financial institution *may* have adverse effects on systemic stability (see below), *and* cause losses to individual (retail) depositors, who are (after the event at least) regarded as incapable of looking after their own interests (i.e. *caveat emptor* does not hold). While we do *not* think that financial institutions should be rescued (bailed out) just because they are financial institutions, nevertheless the impact of their failure on their clients[8] (and on systematic stability) means that regulators are almost inevitably bound to have a prudential concern with the liquidity, solvency, riskiness and general health of individual institutions, both firms and markets. In this respect, both prudential and systemic regulation require the regulation and supervision of *institutions* rather than of the *functions* they perform. Conduct of business regulation, on the other hand, focuses on functions, irrespective of which institutions are involved.

Prudential and *systemic* regulation need to be distinguished, although both adopt a similar approach. Systemic regulation is about the safety and soundness of financial institutions for purely systemic reasons (i.e. because the social costs of the failure of an institution exceed the private costs). On the other hand, prudential regulation is about the safety and soundness of financial institutions *vis-à-vis* consumer protection, in that the consumer loses when an institution fails, even if there are no systemic consequences.

a. Prudential regulation

The case for prudential (rather than systemic) regulation and supervision is that consumers are not in a position to judge the safety and soundness of financial institutions. Prudential regulation is necessary because of imperfect consumer information and agency problems associated with the nature of a firm's business. There is, therefore, a case for prudential regulation (of, say, insurance or life assurance companies) even in the absence of any systemic dimension, where:

- there is a fiduciary role of the institution;
- consumers are unable to judge the safety and soundness of institutions with which they are dealing;
- the value of contracts to the consumer is determined by the subsequent behaviour of the institution, and where the company (e.g. life assurance company) may become riskier because of a change in behaviour after a long-term contract has been taken out by customers;
- there is a potential claim on a compensation or deposit insurance fund.

Prudential and systemic regulation are needed to protect not only consumers (and in the latter case, the system), but also those who finance the safety net or compensation scheme, especially when the premiums levied on the members of such schemes cannot be (or are not) closely related to their relative riskiness.

While the regulations imposed for systemic and prudential reasons may be similar (e.g. the establishment of capital requirements), they do not need to be (nor should they be) conducted by the same agency. The focus should be on the objectives of regulation. The danger is that, if a single regulatory agency conducts both systemic and prudential regulation, it might converge on the same requirements for different institutions, although the objectives might require different approaches.

b. Conduct of business regulation

Conduct of business regulation focuses on how firms conduct business with their customers. It includes information disclosure, the honesty and integrity of firms and their employees, the level of competence of firms, fair business practices, the way financial services and products are marketed, etc. Conduct of business regulation can also establish guidelines for the objectivity of advice, with the aim of minimising the potential principal–agent problems associated with financial advice when principals and agents are not equally well informed. This area can also include procedures for compensation in the event that the interests of a customer have been compromised by the behaviour of a financial institution. Overall, conduct of business regulation is designed not to ensure the safety and soundness of institutions but to establish rules and guidelines about appropriate behaviour and business practices in dealing with customers. The rationale for such regulation is considered in Llewellyn (1995a).

In some respects, concerns about customer protection in the financial field closely mirror those in other professions. Poor-quality or self-serving advice can be as dangerous, and possibly as prevalent, in finance as in other professions.

Many of the techniques used to mitigate principal–agent conflict of interest are also widely used among the professions; they include entry qualifications to undertake certain skilled roles, standards of good behaviour and ethics, the appointment of an 'ombudsman' to whom an aggrieved customer can appeal, and (limited and partial – to avoid moral hazard) insurance against failure. Usually, in most professions and in most countries, such measures are enforced by privately run professional organisations, e.g. the national medical association or legal association. Unfortunately, such an organisation can become a monopoly/oligopoly and can use its command over entry and over the actions of members to enforce anti-competitive behaviour, by limiting price competition and advertising, by enforcing excessively high entry qualifications, etc. Methods for reasserting the public interest include insisting on a majority of non-practitioners and consumer representatives being on the boards of the self-regulatory organisations (SROs), or transferring responsibility for consumer protection to a publicly appointed (statutory) body. Whatever the solution, the regulatory body *has* to work closely with the profession involved (no other course of operation is really feasible), and the boundary between appropriate accommodation of practitioner objectives on one side, and regulatory capture on the other, inevitably becomes blurred.

Problems of customer protection within the financial services field are more severe than in other professions; the amount of money at risk and the opportunity for principal–agent conflicts of interest are generally as high, or higher than, elsewhere. In addition, the very nature of the service offered, to handle the client's money, makes straight fraud more likely. Moreover, the confidentiality (even secrecy) typically associated with financial services contributes to the greater likelihood of fraud. Ponzi games, and the kinds of abuse of fund management observed in a couple of well-publicised cases in 1996, are examples.

Similar abuses were responsible for the Gower Report[9] and the subsequent Financial Services Act (1986) in the UK. Indeed the greater part of statutory regulation in the financial field usually relates to customer protection, including separation of client funds, depositor insurance, and who can advise on what (polarisation). Nevertheless, we shall for the most part abstract from such customer protection issues in the remainder of this monograph. Our own main focus and concern, like most central banks, relates particularly to the banking system, whereas consumer protection issues arise throughout the whole field of financial services, including brokerage, insurance and (especially) fund management.

c. Wholesale v. retail   Homogeneity

Consumers of financial services are not a homogeneous group, and their requirements for conduct of business regulation (and willingness to pay the costs of regulation) are also likely to be heterogeneous. Therefore, it is appropriate to have a different regulatory regime for conduct of business issues for retail as opposed to wholesale business. In particular, the case for regulating retail business (involving the purchase of financial products, services and contracts by individuals) is considerably stronger than the case for wholesale business (Llewellyn, 1995b). In brief, this is because market failures and imperfections are likely to be more powerful in the retail sector than in wholesale business.

With respect to conduct of business, the case for regulation in the retail financial sector is especially powerful because:

- The small-volume retail customer does not make frequent repeat orders of financial contracts, and therefore has a limited ability to learn from experience.
- Problems of asymmetric information are greater at the retail level than in professional wholesale markets. The costs of acquiring information are particularly high for small purchases by retail customers.
- The individual consumer has only a limited ability and opportunity to

acquire the necessary skills to enter into complex financial contracts and to assess information.

- The parties to financial contracts are considerably less equal in the retail sector than in professional wholesale markets. The retail sector juxtaposes the uninformed and unskilled consumers on the one hand and the much better informed and more skilled suppliers of financial services on the other.
- A retail consumer may find it difficult to ascertain the value of a contract at purchase. Moreover, because long-term contracts are often involved, a contract's value is determined in part by the behaviour of the supplier after the point of purchase. This requires continuous monitoring of the behaviour of the supplier, and individuals are not in a position to do the monitoring. Even if the individual consumer had the skills, because the supplier's commitment to him or her is relatively small, he or she would not have sufficient power to influence the supplier's subsequent behaviour. Thus, economies of scale are important in monitoring.
- To the individual, a contract (e.g. a personal pension plan) may represent a high proportion of his or her wealth. If the contract fails (or it does not produce what the consumer wanted), the cost to the individual can be very substantial.
- The purchase of financial contracts is often based on advice given by professional advisers, which raises potential principal–agent problems.
- Retail consumers are rarely in a position to judge the safety and soundness of the institutions with which they are dealing.

So, market imperfections are more pervasive in the retail sector than in the wholesale sector and, because the ultimate rationale for regulation centres on questions of market imperfections, retail financial services should generally be regulated more explicitly than wholesale business. If the distinction between wholesale and retail sectors is not made, there is a danger that wholesale markets will be overregulated owing to the need for a higher level of regulation at the retail level.

Where professionals are dealing with professionals, the need for conduct of business regulation is less evident. The regulation of wholesale business is often best left to self-generated codes of conduct, and the role of the regulatory agency, if any, is to facilitate the generation of such codes, to monitor them, and to impose sanctions when infringements occur.

(iii) Systemic issues

Systemic regulation is necessary when the social costs of the failure of a financial institution (particularly a bank) exceed the private cost and such potential social costs are not incorporated in the decision making of the firm. Yet, systemic issues do not relate to all institutions. The key point is that banks are subject to runs, which have contagion effects, and which can throw solvent banks into insolvency both because a large proportion of their assets are not easily marketable and, probably to a lesser extent, because the panic drives down the current value of marketable assets. The value of a bank's loans is based on inside information possessed by the bank that cannot credibly be transferred in a secondary market. Put another way, a bank's assets are usually more valuable on a going-concern basis than on a liquidation (break-up of the bank) basis. In particular, failure (losses) in one bank will (rightly or wrongly) cause outsiders to revise their view of the value of other banks' assets (see Docking *et al.*, 1997; Schoenmaker, 1996). Governor Kelly of the Federal Reserve Board restated this concern (1997) when he said:

> It is probably fair to say that there is considerable agreement among central bankers and other economic policy makers that [banks'] unique balance sheet structure creates an inherent *potential instability in the banking system*. Rumours concerning an individual bank's financial condition [can spread] if the distressed institution is large or prominent; the panic can spread to other banks, *with potentially debilitating consequences for the economy as a whole*.
>
> (emphasis added)

Some analysts (notably Kaufman and Benston)[10] challenge the basic premise that banks are prone to runs that create systemic hazards. In addition, they argue that the negative effects of bank failures and bank runs (on the limited number of occasions that they have occurred) have generally had no larger impact on the economy than other business failures. This is not the place to review this challenge in any detail[11] or to consider the empirical evidence. However, there is a particular dimension to the debate that is worth noting: the risk v. seriousness of the issue. The probability that the failure of a single bank will induce a systemic problem may be low, but, if systemic failure were to occur, it could be serious and the costs could be high. Thus, regulation to prevent systemic problems may be viewed as an insurance premium against a low-probability occurrence. As Greenspan (1996b) said: 'There will always exist a remote possibility of a chain reaction, a cascading sequence of defaults that will culminate in financial implosion if it is allowed to proceed unchecked'. Low-probability/high-seriousness risks are always hard to handle.

C Economies of scale in monitoring

Potentially substantial economies of scale can be secured through collective regulation and supervision (or monitoring) of financial firms. So a further rationale for regulation is the efficient conduct of the monitoring process. Because some investment contracts are long term, and often involve a fiduciary role in a principal–agent relationship, continuous monitoring is required. Monitoring is also needed because, unlike the value of most goods and services, a financial contract's value to the consumer is often determined by the behaviour of the financial institution *after* the point of purchase. This is particularly true for long-term contracts, since the consumer is unable to exit the contract at low cost. To some extent it may also apply to bank depositors; although they can exit at low cost, consumers may not have the necessary information to make such a decision. Thus, while continuous monitoring is needed, a question arises about who is to undertake the monitoring.

In the absence of regulation and supervision by a specialist agency that offers certain minimum standards, consumers are required to spend time, effort and resources investigating and monitoring firms supplying financial services and contracts. This involves two sets of costs:

1 substantial duplication and hence excessive social costs,
   since all consumers would be duplicating the same processes; and
2 the loss of the economies of scale that are derived through a specialist regulator's/supervisor's acquiring expertise and establishing effective monitoring systems.

In the absence of a specialist agency, an intermittent consumer would find the cost of investigating and monitoring firms excessive, and 'free-rider' problems are likely to emerge. With a specialist agency, consumers delegate to the regulator/supervisor at least some of the monitoring responsibilities and, in the process, reap the benefits of economies of scale. This is rational and economic, since intermittent and occasional consumers are unable to appropriate the full benefits of the costs of supervision when it is undertaken on an individual basis, and the investment of time and resources is inordinately large for small, infrequent purchases. However the advantages of delegation must be set against the costs of regulation (see Dewatripont and Tirole, 1994).

D. Why banks are special

The rationale for regulation, and the form that the regulation should take, differs significantly between banking and non-banking financial services, especially (as with pensions, insurance and life assurance) when long-term contracts are involved. In particular, *systemic* issues are central in the regulation of banks,[12] but they are much less significant for non-bank financial services, whereas consumer protection issues are comparatively more important in the latter.

The traditional rationale for bank regulation and supervision is based on four main considerations:

1 the pivotal position of banks in the financial system, especially in clearing and payments systems;
2 the potential systemic dangers resulting from bank runs;
3 the nature of bank contracts;
4 adverse selection and moral hazard associated with the lender-of-last-resort role and other safety net arrangements that apply to banks.

Banks have a pivotal position in the economy for two main reasons: they are the only source of finance for a large number of borrowers (Bernanke, 1983), and more importantly they manage the payments system. If the banking system is placed in jeopardy, the resultant financial disruption is likely to be more serious than it would be with other sectors of the financial system. Because of the nature of banks' deposit contracts (full-money certainty on the basis of assets with an uncertain value), and the potential for contagion, banks are prone to runs where the failure (or perceived threat of failure) of one bank may induce customers to withdraw deposits from other banks. (See, amongst others, Diamond and Dybvig, 1983; Baltensperger and Dermine, 1987b; Postlewaite and Vives, 1987; Bhattacharya and Jacklin, 1988; Chari and Jagannathan, 1988.) The interconnectedness of banks (e.g. in their gross positions with each other in clearing systems, in interbank deposits, etc.) is much greater than that in most other industries, so the failure of one bank can directly cause immediate losses to other, interconnected banks.

The nature of bank contracts is relevant: banks offer contracts for liquid deposits (where the redemption value of the deposit is independent of the per-formance of the bank and the value of its assets) that finance the acquisition of illiquid assets of uncertain value. The potential hazard is that even a solvent bank may be forced to sell assets at a loss. Bank loans are difficult to sell in the absence of a secondary market (although secondary markets for some cate-gories of loans are starting to be established) because it is difficult for potential purchasers to evaluate customer-specific information.[13] Distress selling of assets may therefore induce insolvency in what would otherwise be a solvent bank because, owing to problems of asymmetric information, the market is unable to assess the quality of the assets being sold (Lewis and Davis, 1987; Benston and Kaufman, 1988). Moreover, the sale of marketable assets drives down prices, and in panics the general fall in asset values can be large.

In summary, regulatory capital is required for banks in order to reduce the probability of insolvency. In the final analysis, risks arise in banking because of the nature and asymmetry of banking contracts and because there is still no well-established secondary market in bank loans (but see Chapter 5 for a discussion of the regulatory implications of the developing markets in credit derivatives).

The issues involved in the regulation of non-banking financial services are different:

- Systemic risk is considerably less evident than in banking (and often does not exist at all).
- Contagion is less likely.
- The potential disruption of the payments system does not arise.
- So long as there is no perceived lender of last resort, problems of moral hazard do not arise (see also Chapter 7).
- Securities firms hold liquid assets that can be rapidly traded in (often liquid) secondary markets.

- The time-scale of adjustment to balance sheet positions is much shorter for securities firms than for banks. Securities firms have substantial asset turnover through their market-making, underwriting and regular trading activities. They also tend to take a short-term time horizon in their investment strategy. (Banks, on the other hand, have longer-term commitments to customers and are less able to adjust their balance sheets quickly in response to adverse developments.)
- Banks rely on potentially volatile, unsecured short-term deposits for the bulk of their funding, whereas securities firms have a much higher proportion of secured funding.
- The risks faced by banks and securities firms also differ significantly. In general, bank risks are credit risks, whereas securities firms are more subject to market risk.
- Because the assets of a securities firm consist mainly of marketable securities, their value on a going-concern basis differs little from their value in liquidation.
- The valuation of securities firms is on a liquidation basis; hence accountancy is on a marked-to-market basis. On the other hand, banks are valued on an ongoing basis, and accountancy procedures are based on original cost. The absence of a secondary market for the bulk of bank assets also makes it difficult to place a true market value on bank loans.[14] Therefore, the valuation of securities firms is more accurate than that of banks.
- Again because of the nature of their assets and the type of business undertaken, the way banks and securities firms respond, and are expected to respond, to shocks is fundamentally different. A securities firm with impaired capital is expected to contract its balance sheet immediately in order to comply with its regulatory capital requirements. This is possible because its assets have a secondary market. As a result, the regulator is more concerned about securities firms' liquid capital. On the other hand, banks are not expected to respond to shocks by contracting or withdrawing from the market.
- The overall valuation of a securities firm is easier to determine than that of a bank, because the value of its assets is readily ascertainable in secondary markets. In fact, forced contraction and even closure are the regulator's major weapons in dealing with financially vulnerable securities firms (Dale, 1996).

E. Do securities firms or insurance companies pose any systemic dangers?

In general, the requirement for regulation (most especially with respect to capital adequacy) is less evident for securities firms than for banks. The question is whether there is any need to regulate securities firms for systemic reasons, and whether it is necessary to stipulate capital adequacy requirements, especially if investors' cash (pending investment) and securities are held in a separate account so that they cannot be used to pay off creditors in the event of insolvency of a securities firm.

These questions arise because most, if not all, of the special characteristics of banks that support the case for regulation do not apply to securities firms: as already noted, in the absence of deposit insurance and a lender of last resort, there is no moral hazard to be protected against; the systemic risk is less evident and often does not exist at all (Mayer, 1993); contagion is less likely; and disruption of the payments system does not occur with failure of securities firms. Since securities firms' assets are readily marketable, they can be liquidated, albeit at the risk of a fall in prices, in the event of difficulty. Ultimately, the option exists to contract the balance sheet. Above all, securities firms are not subject to the asymmetric asset and liabilities contracts that are a feature of banking. As noted by Dale (1996), 'an important answer to the question regarding the relative importance of bank insolvency compared with that of non-banks is that it is the possibility of systemic crisis that distinguishes the two'. In practice, however, securities firms *are* regulated (albeit differently under different national regimes) and capital adequacy requirements are imposed on their gross and net positions.

Even so, securities firms may under *some* circumstances pose systemic threats. One obvious case is the potential impact on banks when securities operations represent part of the banking group.[15] Even if a firewall arrangement establishes its legal independence, the default of a bank subsidiary would inevitably damage the credit standing of its owner bank.[16] On the other hand, this argument should not be pressed too far, since the same could apply to any bank subsidiary. Similarly, while a bank may be potentially vulnerable owing to its securities firm subsidiary, it is equally vulnerable to many other types of exposure. Care is needed when isolating securities business as a special focus of vulnerability.

On the other hand, as a recent official study states:

the rising importance of securities markets in the financial systems of OECD countries, the growing concentration in the securities industry, the effects of new technologies, the nature of the risks now being borne by securities market intermediaries and the links between the securities market and the banking and payments system all suggest that the occurrence of serious misfunctions in the securities markets would have the potential to destabilise the entire financial system.

(OECD, 1993)

So, the extent of the systemic threat posed by securities firms, whether or not they are part of a wider banking group, remains a matter of debate. The prudential regulation of insurance companies, and especially life assurance companies, raises different issues. The general case for *prudential* regulation is as stated above: information problems for the consumer, agency costs, and the fact that, as such companies issue long-term contracts, the value of the contracts to the consumer is determined by the institution's behaviour and performance after the contract has been signed. However, the purely systemic dimension is considerably less of an issue:

1 insurance companies' liabilities are long term and are not prone to runs;
2 as noted by Thompson (1996), insurance companies do not have linkages with each other through market trading and the payments system;
3 their assets are readily marketable;
4 the company's commitment to its contractual liabilities is determined by the performance of its assets;
5 insurance companies are not involved directly with the payments system.

Over all, insurance companies are not engaged in the type of asset transformation that banks engage in and that give the latter a particular systemic dimension. In fact, an insurance company engages in the opposite type of asset transformation: it effectively transforms illiquid liabilities into liquid assets (in contrast to banks, which transform liquid liabilities into illiquid assets).

Thus, while there is a case for prudential regulation of insurance companies, it is not because they raise potential systemic issues. On the other hand, to the extent that insurance companies are owned by banks, a bank could be threatened, either directly or through a reputation effect, by the insolvency of its insurance company subsidiary. For this reason, the regulation of insurance companies is not irrelevant to bank regulators. However, this does not mean that the most appropriate structure is for insurance companies to be supervised by the same prudential regulator as banks.

F. Conclusion

The theme of this chapter, and subsequently, especially in Chapter 4, is that regulators supply regulatory services for which there is a consumer demand. But there is a cost to regulation, and, one way or another, the consumer pays that cost. However, regulation is not supplied through a market process; and hence, the consumer is not able to indicate what type of regulation is required, how much regulation is desired, and what price will be willingly paid. Regulation is always about making judgements and trade-offs, particularly when considering costs and benefits. For this reason, occasional regulatory lapses and failures must be regarded as the necessary cost of devising an effective system of regulation. The degree of regulatory intensity that removes all possibility of failure would almost certainly be excessive, in that the costs would outweigh the benefits.

There needs to be a recognition of the limitations of regulation and supervision that not all risks are covered, and that the optimal level of regulation falls short of eliminating all possibility of consumers making the wrong choices in financial contracts. Finance is necessarily about risk, and to attempt a level of regulation that removes all risk from the investor would mean regulating away the very function of finance and financial contracts.

Public policy arrangements should never eliminate the incentive for consumers of financial services to exercise due care.

At various points in this monograph, reference is made to potential moral hazards created by regulation. A particular moral hazard should be highlighted here. When a regulatory or supervisory authority is created and establishes regulatory requirements, a danger arises that an implicit contract is perceived as having been created between the user of financial services and the regulator (i.e. the consumer assumes that, because there is an authorisation procedure, specific aspects of regulation are established, the supplier of financial services is authorised and supervised, and the institution is therefore safe). The obvious danger is that an *implicit contract* creates the impression that the consumer need not take care with respect to the firms with which he or she deals in financial services. This is the moral hazard of regulation: regulation itself creates the image that less care need be taken. This point was made by the Wallis Committee of Inquiry in Australia (April 1997: 300):

> a prudential regulator is required to strike a difficult balance between increasing the likelihood that financial promises are kept and being perceived as the underwriter of those promises . . . . The investing public may perceive the regulator as implicitly guaranteeing the creditworthiness of regulated institutions. Ironically, the regulator is perversely exposed in this respect to its own performance – the better its track record in preventing failure, the more likely the public is to regard the regulator as guaranteeing the underlying promises.

This is a fundamental moral hazard in all forms of externally imposed regulation, and it can create adverse incentives on the part of both the consumer and the regulated institutions. The twin danger is that the consumer assumes that regulation guarantees safety and good conduct, and the regulated firm judges that all it need do is obey specific aspects of the regulator's requirements.

There needs to be public policy recognition of, and encouragement of consumer awareness of, the limitations of regulation and supervision – that they have only a limited role, that even in this restricted dimension they can fail, that not all risks are covered, and that the optimum level of regulation and supervision falls short of eliminating all possibility of consumers making the wrong choices in financial contracts. Consumers must recognise that regulation and supervision do not protect them against all possibility of loss.

Appendix

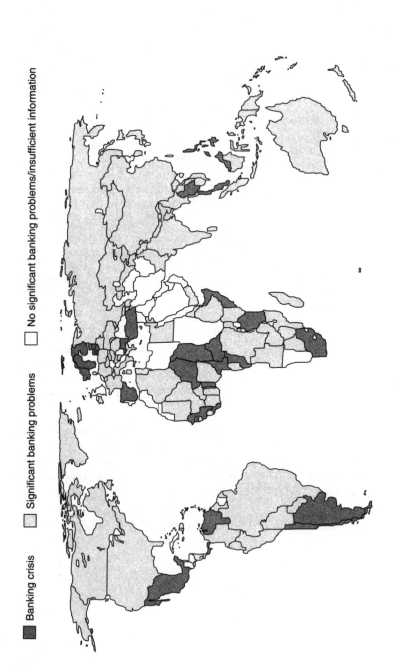

Figure A1.1 Banking problems worldwide, 1980–96

Table A1.1 Survey of banking problems: 1980 to spring 1996[1]

Country	Type of problem	Measure of extent
Albania (1992–present)	Significant	Thirty-one percent of 'new' (post-July 1992 cleanup) loans are nonperforming; some banks are facing liquidity problems owing to a logjam of interbank liabilities.
Algeria (1990–92)	Significant	Fifty percent of loans were nonperforming and were taken over by the treasury; operations covered all the 5 commercial banks, and were followed by ongoing structural reforms.
Angola (1991–present)	Significant	The two-tier banking system (established in 1991) is still not consolidated; 2 commercial banks (state-owned) are experiencing solvency problems.
Argentina (1980–82)	Crisis	Nine percent of loans were non-performing in 1980 and 30% in 1985; 168 institutions were closed.
(1989–90)	Crisis	Nonperforming assets constituted 27% of the aggregate portfolio and 37% of the portfolios of state-owned banks. Failed banks held 40% of financial system assets.
(January to September 1995)	Crisis	Through September 1995, 45 of 205 institutions were closed or merged.
Armenia (1994–present)	Significant	The central bank has closed half of the active banks since August 1994, but the nonperforming asset problem of the large banks remains to be tackled. The Savings Bank has negligible capital.
Australia (1989–92)	Significant	Nonperforming loans rose to 6% of total assets in 1991–92. State-owned banks, especially in Victoria and South Australia, had to be rescued at a cost to the state governments of 1.9% of GDP. A large building society failed.
Azerbaijan (1995–present)	Significant	One large state-owned bank is facing a serious liquidity problem; new management has been appointed; 12 private banks have been closed owing to noncompliance with regulations; 3 large state-owned banks will be insolvent if loan losses are written off.
Bahrain		The system withstood deposit withdrawals from the offshore center during the Persian Gulf war.
Bangladesh (1980s–present)	Significant	In 1987, 20% of the loans of 4 major banks, whose assets accounted for 70% of all lending, were nonperforming.
Belarus (1995–present)	Significant	Many banks are undercapitalized; forced mergers have burdened some banks with poor loan portfolios; the regulatory environment is uncertain.
Benin (1988)	Crisis	All three commercial banks collapsed; 78% of loans were nonperforming at the end of 1988.

Table A1.1 Cont.

Country	Type of problem	Measure of extent
Bhutan (Early 1990s–present)	Significant	Nonperforming loans amount to approximately 7% of total loans.
Bolivia (1986–87)	Significant	Nonperforming loans reached 30% of banking assets.
(1994–present)	Significant	Two banks with 11% of assets were closed in November 1994. Four of 15 domestic banks, with 30% of assets, were undercapitalized and had liquidity problems and high levels of nonperforming loans in 1995.
Bosnia-Herzegovina (1992–present)	Significant	There has been no major bank closure. Loans made in the late 1980s and early 1990s are in default owing to the breakup of the former Yugoslavia and the war; this also translates into unrepayable commercial bank debt to international lenders.
Botswana (1994–95)	Significant	One problem bank was merged in 1994, a small bank was liquidated in 1995, and the state-owned National Development Bank was recapitalized at a cost of 0.6% of GDP.
Brazil (1994–present)	Significant	Twenty-nine banks, holding 15.4% of total deposits, were subjected to official intervention, placed under special administration, or received assistance to merge.
Brunei Darussalam (Mid-1980s)	Significant	Several financial firms failed in the mid-1980s. The second largest bank failed in 1986. In 1991, 9% of loans were past due; the level of such loans has subsequently declined.
Bulgaria (1991–present)	Crisis	About 75% of nongovernment loans were nonperforming in 1995, leaving many banks insolvent. Runs on banks have been reflected in pressure on reserve money and a queue of unsettled interbank payments.
Burkina Faso (1988–94)	Significant	Thirty-four percent of loans were nonperforming.
Burundi (1994–present)	Significant	Twenty-five percent of loans were nonperforming in 1995; one bank was liquidated.
Cambodia (Ongoing)	Significant	Commercial banks have rapidly expanded in the past two years. A number of banks do not meet prudential regulations. As supervisory capacity is rudimentary, there is no current information on the quality of the banks' portfolios.
Cameroon (1989–93)	Crisis	In 1989, 60–70% of loans were nonperforming.
(1995–present)	Crisis	About 30% of loans were nonperforming in 1996.

Table A1.1 Cont.

Country	Type of problem	Measure of extent
Canada (1983–85)	Significant	Fifteen members of the Canadian Deposit Insurance Corporation, including 2 banks, failed.
Cape Verde (1993–present)	Significant	In September 1993, the central bank was separated from the principal commercial bank. An estimated 30% of loans of the commercial bank were nonperforming at the end of 1995. This is in addition to nonperforming loans of public enterprises amounting to about 7% of GDP that remained with the central bank and were transferred to the government in September 1994.
Central African Republic (1976–92)	Crisis	Four banks were liquidated.
(1995–present)	Significant	Forty percent of loans are nonperforming; one state-owned bank is being taken over by a private group.
Chad (1979–83)	Crisis	Full banking operations were resumed after the 1979 civil war, with a moratorium on some loans and deposits.
(1992)	Significant	Thirty-five percent of loans to the private sector were nonperforming. The central bank consolidated those loans held by the 3 main commercial banks.
Chile (1981–87)	Crisis	The authorities intervened in 4 banks and 4 nonbank financial institutions (with 33% of outstanding loans) in 1981; 9 other banks and 2 more nonbanks (with 45% of outstanding loans) were subject to intervention in 1982–83, and many others were assisted. At the end of 1983, 19% of loans were nonperforming.
China[2] (1980s–present)	Significant	Problems have been recognized, but their size is very unclear; official estimates suggest that between 10% and 20% of bank loans could be nonperforming.
Colombia (1982–85)	Significant	The authorities intervened in 6 major banks and 8 finance companies; 15% of loans were nonperforming in 1984–85 (5.5% in 1980, 6.6% in 1988). Some insolvent banks were nationalized in 1985–86.
Congo, Republic of (1994–present)	Crisis	Seventy-five percent of loans to the private sector are nonperforming; 2 state-owned banks are being liquidated and 2 other state-owned banks are being privatized.
Costa Rica (Mid-1994– present	Significant	One large state-owned commercial bank was closed in December 1994. The ratio of overdue loans (net of provisions) to net worth in state commercial banks exceeded 100% in June 1995.

Table A1.1 Cont.

Country	Type of problem	Measure of extent
Côte d'Ivoire (1988–90)	Significant	Five specialized financial institutions and one commercial bank were restructured. Nonperforming loans reached 12% of bank credit.
Croatia (1995)	Significant	Banks accounting for 47% of bank credit have been found to be unsound and have been, or are scheduled to be, taken over by the Bank Rehabilitation Agency during 1996.
Czech Republic (1991–present)	Significant	In 1994–95, 38% of loans were nonperforming. Several banks have been closed since 1993.
Denmark (1987–92)	Significant	Cumulative loan losses over the period 1990–92 were 9% of loans; 40 of the 60 problem banks were merged.
Djibouti (1991–93)	Significant	Two of 6 commercial banks ceased operations in 1991 and 1992; their bankruptcy is being finalized. Another bank experienced difficulties.
Dominican Republic (1992–present)	Significant	More than 5% of the total loans of the financial system are estimated to be nonperforming. In the past three years, 3 small banks have been liquidated. In April 1996, the Monetary Board intervened in the third largest bank, which represents 7% of the assets of the banking system.
Ecuador (1995–present)	Significant	High levels of nonperforming loans; the authorities intervened in several smaller financial institutions in late 1995 to early 1996 and in the fifth largest commercial bank in March 1996.
Egypt (1991–95)	Significant	Four main public sector banks were given capital assistance.
El Salvador (1989)	Significant	Nine state-owned commercial banks (later privatized between 1991 and 1993) had 37% of loans nonperforming in 1989.
Equatorial Guinea (1983–85)	Crisis	Two of the country's largest banks were liquidated.
(1995)	Significant	The principal bank's main shareholder has been placed in liquidation.
Eritrea (1994)	Significant	State-owned banks were undercapitalized, but information on the quality of bank portfolios is scarce.
Estonia (1992–95)	Crisis	Insolvent banks held 41% of banking system assets. The licenses of 5 banks have been revoked, 2 major banks were merged and nationalized, and 2 large banks were merged and converted to a loan-recovery agency.

Table A1.1 Cont.

Country	Type of problem	Measure of extent
Ethiopia (1994–95)	Significant	A government-owned bank was restructured, and its nonperforming loans were taken over by the government.
Fiji (1995–present)	Significant	Ten percent of the loans are nonperforming. The problems are concentrated in one large bank that has 30% nonperforming loans.
Finland (1991–94)	Crisis	Nonperforming loans and credit losses reached 13% of total exposure at their peak in 1992; there was a liquidity crisis in September 1991.
France (1991–95)	Significant	Nonperforming loans were 8.9% of total loans in 1994. Fifteen percent ($27 billion) of Crédit Lyonnais' loans were nonperforming, and some other banks have posted large losses.
Gabon (1995–present)	Significant	Nine percent of loans are nonperforming; one bank was temporarily closed in 1995.
Gambia, The (1985–92)	Significant	Ten percent of bank credit was nonperforming in 1992. A government bank was restructuring and privatized in 1992.
Georgia (1991–present)	Significant	About a third of banks' outstanding loans are nonperforming; most large banks would be insolvent if adequate provisions were made for all nonperforming assets.
Germany (1990–93)	Significant	There were major problems at state-owned banks in East Germany following unification. The costs were handled by an extrabudgetary fund.
Ghana (1983–89)	Significant	Forty percent of bank credit to nongovernment borrowers was nonperforming in 1989; one bank was closed and two were merged.
Greece (1991–95)	Significant	There were localized problems that required significant injections of public funds into specialized lending institutions.
Guatemala		Two small state-owned banks had high nonperforming assets; these banks discontinued operations in the early 1990s.
Guinea (1980–85)	Crisis	The state-owned banking system collapsed; 80% of loans were nonperforming.
Guinea-Bissau (Ongoing)	Significant	After transition to a system in which the central bank and private commercial banks operate separately, sizable nonperforming loans (equivalent to 3.5% of GDP) were assumed by the treasury in early 1996.
(1988–present)	Significant	In August 1995, 26% of loans were nonperforming.

Table A1.1 Cont.

Country	Type of problem	Measure of extent
Guyana (1993–95)	Significant	One public bank was liquidated and merged with another public bank, holding more than one third of financial sector deposits. The surviving bank is to be restructured because of high levels of nonperforming loans. In 1993–94, US$28 million (approximately 7% of GDP) in nonperforming loans were written off.
Haiti (1991–present)	Significant	The political situation in 1994 resulted in a disruption of normal banking and a run on banks.
Hungary (1987–present)	Significant	Eight banks, accounting for 25% of financial system assets, became insolvent. At the end of 1993, 23% of total loans were problematic.
Iceland (1985–86)	Significant	One of three state-owned banks became insolvent and was eventually privatized in a merger with 3 private banks.
(1993)	Significant	The government was forced to inject capital into one of the largest state-owned commercial banks after it had suffered serious loan losses.
India (1991–present)	Significant	The nonperforming domestic assets of the 27 public sector banks were estimated at 19.5% of total loans and advances of these banks as of the end of March 1995. At that time, 15 banks did not meet Basle capital adequacy standards.
Indonesia (1992–present)	Significant	Nonperforming loans, which were concentrated in state-owned banks, were over 25% of total lending in 1993 but declined to 12% in September 1995. A large private bank was closed in 1992.
Ireland (1985)	Significant	One of the four clearing banks wrote off one fourth of its capital when its insurance subsidiary sustained losses and was placed under administration.
Israel (1983–84)	Significant	The government nationalized major banks accounting for 90% of the market; there had been an undercapitalization problem exacerbated by a crisis in the stock market.
Italy (1990–95)	Significant	Problems were concentrated in the south, affecting particular institutions. Systemwide, nonperforming loans were 10% of total in 1995. During 1990–94, 58 banks (accounting for 11% of total lending) were in difficulties and were merged with other institutions, and 3 of the 10 largest banks received significant injections of public funds; 10 banks were undercapitalized in 1994.
Jamaica (1994–present)	Significant	A merchant banking group was closed in December 1994; a medium-sized bank was supported in 1995.

Table A1.1 Cont.

Country	Type of problem	Measure of extent
Japan (1992–present)	Significant	In early 1996, the Ministry of Finance estimated problem loans at around 8% of GDP.
Jordan (1989–90)	Crisis	The third largest bank collapsed in August 1989; six other financial institutions encountered difficulties. The central bank provided overdrafts equivalent to 10% of GDP to meet a run on deposits and allow banks to settle foreign obligations.
Kazakstan (1991–95)	Significant	Forty percent of assets are to be written off; 80% of banks would be insolvent if all loan losses were written off.
Kenya (1993)	Significant	About 66% of loans of one third of the commercial banks were nonperforming. The local subsidiary of Meridien BIAO was closed in 1995 with little spillover.
Korea (Mid-1980s)	Significant	Nonperforming loans of deposit money banks rose significantly in the first half of the 1980s, exceeding 7% of total assets in 1986. The ratio of nonperforming loans to total assets declined subsequently to 0.9% in 1995.
Kuwait (Mid-1980s)	Crisis	There was a banking collapse associated with problems in the informal stock market. An estimated 40% of loans were nonperforming in 1986.
(1990–91)	Significant	A large part of the private sector's loan portfolio became nonperforming due to the loss of property and collateral.
Kyrgyz Republic (Ongoing)	Significant	Eighty to ninety percent of all loans are doubtful; 4 small commercial banks were closed in the past year and 2 large state banks are facing problems.
Lao People's Democratic Republic (Early 1990s)	Significant	Nonperforming loans dominated the portfolios of the state-owned commercial banks. In 1994, these banks were recapitalized and an injection of cash and bonds equivalent to 1.5% of GDP.
Latvia (1995–present)	Crisis	Two thirds of audited banks recorded losses in 1994. Eight bank licenses were revoked in 1994 and 15 more were revoked during the first seven months of 1995. The subsequent closure of the largest bank (with 30% of deposits) and two other major banks triggered a banking crisis in the spring of 1995.
Lebanon (1988–90)	Crisis	Four banks became insolvent; 11 banks had to resort to central bank lending.

Table A1.1 Cont.

Country	Type of problem	Measure of extent
Lesotho (1988–present)	Significant	Of 4 commercial banks, 1 that serves mostly the agricultural sector and has only a small share of bank assets has had a large portfolio of nonperforming loans. Banking services were disrupted for two months in 1991 owing to a strike.
Liberia (1991–95)	Crisis	Seven out of 11 banks are not operational; their assets were equivalent to 60% of total bank assets at mid-1995.
Lithuania (1995–present)	Crisis	Of 25 banks, 12 small ones are being liquidated and 4 larger ones do not meet the capital adequacy requirements. The fourth largest bank was closed. The operations of 2 banks, which accounted for 15% of deposits, were supported in 1995.
Macedonia, former Yugoslav Republic of (1993–94)	Crisis	Seventy percent of loans were nonperforming. The government took responsibility for banks' foreign debts and closed the second largest bank.
Madagascar (1988) (1991–95)	Significant Significant	Five major banks had nonperforming loans ranging from 45% to 75% of their portfolios. There were severe management problems in the 2 remaining state-owned banks. Loan losses resulted in reserve deficiencies and the need for substantial provisions in 1994.
Malaysia (1985–88)	Crisis	The largest domestic bank wrote off nonperforming loans equivalent to approximately 1.4% of GDP in 1983. Nonperforming loans were estimated at 32% of total loans in 1988.
Mali (1987–89) (1995)	Significant Significant	The largest bank was nearly illiquid, with 75% of its loans nonperforming; it was restructured in 1989 with equity injection and government loan guarantees. The government made an 'equity' loan to strengthen the capital of one bank following the collapse of Meridien Bank.
Mauritania (1991–93)	Significant	The Development Bank ceased operations and was liquidated in 1994; 3 of the 4 commercial banks required substantial recapitalization.
Mauritius		The central bank closed 2 of 12 commercial banks for fraud and other irregularities in 1996.
Mexico (1982) (1994–present)	Crisis Crisis	The government took over the troubled banking system. The ratio of nonperforming to total loans rose from 9% at the end of 1994 to 12% in December 1995. The authorities intervened in 2 banks in September 1994 and 4 of the remaining 35 banks (holding 17.5% of total end-1994 assets) in 1995.

Table A1.1 Cont.

Country	Type of problem	Measure of extent
		An additional 2 were taken under the administration of FOBAPROA (the deposit insurance agency). The overall cost of the several programs to support the banking system is estimated (in present value) at 6.5% of GDP.
Moldova (1994–present)	Significant	A significant stock of nonperforming assets has built up in most banks, largely resulting from earlier directed credits. Audits of the 4 largest banks will help quantify the extent of the problem.
Mongolia (1991–present)	Significant	Twenty-five percent of loans were nonperforming in 1995.
Mozambique (1988–93) (1994–95)	Significant Significant	Most of the loans outstanding at the end of 1988 were written off with central bank assistance. The 2 dominant state-owned banks became increasingly dependent on central bank support, pending privatization.
Myanmar (Ongoing)	Significant	The banking system is dominated by 4 state-owned commercial banks, the largest of which is experiencing heavy losses and has a large portfolio of nonperforming loans. The other state-owned banks are widely recognized to be undercapitalized, but information on the quality of these banks' portfolios is scarce.
Nepal (Late 1980s–present)	Significant	Official estimates indicate that nonperforming loans amount to between 10% and 15% of total loans in the two large public banks, which account for nearly 70% of total bank deposits.
Netherlands		Banks overcame problems with mortgage loans in the late 1970s.
New Zealand (1989–90)	Significant	Of 4 large banks, 1 that was state-owned and accounted for one fourth of banking assets required a capital injection of almost 1% of GDP because of bad loan problems.
Nicaragua (Late 1980s–present)	Significant	Two large state-owned banks have had long-standing financial problems. About 50% of loans are nonperforming.
Niger (1983–present)	Crisis	In the mid-1980s, 50% of loans were nonperforming. Four banks were liquidated and 3 restructured in the late 1980s. Reform was initiated in 1987–90, and the restructuring process is still under way.
Nigeria (1991–95)	Significant	In 1991, 77% of loans were nonperforming. Of 115 banks, 34, accounting for 10% of deposits, were technically insolvent at the end of 1994.

Table A1.1 Cont.

Country	Type of problem	Measure of extent
Norway (1987–93)	Crisis	Six percent of commercial bank loans were nonperforming. Heavy losses and insolvencies led to a crisis at the end of 1991. The government became the principal owner of the three largest banks, whose share of total commercial bank assets was approximately 85%.
Pakistan (1980–present)	Significant	Nonperforming loans are estimated to be 10% of bank assets.
Panama (1988–89)	Crisis	A bank holiday that lasted for nine weeks was declared in March 1988. As a result of uncertainty and loss of confidence caused by a political crisis, the public banks were particularly affected by a loss of deposits and a rapid deterioration in their loan portfolios that stemmed from poor lending decisions and the sharp contraction of the economy. The financial position of most commercial banks also weakened, and 15 banks ceased operations.
Papua New Guinea (1989–present)	Significant	A severe economic downturn in 1989 led sharp increases in loan losses at commercial banks. Eighty-five percent of the savings and loan associations ceased operations as a result of the economic problems, mismanagement, or fraud. The public lost confidence in the banking system and withdrew deposits in 1994.
Paraguay (1995–present)	Significant	The authorities intervened in institutions accounting for some 10% of financial system deposits during the summer of 1995. There have been interventions in 6 other financial institutions since then. Depositor restitution and operations to facilitate borrowing by distressed institutions cost an estimated 4% of GDP by the end of 1995.
Peru (1983–90)	Significant	Two large banks failed. There were high levels of nonperforming loans and financial disintermediation following nationalization of the banking system in 1987.
Philippines (1981–87)	Crisis	Banks accounting for 1.6% of banking system assets failed in 1981. Through the mid-1980s, a number of institutions failed or were taken over by government financial institutions. Nonperforming assets of two state-owned institutions were transferred to a government agency. These assets accounted for nearly 30% of total banking assets. In 1986, 19% of loans were nonperforming.
Poland (1991–present)	Significant	Sixteen percent loans were classified as losses, 22% as doubtful, and 24% as substandard in 1991.

Table A1.1 Cont.

Country	Type of problem	Measure of extent
Romania (1990–present)	Significant	Five major state-owned commercial banks had 35% of their accrued interest receivables overdue as of June 30, 1994.
Russia (1992–present)	Significant	Official estimates of loan arrears were 40% of total credit to the private sector at the end of 1995.
Rwanda (1991–present)	Significant	There is a substantial amount of nonperforming loans. One bank, with a well-established network, has been closed.
São Tomé and Principe (1980–present)	Crisis	Over 90% of loans of the monobank were nonperforming in 1992. In 1993, a new central bank began operations. The commercial and development departments of the former monobank were liquidated, as was the only other financial institution. At the same time, 2 new banks were licensed and took over many of the assets of their predecessors. The credit operations of one newly created bank have been suspended since the end of 1994.
Senegal (1983–88)	Crisis	In 1988, 50% of loans were nonperforming. Reform was implemented in 1988–91; 8 banks were liquidated and the remaining 8 were restructured.
Sierra Leone (1990–present)	Significant	In 1995, 40–50% of loans were nonperforming. Recapitalization and restructuring is ongoing. The license of one bank was suspended in 1994.
Singapore		Nonperforming loans at domestic commercial banks reached 0.6% of GDP in 1982.
Slovak Republic (1991–95)	Significant	Loans classified as nonstandard were high at the end of August 1995. There were no runs or major bank closures, but all 5 major banks required government-sponsored restructuring operations.
Slovenia (1992–94)	Significant	Three banks, with two thirds of banking system assets, were restructured during this period. The percentage of bad loans is not known. Bank rehabilitation was completed in 1995.
Somalia (1990)	Crisis	There were nonperforming claims on both private and public sector borrowers during the civil unrest.
South Africa (1985)	Crisis	Banks built up large short-term foreign liabilities owing to high domestic interest rates. When foreign banks began to reduce their exposure, in part owing to political factors, the exchange depreciation and liquidity squeeze on banks resulted in an official moratorium on external capital repayments.

Table A1.1 Cont.

Country	Type of problem	Measure of extent
South Africa (1989–present)		In 1989–90, one major bank, which held about 15% of banking assets, was recapitalized and reorganized after suffering loan losses and management problems. Since 1991, several small banks have been liquidated or put into curatorship, with no systemic repercussions.
Spain (1977–85)	Crisis	From 1978 through 1982, 110 banks, accounting for 20% of deposits, were rescued. In addition, in 1983 one group that controlled 100 enterprises and 20 banks was nationalized.
Sri Lanka (Early 1990s)	Significant	Thirty-five percent of the portfolios of the two state-owned commercial banks, which accounted for over 60% of banking system assets, were non-performing. In March 1993, bonds equivalent to 4.8% of GDP were issued to recapitalize these banks.
St. Vincent and the Grenadines (1994–present)	Significant	The only domestic bank is a state-owned commercial bank, which accounts for 30% of deposits. About 10% of its assets are nonperforming.
Sudan		Smaller banks are being encouraged to merge with larger banks to ensure compliance with the Basle capital standards before June 1997.
Swaziland (1995)	Significant	Meridien BIAO Swaziland was taken over by the central bank. The central bank also took over the Swaziland Development and Savings Bank (SDSB), which faced severe portfolio problems; the government is now expected to sign an agreement that will allow a foreign bank to take over the management of the SDSB.
Sweden (1990–93)	Crisis	Eighteen percent of total unconsolidated bank loans were reported lost and the two main banks were assisted.
Tajikistan (Ongoing)	Significant	One of the largest banks is insolvent; 1 small bank has been closed and another (out of 17) is in the process of liquidation.
Tanzania (1988–present)	Crisis	State-owned commercial banks, accounting for over 95% of the system, were insolvent. At the end of 1994, 60% of all loans were nonperforming and the losses of the largest bank were equivalent to 70% of deposits.
Thailand (1983–87)	Crisis	Fifteen percent of bank assets were nonperforming. There were runs during the crisis of 1983–85 and 15 finance companies failed. More than 25% of the financial system's assets were affected.

Table A1.1 Cont.

Country	Type of problem	Measure of extent
Togo (1989–91)	Significant	One of 10 commercial banks with 7% of bank credit was insolvent and liquidated and its credits were taken over by the government.
Trinidad and Tobago (Early 1982–93)	Significant	The banking sector expanded rapidly in the mid-1970s in a time of lax supervisory and prudential controls. With the onset of the general downturn in the economy in the early 1980s, some financial institutions experienced solvency problems, resulting in the merging of three government-owned banks in 1993 as an intermediate stage to the planned privatization of the merged bank.
Tunisia (1991–95)	Significant	Introduction of new loan classification and provisioning standards and capital adequacy requirements in 1991, coupled with extensive portfolio audits in 1992, made clear that most commercial banks were undercapitalized. (State-owned banks accounted for over 65% of total lending.) From 1991 to 1994, the banking system raised equity equivalent to 1.5% of GDP and made provisions equivalent to another 1.5%. Thus recapitalization through 1994 required at least 3% of GDP, and some banks remained under-capitalized; recapitalization continued through 1996.
Turkey (1982) (1991) (1994)	Crisis Crisis Significant	Several small banks and most brokerage houses collapsed. The start of the Persian Gulf war led to bank runs. Depositor runs in the spring of 1994 resulted in the closure of 3 medium-sized banks. To stem further runs, the government introduced full deposit insurance in May 1994.
Uganda (1990–present)	Significant	A small bank failed in early 1993. Several other banks are in difficulty or insolvent, including state-owned banks accounting for more than 40% of banking system assets.
Ukraine (1994–present)	Significant	In 1994, many banks did not meet capital and other prudential requirements. Audits indicated that one of the five largest banks was insolvent. Approximately 30% of loans outstanding were in arrears. The authorities intervened at 20 small to medium-sized banks in 1995.
United Kingdom[3]		No systemic problems, but several notable bank failures, including Johnson Matthey (1984), Bank of Credit and Commerce International (1991), and Barings (1995), have occurred.

Table A1.1 Cont.

Country	Type of problem	Measure of extent
United States (1980–92)	Significant	During the period, 1,142 savings and loan (S&L) associations and 1,395 banks were closed; 4.1% of commercial bank loans were nonperforming in 1987.
Uruguay (1981–85)	Crisis	Eleven percent of loans were nonperforming in 1982; 59% in 1986.
Uzbekistan (1993–present)	Significant	Almost 10% of loans were reported to be overdue in October 1995.
Venezuela (1994–present)	Crisis	In 1993, before the crisis started, 8.5% of loans were reported as nonperforming. The authorities intervened in 13 of 47 banks, which held 50% of deposits, in 1994, and 5 additional banks in 1995. Support by the government and the central bank to the banking system amounted to almost 17% of GDP in 1994–95.
Vietnam (Ongoing)	Significant	State-owned banks are widely recognized to be undercapitalized, but information on the quality of their portfolios remains scarce.
Yemen Arab Republic (Ongoing)	Significant	Banks have extensive nonperforming loans and heavy foreign currency exposure.
Zaire (1991–present)	Significant	Four state-owned banks are insolvent; a fifth bank is to be recapitalized with private participation.
Zambia (1994–present)	Significant	One of the largest commercial banks, the local Meridien BIAO subsidiary, failed in early 1995 and received official support equivalent to approximately 1.5% of GDP. Two small banks failed in late 1995, and several others are fragile.
Zimbabwe (1995–present)	Significant	Two of the 5 commercial banks are unable to meet their statutory reserve requirements owing to a high percentage of nonperforming loans.

[1] Under 'Problems', a blank space indicates that there was a problem but that it was neither 'significant' nor a 'crisis'. Years in parentheses denote the period of banking problems.
[2] In 1995, fraud resulted in major losses and depositor runs at two institutions in Taiwan Province of China; one was taken over by a state-owned bank and the other supported by the central bank and a state-owned bank. The large state-owned banks are reported to have an overhang of bad loans to real estate projects.
[3] From 1982–86, 16 Hong Kong banks and other deposit-taking institutions failed, were liquidated, or were taken over. The closure of the BCCI subsidiary in Hong Kong in 1991 led to minor runs on several local banks.

Source: C.-J. Lindgren, G. Garcia and M. I. Saal (1996), *Bank Soundness and Macroeconomic Policy* (Washington, DC: International Monetary Fund). (Reproduced by kind permission of the International Monetary Fund.)

Table A1.2 The impact of bank unsoundness on the real sector[1]

Argentina (1980–82): Interest rate spreads were high. Credit and payments systems were disrupted. Growth was reduced after the 1980–82 crisis. There was a substantial redistribution of wealth in favor of debtors.
(1995): The sharp growth in real GDP following convertibility was reversed to a recession in 1995.

Bangladesh (1980s–present): Spreads are wide and reduce intermediation.

Bolivia (1986–87): High interest rates and heightened caution on the part of liquid banks limited the access of small businesses to credit.

Brazil (1994–present): High interest rates and increased caution on the part of the banking system limited access to credit.

Chile (1981–87): Growth was reduced from an average of 8% a year in the five years before the crisis to 1% in the five years after it. The payments system was disrupted.

Czech Republic (1991–present): There were high spreads between domestic deposits and loan rates and between rates on domestic and foreign funds. High levels of nonperforming loans reduced banks' ability to extend credit.

Egypt (1991–95): Interest rate spreads were high.

Estonia (1992–95): There was already a severe recession before the banking crisis occurred; it is not clear whether the banking problems exacerbated the downturn.

Finland (1991–94): Growth averaged 4.5% in the three years before 1990, zero for 1990, and –4.0% in the following three years. Unemployment reached a peak of 18.4% in 1994.

France (1991–95): No apparent impact.

Ghana (1983–89): Low levels of intermediation, inadequate resource mobilization, and a large stock of nonperforming assets reduced banks' flexibility to lend to new customers. Favorable returns on risk-free investments also discouraged lending. Economic growth fell from 3% in the five years before the crisis to 2.5% in the three years after it.

Hungary (1987–present): Stabilization and growth were impeded. Despite enacting bankruptcy legislation, enterprise restructuring was hampered by inadequate reforms to bank lending policies.

Indonesia (1992–present): High spreads led to disintermediation and a growth in nonbank financial institutions.

Japan (1992–present): Weak bank balance sheets have tended to undermine public confidence and may have limited the speed of economic recovery. Loan rates rose relative to funding costs.

Kazakstan (1991–95): Real interest rates became positive. A lack of competition and perceived weakness in the banking system induced very high interest rate spreads.

Kuwait (1990–91): Banks' hesitancy to lend and uncertain domestic investment prospects reduced growth.

Latvia (1995–present): There was a decline in economic activity, but it was not as sharp as the 20% decline observed in the monetary aggregates.

Lithuania (1995–present): There was a credit crunch, especially in the agricultural and energy sectors.

Table A1.2 Cont.

Malaysia (1985–88): A secondary mortgage market to aid bank liquidity was established. The crisis caused high real interest rates as banks increased their margins to cover the cost of their nonperforming loans. This contributed to disintermediation and impeded investment.

Mexico (1994–present): Real interest rates are high and are affecting the repayment capacity of borrowers. It is estimated that credit to the private sector declined by about 20% in real terms during 1995.

Norway (1987–93): Growth fell from an average of 3.2% in the five years before the crisis to 1.7% in the two years after it, but not solely as a result of the banking crisis.

Pakistan (1980–present): High interest rates and credit shortages for the private sector diminish investment and growth.

Paraguay (1995–present): There was a flight to qualify, reducing the availability of bank funding. Economic growth slowed toward the end of 1995 owing in part to the disruptive effects of the banking problems.

Philippines (1981–87): Real interest rates rose and there was a recession and a credit crunch. Growth fell from an average of 6% a year in the five years before the crisis to − 1.25% in the following five years.

Poland (1991–present): Lending to enterprises was viewed as risky and banks preferred to lend to the government. Thus financing to the real sector declined sharply from 1991 to 1993. Banks raised interest rate spreads in an attempt to earn their way out of trouble.

Russia (1992–present): The weak banking system has not mobilized savings efficiently and has a limited ability to intermediate savings to private sector investors. Banks have focused on short-term investments in foreign exchange and government securities.

Spain (1977–85): Financial intermediation costs rose (both interest margins and operating expenses), imposing an increased burden on enterprises.

Sweden (1990–93): Small borrowers complained of high interest rates and restricted access to credit. There was an economic downturn, but it is difficult to separate the effects of the banking crisis from those of the currency crisis and the broader European recession.

Tanzania (1988–present): The cash-based economy has hindered growth. There is little intermediation. The deposit-to-GDP ratio declined from 1980–88 and much of those funds that were available were misallocated. The payments system is slow.

Thailand (1983–87): Bank spreads fell, and there was a sharp decline in finance company loans to the private sector. The effects are difficult to gauge but growth slowed in 1984–85.

Turkey (1994): Real rates are high and a flight to quality and tiering have occurred. Responding to a number of factors, output contracted sharply in 1994, but recovered quickly in 1995.

United States (1980–92): The real estate markets in several areas of the country experienced a cutback in credit supplies as a result of the problems in the thrift industry, which may have contributed to the decline in property prices in the early 1990s. The credit crunch arising from weak bank capitalization slowed recovery from the 1990–92 recession.

Table A1.2 Cont.

Venezuela (1994–present): Interest rates turned sharply negative following the reintroduction of exchange controls; nevertheless, the fall in imports disrupted production. The demand for credit remaining strong.

Zambia (1994–present): The wealth effect of deposit losses diminished demand and growth. There was a credit crunch for some borrowers, but intermediation in general and the payments system were not impaired.

[1] Years in parentheses denote the period of banking problems.

Source: C.-J. Lindgren, G. Garcia and M. I. Saal (1996), *Bank Soundness and Macroeconomic Policy* (Washington, DC: International Monetary Fund). (Reproduced by kind permission of the International Monetary Fund.)

Table A1.3 Summary of banking problems for country groupings

Country group	'Crisis' (#%)(1)		'Significant' problems (#%)(2)		Other problems (#%)(3)		(1)+(2)+(3) (#%)		No problems reported (#%)		Total number
Industrial countries	4	17	12	52	2	9	18	78	5	22	23
Developing countries (without twenty-two mini states)	33 (32)	20 (23)	86 (82)	53 (59)	4 (3)	2 (2)	123 (117)	76 (84)	38 (22)	24 (16)	161 (139)
Emerging markets	10	63	5	31	1	1	16	100	0	0	16
Transition economies	4	17	19	79	0	0	23	96	1	4	24
Oil exporters	1	8	2	15	0	0	3	23	10	77	13
ALL COUNTRIES	37	20	98	53	6	3	141	77	43	23	184

Notes: Total number of countries (184) is larger than that reported in Lindgren et al. (1996) since we added Hong Kong, North Korea and Taiwan – which are not full IMF members – as independent countries

Emerging markets: Argentina, Brazil, China, Hong Kong, Indonesia, Korea (South), Malaysia, Mexico, Philippines, Singapore, South Africa, Taiwan, Thailand, Turkey, Venezuela

Transition economies: Albania, Armenia, Azerbeijan, Belarus, Bulgaria, Croatia, Czech Republic, Estonia, Georgia, Hungary, Kazakstan, Kyrgyz Republic, Latvia, Lithuania, Moldova, Poland, Romania, Russian Federation, Slovak Republic, Slovenia, Tajikistan, Turkmenistan, Ukraine, Uzbekistan

Oil exporters (IMF definition): Algeria, Indonesia, Iran, Iraq, Kuwait, Libya, Nigeria, Oman, Qatar, Saudi Arabia, Syria, United Arab Emirates, Venezuela

Sources: IMF (1996), Lindgren et al. (1996), own calculations

Table A1.4 Deficiencies in internal governance[1]

Agentina (1980–82): Banks knew little about their clients and allowed speculative and distress borrowing. Accounting was weak.
(1989–90): Portfolios were not diversified, and banks lent heavily to the public sector. Public sector banks were inefficient and had very high levels of employment. Accounting was still weak. Banking was subject to political direction.
(1995): State banks were still weak. Banks were not diversified or automated and they made a large share of their loans in dollars. Accounting improved only in 1994.

Bangladesh (1980s–present): There is poor corporate governance with weak accountability and extensive insider lending. State-owned banks that account for two-thirds of deposits have very weak management and accounting systems. Political interference in lending occurred throughout the period.

Bolivia (1994–present): Troubled banks have several problems: concentrated ownership, extensive insider and related-party lending, weak internal controls, a lack of a clear division of internal responsibilities, low efficiency, and high costs.

Brazil (1994–present): Management was poor at some state banks that were not run on a commercial basis. The same applied to some private banks that did not diversify risks well. Some banks did not adjust quickly to the postinflationary environment.

Chile (1981–86): Banks were undercapitalized with respect to their historic averages. Loans to controlled companies were used to finance speculative asset purchases. From 1980, there was a sharp increase in 'distress borrowing', rolling over bad loans, and capitalizing interest due.

Czech Republic (1991–present): Banks are inefficient and overstaffed, and shareholders exert pressure to obtain preferential terms. Some small banks funded their loans in the overnight interbank market.

Egypt (1991–95): Domination of banking activities by 4 state-owned commercial banks is a problem.

Estonia (1992–95): Banks were not diversified and extended insider loans to owners. Credit-assessment skills were undeveloped and banks had weak accounting systems and inadequate classification and provisioning systems for bad debts.

Finland (1991–94): Banks had low capital, were not diversified, and engaged in aggressive, concentrated lending. Management focused on gaining market share rather than on risk analysis. Corporate lending to a large extent was in foreign currency. Auditing was lax.

France (1991–95): Internal controls have improved markedly in recent years and are broadly appropriate, although increased separation of back-office operations is still desirable. More generally, state shareholding in several banks (e.g. Crédit Lyonnais) poses specific problems.

Ghana (1983–89): Inadequate management, information, and internal control systems led to high operating expenses and even fraud. Loan losses were not recognized. There was no uniform system of asset classification or provisioning. Accounting standards were not uniform or were inappropriate.

Hungary (1987–present): Fraud occurred at 2 failed banks. Banks have too many branches and are overstaffed. There is adverse selection of borrowers at state-owned banks.

Indonesia (1992–present): State banks have been poorly managed in the past and have been subject to political interference. Industrial ownership of private banks

Table A1.4 Cont.

---

has sometimes led to intragroup lending in excess of the legal limits on large exposures.

Japan (1992–present): The main bank system has led to selected lending. Accounting systems and internal controls were weak at some banks (e.g., Daiwa Bank). Banks' financial technology lagged behind their growth. They were not diversified, made inadequate provisions for problem loans, and grew rapidly in a quest for market share.

Kazakstan (1991–95): Management has no clear strategy. Speculation in foreign exchange produced profits but banks have no concept of how to grant and manage credits. Loans are rolled over and interest is capitalized. Lending is often concentrated or extended to related parties.

Kuwait (1990–91): Internal governance appears to have been adequate.

Latvia (1995–present): Risk-assessment skills are lacking; management is poor and accounting systems are weak. Major problems have been high foreign exchange exposure, insider lending, and fraud.

Lithuania (1995–present): The country's banks suffered from political interference in lending, inherited from Soviet times. Management is poor at state-controlled banks and private banks alike. In some cases, shareholders have seriously misused their rights.

Malaysia (1985–88): Banks were often under family control. Some smaller institutions lacked a code of ethics, internal controls, audit committees, and Chinese walls, so that fraud occurred. Institutions engaging in new activities (such as finance companies) often lacked professional expertise and fast growth overstretched their managerial resources. Risks increased rapidly (the loan-to-deposit ratio reached 90%) and distress borrowing was permitted. Management was not used to dealing with bad loans in an expanding, inflationary economy.

Mexico (1994–present): After many years of nationalized banking (from 1982 to mid-1992), commercial banks lacked the experience and organizational and information systems to adequately assess credit and other market risks and to monitor and collect loans. Accounting practices did not follow international standards. Concentration of loans and loans to related parties was a problem in those banks that were subsequently subject to official intervention.

Norway (1987–93): There were problems with high leverage, fast and concentrated growth in risky assets (especially in real estate), and lax auditing.

Pakistan (1980–present): State ownership has been a problem – state banks have been subject to political pressure to lend and to withhold debt-recovery efforts. Political interference in lending and weak collection have hurt banks.

Paraguay (1995–present): Insider lending and risk concentration was high and there was excessive illegal (off the books) deposit taking by banks.

Philippines (1981–87): There were weak banking and accounting practices and portfolios were not diversified. State banks owned 36% of banking assets. Commercial ownership through groups was high, leading to connected lending, interlocking directorships, and excessive risk taking.

Poland (1991–present): Political interference has occurred at some state banks. Banks were overstaffed and had poor management and information systems. New accounting standards were introduced in 1995.

Table A1.4 Cont.

Russia (1992–present): Weak internal controls and management practices have contributed to falling profitability and fraud. Accounting standards are weak. The central bank has introduced improved reporting requirements but the underlying chart of accounts is inadequate.

Spain (1977–85): Banks were not diversified, and credit was politically directed, which discouraged the development of credit-evaluation skills. Accounting was not consolidated.

Sweden (1990–93): Loan administration was poor and systems for credit monitoring were lacking. Pricing did not adequately reflect risk. There was an overdue concentration of bank portfolios on real estate, and competition to lend to the real estate sector was destructive.

Tanzania (1988–present): Management and internal controls at state banks were weak. These banks were inefficient, overstaffed, and not run for profit. There was political interference in bank structure and lending for most of the period from 1967 to 1994. Accounting, auditing, reporting, and credit assessment were weak.

Thailand (1983–87): Banks were run by a few families, who were not professional bankers. Management weaknesses were pronounced especially at finance and securities companies. Ownership was concentrated, with little outside shareholder discipline. Internal controls were inadequate and there was heavy insider lending and high expenditure on banks' offices. Accounting was weak.

Turkey (1994): Industrial owners of banks pressured for subsidized loans. Accounts were not adjusted for inflation. There were deficiencies in risk analysis and risk management especially regarding foreign positions, leading to speculation. Banks had poor (unaudited) information on their borrowers. Banks are overstaffed and overbranched. There has been fast growth, especially in the off-balance-sheet activities.

United States (1980–92): In general, management and internal controls were inadequate at the banks that survived, but they were seriously deficient at many banks and thrifts that failed. Savings-and-loan regulators encouraged 'phoney' accounting to hide net worth deficiencies. There was also political interference in lending in the thrift industry. Accounting even at banks ignored off-balance-sheet activities until the late 1980s and was slow to acknowledge the importance of market valuation.

Venezuela (1994–present): Banks had inefficient operations with high costs and extensive branch networks and offshore operations. There was weak accounting, extensive insider lending, and rampant fraud.

Zambia (1994–present): Banks had weak management and internal controls. They engaged in risky activities, including derivatives, and experienced very fast growth (assets quadrupled in two years). There has been political interference in banking, and incentives for performance at the large state bank are weak.

[1] Years in parentheses denote the period of banking problems.

Source: C.-J. Lindgren, G. Garcia and M. I. Saal (1996), *Bank Soundness and Macroeconomic Policy* (Washington, DC: International Monetary Fund). (Reproduced by kind permission of the International Monetary Fund.)

2 Barings and the need to recast the form of external regulation in developed countries

In the past, regulatory objectives have been achieved largely by regulators' external imposition of certain required common (one-rule-fits-all) ratios on the regulated. Here we discuss why this approach to regulation may need recasting, at least in developed financial systems.[1]

The main regulatory problems in *developing* countries are still mostly the traditional ones, involving undue credit risk, lack of appropriate diversification, connected lending, politically directed lending, etc. The standard approach to such credit risks, developed over recent decades, involves inspection of banks' loan books and a requirement for adequate capital as a protection against non-performing and impaired loans, and it remains an appropriate approach, although it is often difficult to enforce in circumstances of weak external auditing and volatile macroeconomic conditions.

In some emerging countries the potential role for regulation and supervision may be circumscribed by a lack of skilled personnel and the comparatively great political influence of the main indigenous financial institutions (see also Chapter 6). There may also be problems with standards of accounting and auditing, and therefore also with the transparency and accuracy of the available data on the condition of financial entities. As a result, there is a general need for higher standards among regulators, the regulated and accountants, as well as in the legal infrastructure (see, for example, *The Economist*, 1997a; Goldstein, 1997). The most efficient ways of achieving this are addressed at greater length in Chapter 6.

In the *industrialised* countries, however, financial developments have led to shifts in bank business. With the credit ratings of larger non-financial companies rising relative to those of banks (owing in part to the capital erosion suffered by banks, until that was reversed by the Basle Accord of 1988), the relative market share of bank financing has tended to fall.[2] Instead, non-financial companies have been directly accessing capital markets. Meanwhile, partly in order to economise on scarce capital, banks have been increasingly securitising other parts of their previous loan book, notably mortgages.

So banks have been shifting from their role as direct intermediaries, taking and holding borrowers' loans on their own books, into acting as expert facilitators in arranging the financing needs of their clients, in large part via capital market operations. These market operations have involved, and required, trading in derivative markets, in order to obtain the best available balance of risk and return for banks' clients and for themselves. This has led to a manifold expansion in the market trading activities of the larger banks in industrialised countries, relative to their original function of pure intermediation. The globalisation of financial markets and the continuing interpenetration of multinationals have also led to the major banks being represented in, and acting on, financial centres and markets around the world.

These trends have had several consequences. First, the dividing line between commercial banks and investment banks has become increasingly blurred, and now hardly exists.[3] (The dividing line between banking and insurance remains clearer, but is also beginning to erode under the pressure of competition.) Second, the complexity of banks' business has increased, and the legal, operational and geographical structure of banks has also become more complicated.[4] Third, the greater use of derivatives and off-balance-sheet positions has made the use of occasional (e.g. monthly) balance sheet data less reliable as a guide to the bank's state of health (over the next few succeeding weeks).

For all these reasons, external regulation, both in its regulatory mode of seeking to lay down, *ex cathedra*, common rules and ratios that all banks should follow, and in its supervisory/monitoring mode of checking whether banks are complying with the rules, is becoming both less effective and less feasible.[5] This is nicely stated by the BIS (1997: 151):

> Given the greater reach and vigour of market forces, in implementing policies *diktat* increasingly had to give way to inducement. Markets could not be told what to do, they had to be given good reasons for doing it. Hence the progressive shift towards transparency and attention to incentives and credibility.

Although the Barings failure produced the standard reaction among (less informed) observers that supervision needed to be increased and improved, among the more perspicacious commentators, and among most of the supervisors themselves, and certainly among most practitioners, the lesson that was drawn was that the *external* regulation required to prevent such cases of fraud (when it had escaped internal management) would have had to be so pervasive, so intrusive and so expensive as to be practically impossible. The Barings failure arose from poor internal monitoring and supervision, not from a failure of regulation. The problems included a lack of internal control systems, the failure of management to monitor its staff, the failure of the bank to enforce its own rules, and insufficient mechanisms for effective monitoring or supervision.[6] Indeed, we would argue that the majority of so-called regulatory failures are actually failures of *internal* monitoring and supervision.

There is really no alternative to placing the primary responsibility for risk control on internal management, and on its auditors. The major banks in industrialised countries, with large trading books, need to shift their emphasis towards the reinforcement of internal managerial risk-control mechanisms, and the nature and functions of external regulation must be turned away from generalised rule setting and towards establishing incentives/sanctions to reinforce internal control mechanisms.[7] The incentives/sanctions should include disclosure requirements and fiduciary rules for internal management (i.e. rules establishing the responsibilities of directors, managers, and legal advisers).[8]

This may lead to a divergence between the focus and needs of the regulatory authorities in emerging and transitional countries, who need to enforce the old, traditional lessons of credit control and properly diversified and arm's-length lending, and those of the authorities in more industrialised countries, who are beginning to experiment with placing more reliance on the new techniques of internal risk control, and are encouraging good practice in these new fields. These techniques (e.g. VaRs, pre-commitment and credit derivatives) are the main subject of Chapter 5, but at present these techniques are really only used by, and therefore relevant to, the larger multinational banks with sizeable trading desks.

The problem for regulators is that the complexity and speed of adjustment make the application of common external rules to multinationals increasingly suboptimal. The objective, instead, is to reinforce and monitor internal mechanisms of managerial self-control, but there are several difficulties with this approach. The first is that managers'/owners' self-interest does not exactly square with the regulators' objectives; otherwise, the regulators could encourage best practice and then leave control to a combination of transparency, market pressures and internal risk control (as is true in New Zealand now, at least in theory, since in practice most banks there are subject to consolidated supervision elsewhere).

The second major difficulty for the supervisors is that they are working in the context of national laws and regulations, whereas the core institutions of their financial systems are now mainly global in coverage. This is a central concern of the Group of Thirty Report (1977: 12) which states that:

> Even with full understanding of these new challenges and the best of intentions to address them, supervisors find themselves hemmed in by national legislative mandates and agency practices, often based on a sectoral approach. They face political constraints arising from the issues of the moment when legislation is drafted. Such legislation may compel supervisors to act in a fashion which is unnecessarily at odds with the market unless they receive specific legislative authority to change the way they do business.
>
> So cooperation among national and functional supervisory agencies alone is unlikely to produce adequate oversight of global institutions on the time scale that the problem demands. As new issues arise, each supervisor will adopt its own reporting requirements to deal with them. Not only will

reporting vary from country to country as it has in the past, but it may also be inconsistent with the practices of private managements and markets.

Given differences in national structures, history, culture, interests and viewpoints, any international harmonisation will inevitably be a compromise; and like most compromises, it probably will be both unsatisfactory (from the outset) and simultaneously difficult to amend in the light of changing circumstances (see, for example, Scott, 1992). This suggests that the formulation and application of 'standards' might be better assigned to private sector institutions, as has now indeed been advocated by the G-30 Report;[9] but that raises again the question of what (credible) sanctions could be imposed (for backsliding) by self-regulating practitioners without having self-regulating practitioners' organisations become anti-competitive and detrimental to the wider public interest. (We discuss the issue of the proper structure of international regulation in Chapter 8, Section D.)

The third main difficulty is that internal risk-control mechanisms, however technically advanced, cannot be any more reliable than the humans who manipulate them (for a variety of personal ends). Even if the objectives of the financial institution as an entity matched exactly those of the regulators, and its risk-control models were state of the art, the outcome would still depend on the validity of the data being input, and on the understanding and appropriate use of such techniques by management. Barings is understood to have had an excellent VaR model in operation. Both Barings and Daiwa suffered mostly from failure to enforce the oldest and most essential control mechanism: the separation of front and back offices. Technical expertise cannot offset or prevent human failings.[10]

So, the main issue for supervision remains the culture of internal management, rather than its technical sophistication. But how do you measure culture? Since assessment of culture is inevitably a subjective judgement, how can discretionary differential penalties be imposed on the basis of subjective judgements? In an increasingly litigious world, any such imposed penalties may be met by legal challenge. (Everybody may have 'known' that BCCI had a shady reputation, but the Bank of England needed some objective proof before it could be closed.) Discretion and confidentiality may offer some help in imposing differential sanctions on the basis of subjective judgements: the commercial banks involved may submit to sanctions if – and only if – they are kept confidential.[11] As Bisignano (1997) has noted:

> An important aspect of institutional behaviour and operating and normative rules which can at times secure and later undermine survival is information disclosure. Limited disclosure can be used to protect a firm's managers against competition, against takeover, against shareholders and creditors and even regulators.

Various procedures, processes and structures can help to reinforce internal risk-control mechanisms. Internal auditors, internal audit committees and procedures for reporting to senior management, and perhaps to supervisors, can and should be introduced. Supervisors can help to strengthen internal procedures by relating the frequency and scale of their external supervision to the perceived adequacy of the internal control mechanisms (see Chapter 3).[12]

Given the divergence between private and social costs, external regulation also needs to set some (genuinely) *minimum* standards, which should not impinge on the average (well-run) firm, but which will help guard against the unusually incompetent/risk-loving/optimistic. There should remain some independent external oversight to ensure that there are some *ex ante* checks on self-assessment. In other words, there should be driving tests as well as traffic cops (who come in only *after* offences have happened) but we must accept that driving tests cannot be expected to eliminate all accidents.

There is also always the problem of the appropriate sanctions when something goes wrong. Almost by definition, internal management (and external supervision) will have failed. But when is management culpable, and to what degree? Given the limitless range of failure scenarios, it is hardly possible to set down any objective guidelines. For example, when someone new comes into an audit, or a compliance, or a risk-control position, at what exact moment does he or she become fully responsible for all revealed problems?

Whatever the fascination with quasi-objective risk models, the core of the supervisory process will always be primarily concerned with human qualities, both of the regulated and of the regulator. A difficulty is that the role of supervisor is not glamorous, either in commercial firms or among the authorities. In contrast to the glamour of a 'star' trader, the supervisor/auditor is usually paid far less, and when the star misbehaves, the supervisor is almost as likely to be sacked for not preventing the star from undertaking his or her misdeeds.

How, then, will we get sufficiently qualified and motivated people to take on the auditing/compliance role? Again, regulators can help by calibrating the external burden of regulation, e.g. number of visits, frequency of forms, perhaps the range of business permitted, etc., to the perceived quality of the managers charged with risk control within each regulated entity. That would help to demonstrate to top management the tangible value of good internal risk-control personnel and procedures. Such differentiation entails, however, a risk for the external regulators. There are bound to be publicised control failures in entities whose internal regulatory processes were designated good, and which were, therefore, more lightly regulated. That could bring derision, as well as obloquy, down on the heads of the external regulators.

Borrowing from Gilbert and Sullivan, it can be said that the position of an external regulator is not a happy one. He or she can hope at best to be ignored, at worst reviled. Like a dentist, the regulator knows that clients enter fearful and usually are relieved to leave their conferences. To attract well-qualified people to this unpleasant job, regulators' salaries must be set at a proper market rate. What else can be done to maintain the morale of the regulators? Although confidentiality makes possible their successes, these successes still need to be publicised, in order to offset the natural tendency for only their 'failures' to be noticed.

Even so, the built-in tendency is for external regulators to draw unto themselves a poor reputation, since their failures are overt while their successes are covert, is a factor that central banks need to keep in mind during discussions of the appropriate structure of regulation. (We turn to this topic again in our penultimate chapter, Chapter 8.)

3 Incentive structures for financial regulation

Parliaments enact laws, regulators interpret and enforce them through directives and regulations, and supervisors act to prevent financial institutions (especially banks) from taking undue risk. These laws, regulations and supervisory actions provide incentives for the regulated to adjust their own actions and responses, sometimes in the desired manner, sometimes not (an example of the latter being the moral hazard induced by 100 per cent deposit insurance without risk-adjusted premiums, which provides a 'free' put option on deposit insurance funds (Merton, 1977) or, ultimately, on taxpayers' money).

Indeed, laws and regulations can be seen as *contracts*.[1] If they are well designed, they induce bank managers to act in ways that will avoid or reduce systemic risk without (or with little) unintended side-effects on the financial system as a whole. If they are improperly designed, they may fail to reduce systemic risk or have undesirable side-effects on the process of financial intermediation; for example, excessively high, risk-unrelated capital ratios would constrain lending and hence real investment. It is therefore essential that the regulatory contracts anticipate the likely responses of banks and steer them towards the socially desirable solution where systemic risk or the likely payouts of the deposit insurance fund are kept low.[2]

Similarly, we may ask whether there are appropriate incentives for the regulators themselves to adopt well-designed rules when governments – or rather voters (taxpayers) – have less information on the state of the financial system (and the risks involved) than the regulators.

Several economic agents (such as bank owners and managers, depositors, financial regulators, etc.) are involved in the process of financial intermediation, and their actions affect the incidence of systemic risk. This chapter looks at the interactions between these groups and how their interactions affect the effectiveness and efficiency of financial regulation. Whether the different parties involved have the right incentives to act in a socially desirable way is the central issue.

A crucial feature of this analysis is that the behaviour of every agent must be regarded as responsive to the regulatory framework (i.e. 'endogenous' in economists' jargon). This in turn should feed back into the optimal design of regulatory rules. An implicit underlying assumption is that *pure* market forces alone, provided by depositors' choices, are not sufficient to avoid systemic risk or large deposit insurance fund losses. Without a safety net, banks are subject to contagious runs; with full deposit insurance for small depositors and implicit 'too big to fail' guarantees, creditors have little, or at least reduced, incentive to monitor borrowers. It is for these reasons that regulators act on behalf of society (including depositors) to limit excessive risk taking (see Chapter 1).

Until recently, financial regulation was primarily *externally imposed* upon the regulated, as described in Chapter 2. While much external regulation will remain, the increasing complexity of operation and speed of (portfolio) adjustment among financial institutions make it less satisfactory. This raises the question of how a shift from external regulation to internal self-regulation, reinforced by appropriate incentive structures, is to be managed. Although it is now common practice in many industrial countries to invite comments by the financial industry on planned changes in regulatory regimes, nevertheless the regulators (in conjunction with the government) have always had the last say.

For all these reasons, the weight given to the external regulatory mode, at least in the industrialised countries with the most developed financial markets, has recently been declining, and internal managerial control has increasingly become the first, and the most important, protection against imprudent or improper actions and positions. In view of the growing importance of internal control mechanisms, it must be asked whether there are structures that can be put in place to reinforce the incentives for all the parties involved (notably management, but also the auditors and the regulators/supervisors) to limit improper behaviour, excessive risk and systemic instability.

The difficulty and complexity of regulation arise from the fact that each of the parties (e.g. regulator, financial intermediary, borrower, saver) has different knowledge of (i.e. asymmetric information on) their own and the other agents' motives, actions and positions. For example, to what extent can depositors or regulators know the risk-taking behaviour of bank managers? Or, if regulators can observe the portfolio risks of a bank only imperfectly, is it nonetheless possible to introduce regulations that keep systemic risk low?

The distribution of information among the parties involved is affected greatly by technical progress in the financial sector. Computer capacities increase, financial instruments become more numerous and more complex, and it becomes ever more easy to transfer funds across borders. In particular, the risks involved in many financial transactions, like derivatives, become more and more complex and require more and more sophisticated risk management techniques (Chapter 5).

Under these circumstances, traditional accounting practices are too slow and too inaccurate to trace the changes in banks' net worth, leading to an exacerbation of asymmetric information. Hence the ability of external regulators to observe and to control the financial risks taken by other agents may be decreasing. We begin, therefore, with a sketch of the incentive issues raised by asymmetric information. The next section looks at incentives for the regulated, while the following section analyses incentives for the regulators.

A. Principal–agent relations and contracts between the regulators and the regulated

Consider financial intermediaries that accept deposits from households, firms and other financial institutions and invest in loan and trading portfolios in order to make a profit. The business of banking is to manage the risks involved in these activities. However, when making their optimal portfolio choices, managers selecting the optimal risk–return combination for their particular institution do not take the potential social costs of spillovers (contagion) of their own potential failure into account. Financial regulators – the principals – aim to establish a system that limits systemic risk by supervising the risk taking behaviour of single institutions – the agents.[3] As shown above, this principal–agent relationship between the regulators and the regulated is *hierarchical*, since regulators are entitled by law to interfere in banking through directives and rules and, if necessary, direct intervention to ensure the stability of the financial system.

(i) Adverse selection and moral hazard

Regulators face at least three information problems in performing their task. First, they do not know with precision the quality of banks' internal risk management capabilities, such as market experience and financial engineering skills, beforehand. Second, once they have put regulations in place they cannot perfectly observe how far the regulated adhere to the rules imposed. Finally, apart from the quality of their own risk management techniques and the efforts internal managers put into keeping portfolio risks under control, even under the most prudent business practices, there will always be some residual risk. When a regulator learns that an institution has problems, he or she does not always know with certainty whether they are due to one of the first two factors or to residual risk.

The quality of risk management techniques in place differs between financial institutions. A regional savings and loan institution may have less advanced systems than a global investment bank, for example. Nonetheless, both institutions' portfolio value varies with interest rate risk. Should they be regulated in the same way? We argue that one rule cannot fit all cases. Institutions with better techniques can be relied upon more than those with more imprecise techniques. For example, to achieve a given portfolio risk, the minimum capital requirement for the former can be lower than that for the latter. The banking supervisor can accommodate this by offering a *menu of regulatory contracts*, rather than the same regulation for all institutions.

The difficulty is that a supervisor cannot always know whether the risk management of a particular institution is in fact of sufficient quality to merit the less costly option. The supervisor can solve this problem either by examining its risk management systems or by letting the institution choose its contract from the menu. If the contracts have the right incentives, then the regulated bank will *self-select* into the appropriate category and thereby truthfully reveal its risk management type. Of course, a priori all institutions would like to choose the low-capital scheme; bad risk managers would like to mimic good risk managers. How can the regulator prevent an *adverse selection*, in which even bad risk managers self-select into the high-quality/ low-cost contract (a *pooling equilibrium* in the language of economists)?

Consider, for example, regulations to limit portfolio risk arising from interest rate fluctuations. The regulator could include a clause in the high-quality regulation package that a bank has to provide back-testing results on its interest rate risk management techniques and that, if the precision of its model is low (i.e. the realised losses turn out to exceed the predicted losses), minimum regulatory capital would increase automatically. If the expected capital penalty schedule is sufficiently steep, a rational banker with low risk management abilities will self-select into high-risk regulation (i.e. the banker must expect to end up with more capital after penalties in the low-risk contract than he or she would have had by choosing the adequate high-risk contract right away). A menu-cum-incentives approach amounts to (quality) *screening* of bank risk managers.[4]

A closely related, but conceptually distinct, principal–agent problem is *moral hazard*. After the adoption of regulatory rules ('signing' of the regulatory contract) and at given risk management abilities, circumstances might materialise that incite bankers to take on larger risks than the maximum ones compatible with regulations – even though it was optimal *ex ante* to accept the rules. Look at the following example. A bank's bond trader has made an error (or has had bad luck) and has incurred a large loss. If the trader reveals this loss to his or her superior, the trader risks being fired. Therefore, the trader decides to 'gamble on resurrection' by hiding the loss and by taking on positions more aggressively in order to recover the initial loss. If the trader continues losing money and internal controls fail, he or she might even bring down the whole bank, as happened to Barings in February 1995 (Board of Banking Supervision, Bank of England, 1995).[5] This situation can arise even when it has been optimal for the employee to commit to adhering to the regulations and related internal control mechanisms *ex ante*.

The same incentive, to hide a really large loss, may exist for a financial intermediary as an entity, raising some general questions of how to design an incentive structure and sanctions that will encourage firms to confess to the regulator their mistakes/errors/losses, when such confession will of itself have immediate and serious consequences for the firm.

Such a commitment may be *time inconsistent* (Kydland and Prescott, 1977). The *ex ante* incentives to commit can be different from the *ex post* incentives to adhere, once something unexpected happens (Williamson, 1985). Time-inconsistency often leads to implicit or explicit 'renegotiation' of the regulatory contract. We return to this issue in Section B.

(ii) Pay structures, time-inconsistency and internal controls

Agents do not abide by established control procedures if it is not in their own perceived interest to do so. In particular, if the pay-off from their actions makes it in their own self-interest to assume risk, they tend to do so, no matter what the rule book may lay down.[6]

Figure 3.1 Pay-off structure indicating risk

Figure 3.2 Pay-off structure indicating caution

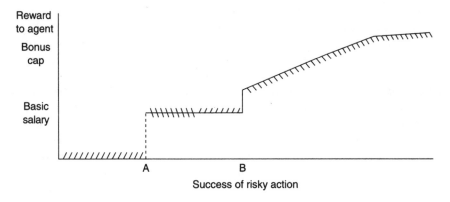

Figure 3.3 Typical pay structure

If the pay-off relating the agent's reward to the success of the risky action being taken by that agent follows the curve shown in Figure 3.1, agents will wish to assume greater risk, since the downside risk is less than the potential upside gain. Equivalently, if the curve is reversed, as in Figure 3.2, agents will be induced to be risk averse.

Therefore, all concerned with risk avoidance (internal or external) must be aware of circumstances where agents who make decisions affecting the institution's assumption of risk face a pay-off structure like that in Figure 3.1. For example, this is well understood in the case of capital adequacy. Limited liability means that owners face no extra penalty once equity vanishes. So the return to equity owners looks like that shown in Figure 3.1, and the nearer owners are to the zero equity point, the greater the incentive to gamble on resurrection.

What is not so well understood is that the typical *pay* structure often incorporates several elements that also rationally will cause some agents to wish at some points to assume risk and at others to avoid it. Assume that an agent can influence the outcome by his or her actions and that the agent's pay is related to the outcome, which can be measured. If the outcome is bad enough, say to the left of point A in Figure 3.3, the agent may be fired. The agent will also, therefore, gamble on resurrection. Any agent doing badly enough to face a serious risk of being sacked will become a risk-lover.

Next, a bonus payment is usually not made until some minimum (good) outcome is reached, and often it is a minimum lump-sum payment, as shown at point B in Figure 3.3. Clearly, in the area below B, the agent will be risk loving. Finally, bonus payments often are capped, to avoid embarrassing payouts (which may disturb internal relativities). As the agent nears the cap (or goes beyond it) he or she will become increasingly risk averse; alternatively, agents may use various strategies for shifting accounting profits from one year to another. Outcomes generating risk-seeking behaviour are marked with ///, and those that are risk avoiding are marked \\\ in Figure 3.3.

The influence of capital adequacy on risk-seeking behaviour is understood by most people, and the consequential rationale for external regulators to enforce (graduated) additional controls over financial institutions with insufficient capital is generally accepted. The isomorphism of the pay structure's effect on risk-seeking behaviour is generally not well understood,[7] and internal management shows little willingness to allow external regulators to have any say in the matter. Indeed, the internal committees and groups that examine risk, and its control, within firms virtually never consider internal pay structures. Equivalently, the (personnel) committees and groups within companies that decide on remuneration virtually never consider, or discuss, the implications of what they are doing for risk-seeking behaviour.

(iii) Signalling, delegation and incentive contracts

Of course, it is impossible for the regulator to control completely and continuously banks' or bank employees' adherence to prudent practices. If regulators behave as if any bank, or any bank employee, might offend at any time, regulation becomes impossibly expensive for both regulators and banks. For example, frequent on-site examinations by the supervisors would be very costly. How could a bank *signal* to its regulators that its internal control systems can prevent employees from acting in detrimental ways, as described above?[8]

One signal is industry standards of best practice, as issued by professional organisations and industry bodies, such as national banking associations, the Group of Thirty (1993), the International Swap and Derivatives Association (ISDA) and the International Securities Markets Association (ISMA). These bodies might also issue guidelines and award risk-control 'trademarks'. Of course, a disadvantage of *self-regulatory* mechanisms is the potential for anti-competitive behaviour (i.e., members of the 'club' might prevent entry of outsiders or they might impose constraints on price setting by insiders).

Industry standards also raise the question of possible sanctions by the issuing body and their legal basis. The recent Group of Thirty (1997a) Study Group Report attempts to overcome this problem by proposing the involvement of regulatory bodies in a new *standing committee* – developing uniform global principles for managing risks in large transnational banks.

The relationship between regulators and banks is ongoing, not 'one shot'. By acting prudently on a continuous basis a bank can build up a positive *reputation vis-à-vis* the regulator. Acting imprudently for a short period might be penalised by increased regulatory intrusion over a longer period of time. For example, the Securites and Futures Authority (SFA), the main regulatory body for UK securities trading firms, fine tunes the number and intensity of on-site examinations to the past behaviour of each institution (Hedges, 1997).

If the SFA has been satisfied by internal controls in the past, it reduces the number of visits. When it discovers problems, the number of visits is increased. US bank regulators have also developed similar risk-adjusted examination schedules (King and O'Brien, 1991).

In its recent consultative paper on RATE (Risk Assessment, Tools of Supervision and Evaluation), the Bank of England (1997) signalled similar intentions for the future.[9] A question asked by that paper is whether and how quantitative (capital ratios etc.) and qualitative (organisation, management culture, etc.) indicators of risk-control quality (including bonus schemes!) could be merged into a single risk scale, say between 1 and 10, which then would translate into more or less intrusive on-site examinations. The SFA already applies a risk rating, with scores varying between 1 and 5.

A bank might also offer a *contract* to the regulator, pre-committing that internal controls will be enforced, that banking or trading book losses will not exceed certain thresholds, and that staff will adhere to conduct of business rules. In order to give the right incentives (to avoid excessive risks) and be credible (i.e. in order to be *incentive compatible*) such a contract should predetermine regulatory interventions and penalties based on *ex post verifiable* events showing the violations of pre-commitments.

This particular solution to asymmetric information problems in banks' adherence to risk regulations is relatively new and is somewhat unusual for financial regulation. A recent proposal (Kupiec and O'Brien, 1995a, 1997b), which has been prominent in the discussion, applies this principle to capital requirements for market risks. This pre-commitment approach is related to the recent progress in market risk management techniques, and therefore it is discussed in greater depth in a separate chapter (Chapter 5).

A bank's reputation and credibility with respect to risk controls may be further improved by means of internal or external *delegation*. It might appoint an internal audit committee. Banks in the City of London, for example, appoint compliance officers for this task, as required by the Financial Services Act. The organisation of the internal auditing function is primarily an issue in corporate governance, and governance structures vary from country to country.[10] The key is to have those responsible for the internal audit function report to a person or a small committee who are independent of the CEO but who have enough seniority and weight to force the CEO to respond to any issues brought to his or her attention. This enables ultimate authority for internal regulatory issues to be identified, so that the locus of responsibility internally is clear. If the internal chain of command and locus of responsibility are clear, then there is no good reason to force internal auditors to report to external supervisors as well, since having to make any such reports will distort the internal auditing function.[11]

The external auditors may also report on the adequacy of the control procedures, and of (potential) failures in their implementation, although the auditors' legal and professional obligations differ from country to country and sometimes between financial institutions (e.g. between banks and non-banks) even in the same country. They report primarily and initially to the company that they are auditing. Questions regularly arise, however, whether and when external auditors should report to the supervisors/regulators, which auditors should report, and what should be reported. This is a large and sensitive subject (as is the legal responsibility, if any, of the auditors for failing to spot control failures). These important questions are a major issue in accounting (and law), but not questions on which economics, *per se*, can help much. So we leave these questions, in full awareness that they deserve much more attention (by others).

If internal management is party to the control failure (fraud?) or unaware of it (negligence?), it will usually be very difficult for external supervisors (or external auditors) to detect it. It is always easier to establish whether the appropriate procedures, rule books and committees are in place, than to see whether the spirit of the procedures is being followed. If the supervisor develops suspicions, or has suspicious circumstances pointed out by others, there must be some mechanism for following up these suspicions. The supervisor may commission a special investigation by an external auditor, who may be the institution's regular external auditor.

The obvious difficulties for external regulators and auditors (in detecting control failures that internal management is either trying to cover up or is simply unaware of) have not stopped much of the press or the creditors damaged by such failures from blaming the regulators and auditors. *Ex post facto*, there will be claims that there was much (semi-public) knowledge of the problems involved. It will be asked whether the supervisors were warned, and, if so, what steps they took. Another question will be, even if they were not specifically warned, should they have known anyway?

B. Forbearance and pre-commitment on closure

Regulatory authorities are agents of governments and, therefore, ultimately of the citizens (or voters) whose wealth may be put at risk in a financial crisis. In general, people with considerable experience and a reputation for stringency should be appointed to this task, because diligent and tough regulators will influence expectations appropriately in the financial sector. If the likelihood of being punished is high, bankers will have stronger incentives to keep their internal controls in good shape.

(i) How serious is regulatory forbearance?

However, is the *ex ante* optimal choice of persons and rules time consistent? What happens if a major bank in a country comes into difficulties (e.g. Crédit Lyonnais in France)? Is it always sensible for regulators to stick to the original rules, to impose stringent measures on the bank, and finally to close it down, especially if there are some prospects of bringing it back to profitability (and there usually are)? A lot of other factors can influence regulatory decisions directly or indirectly. The deposit insurance fund might not have enough resources to reimburse the losses of all depositors affected. The government might already be struggling with a large budget deficit or face elections soon. The disappearance of a large financial institution might weaken the country's status as an important international financial centre. Revelation of a major problem might also entail the public reputation of senior regulators and lead to demands for personal penalties. These are only a few examples; the spectrum of possible factors is wide.[12]

The presence of such considerations can lead to *forbearance*, instead of prompt and stringent action.[13] That does not mean that regulators or other public officials are dishonest or are intentionally misleading the public. However, they may be exposed to pressures from the political or financial sector to deviate from the *ex ante* optimal responses to financial difficulties. In particular, incentives to delay intervention and disclosure can be strong. If the political costs of prompt and rigorous action are high, then it might be easier to avoid early disclosure, to provide the required liquidity to an individual bank, and to hope that it finds its way back to solvency and profitability. By doing this, the regulator implicitly or explicitly enters into a form of *renegotiation* of the originally optimal contract. The likelihood of success can be enhanced by making forbearance and liquidity provisions conditional on certain internal measures taken by the bank.

However, when a relatively quick recovery cannot be achieved, the regulator and the bank(s) may become more and more mutually dependent. The bankers need continued liquidity assistance and confidentiality in order to avoid bankruptcy and the loss of their jobs. If the strategy of forbearance is not successful, the total costs of the failure to the public may well be increased. For example, the additional injections of liquid funds may be lost, and the bank may sink deeper into the mire of its loan losses. As this happens, it may become increasingly difficult for the authorities to reveal the problem, to close the bank, and to realise the losses at the expense of the taxpayer. Both parties can become increasingly 'locked in'.[14] The renegotiation can continue for some time, until either the bank is finally saved or the losses have become so big that they cannot be hidden from the public any more.

The real concern about this is, perhaps, less with the isolated occurrence of such events than with the fact that financial markets are, of course, aware of time-inconsistency and credibility problems. This knowledge will enter into financial markets' expectations about forbearance and public bail-outs, which in turn implies a reduction of incentives to set up better internal controls, itself increasing the likelihood of financial distress. Some credit agencies' practice of giving a counterparty risk score to debtors as well as publishing a rating of the likelihood of public bail-outs in certain countries illustrates the impact of potential forbearance on financial market expectations.

But forbearance is not necessarily wrong. Eisenbeis and Horvitz (1994) set out a number of arguments in favour of forbearance. First, immediate closure of either one large bank or several smaller banks in difficulties might entail *systemic consequences*, which can be more costly than supporting problem cases for a limited period of time and bringing them back to solvency. Second, in some circumstances the forced liquidation, the *fire sale*, of a whole bank (or its assets separately) may earn less than its actual franchise value.[15] Third, certain bank assets may be worth more under the current management than under other banks' management or regulatory administration (*going-concern value*). Fourth, empirical research has shown that bankruptcy costs amount to an important share of liquidated assets, which might be saved with a successful forbearance policy.[16] If one or all of these aspects are important enough, then the benefits of forbearance could outweigh its costs.

Important crises where regulatory forbearance and postponement of intervention have played a role are the US Savings and Loans crisis (1983–5), Banesto in Spain (1993), Crédit Lyonnais in France (1995–today), Banespa in Brazil (1994), and the Japanese banking crisis (1991–today).[17] The more difficult question is whether these and other cases of forbearance have done harm, as reflected by the debate on the US Savings and Loans crisis. For example, DeGennaro and Thomson (1996) claim that forbearance in that episode cost US taxpayers about $16 billion, whereas White (1991: 141) argued that earlier intervention 'could not have saved large sums', and Benston and Carhill (1992) even stated that waiting was on balance beneficial, because of the subsequent rise in US interest rates. However, Crédit Lyonnais and the jusen problem seem to be viewed widely as very costly for the French and Japanese taxpayers respectively.

A final answer on the success of forbearance policies can probably never be given for at least two reasons. First, cost–benefit analyses will always be limited to *ex post* quantifications, but have little to say about whether forbearance was likely to succeed *ex ante* (see Chapter 4). Also, the number of observed financial crises is too low to get any statistically significant results. Moreover, in contrast to the highly publicised major financial failures mentioned above, cases where regulators have used their discretion in adapting to the particular circumstances more successfully remain largely unreported. Hence, so long as these cases remain confidential, estimates of the relative costs and benefits of forbearance will have low power and will be biased in favour of a negative judgement (Quinn, 1996a: 4).

(ii) Accountability

There is a built-in negative bias in the public's assessment of supervisory skills. Supervisory failures have to become public, but supervisory successes in averting crises often have to remain secret, at least for a time. This situation highlights the difficulty of reinforcing transparency and accountability for the regulators while accommodating the confidentiality of their work.

One possible approach is for the external supervisory authority to report on what it is trying to achieve, and on its successes and failures, to an independent person or body with sufficient seniority and weight to force the regulator's CEO to respond to its concerns.[18] The report should *not* be made public at the time. Although publication does violate confidentiality, our view is that such reports *should* be published after an appropriate lag time. But what is an appropriate lag time? Early public reporting raises behavioural and confidentiality difficulties, while delayed publication misses the mark.[19] Is there a solution to this difficult problem?

(iii) Prompt corrective action provisions

Assuming that the previous examples of unsuccessful forbearance provide a presumption against it, what are the possible ways to overcome time-inconsistency in financial regulation? Again, part of the answer is given in the previous section:

1 The regulatory authorities could build up a *reputation* for tough supervision by acting promptly and stringently in any case of financial problems. This would appropriately influence financial market expectations.[20]
2 *Delegation* is already common practice. Governments themselves do not supervise financial institutions, since they would be much too vulnerable to short-term political considerations. However, financial regulators are usually less independent from the government than monetary policy makers. Giving both autonomy in monetary policy (i.e. to set interest rates) and supervisory responsibility to an independent central bank might be viewed as giving too much power to an unelected body (see the discussion in Chapter 8). In several countries with relatively independent central banks, for example, regulatory agencies are separated from the monetary authority and often subordinate to the Ministry of Finance (Goodhart and Schoenmaker, 1995b: 544).
3 Formulating rules for regulatory reactions in the form of an *incentive contract* is again relatively rare.[21]

However, there are examples of more *rules-based regulation*. The most far reaching and now best known is the US Federal Deposit Insurance Corporation Improvement Act (FDICIA, 1991; Mann and Ellis, 1993; Kaufman, 1994). The FDICIA links the intensity of supervision to the capitalisation of banks. Table 3.1 summarises the five capital zones and the related *prompt corrective action* provisions as stipulated by the Act. Although this *ladder of graduated responses* is based on the crude Basle capital ratios for credit risk, it has the potential to enhance the credibility of regulatory intervention.

A second innovative element of the Act is the requirement that bank failures be resolved on a 'least-cost basis' for the deposit insurance fund, unless it threatens to trigger a payment system breakdown, in which case the FDIC and the Fed may recommend a more costly solution.[22] Clearly, this new regulation has been shaped by the lessons drawn from the US Savings and Loans crisis, in particular the forbearance involved.

Table 3.1 Summary of prompt corrective action provisions of the Federal Deposit Insurance Corporation Improvement Act 1991

Zone	Mandatory provisions	Discretionary provisions	Capital ratios (%)		
			Risk based		Leverage
			Total	Tier 1	Tier 1
1 Well capitalised			>10	>6	>5
2 Adequately capitalised	1 No brokered deposits, except with FDIC approval		>8	>4	>4
3 Undercapitalised	1 Suspend dividends and management 2 Require capital restoration plan 3 Restrict asset growth 4 Approval required for acquisitions, branching and new activities 5 No brokered deposits	1 Order recapitalisation 2 Restrict interaffiliate transactions 3 Restrict deposit interest rates 4 Restrict certain other activities 5 Any other action that would better carry out prompt corrective action	<8	<4	<4
4 Significantly undercapitalised	1 Same as for zone 3 2 Order recapitalisation[1] 3 Restrict interaffiliate transactions[1] 4 Restrict deposit interest rates[1] 5 Pay of officers restricted	1 Any zone 3 discretionary actions 2 Conservatorship or receivership if fails to submit or implement plan or recapitalise pursuant to order 3 Any other zone 5 provision, if such action is necessary to carry out prompt corrective action	<6	<3	<3
5 Critically undercapitalised	1 Same as for zone 4 2 Receiver/conservator within ninety days[1] 3 Receiver if still in zone 5 four quarters after becoming critically undercapitalised 4 Suspend payments on subordinated debt[1] 5 Restrict certain other activities				<2

[1] Not required if primary supervisor determines action would not serve purpose of prompt corrective action or if certain other conditions are met
Source: Board of Governors of the Federal Reserve System

In a similar reaction to the current Japanese banking difficulties, a study group set up by the Japanese Ministry of Finance (MoF) issued an interim report in December 1996 (Wolfe, 1997) that proposed a prompt corrective action schedule, similar to the FDICIA, with three capital zones. A revised version of this provisional framework could be introduced, as part of the Japanese 'Big Bang', by April 1998 (Ministry of Finance Japan, 1997).

Besides the role of capital in limiting risk-seeking behaviour and gambling for redemption, the greater the capital, the less the likelihood of insolvency for a given expected risk. For both reasons the less the remaining capital, the greater the danger. But there cannot be a single point value above which the financial institution is safe, and below which it must be closed. Clearly, danger increases gradually as capital diminishes. That fact by itself implies that there should be a graduated series of responses from the external authorities as capital diminishes. Beyond that, the fact that any dividing line (say the 8 per cent minimum level of the Basle Committee) is arbitrary makes it undesirable to put too much weight on any one number. It is preferable to have a series of dividing lines, with the effect of passing through any one of them relatively minor, but the cumulative effect large. In this respect the principle of the graduated sequence of responses in FDICIA seems right.

Regulators often argue that establishing a pre-defined sequence of responses to worsening capital positions involves the application of rules to them. They claim that in practice they do apply a sequential and graduated response to capital impairment, but because their response is discretionary, it can be tailored to each specific case (and all cases differ). There are several arguments that can be made on both sides (e.g. if the response is to be graduated, the present 8 per cent starting point is already probably too low). Our own prejudice in this area is that there is a good general argument that pre-commitment and rules are normally advantageous.[23]

But if an external regulator feels very strongly about a particular case, the regulator should be allowed to override the pre-commitment. However, both the justification for, and perhaps even the existence of, such an override may need to be kept confidential, for obvious reasons. How, then, can one prevent the external regulator from effectively just exercising discretionary control? Our answer is that a report and justification would have to be made to the independent overseeing body, again with full publication after an appropriate lag. Or, in the words of Williamson (1985): 'The contract has to be extended by delegation and independence in its own enforcement'.

(iv) Size and 'too big to fail'

Forbearance is most commonly observed when a really large, or core, bank runs into difficulties, and thus seems to benefit the larger banks most. But most really big financial intermediaries, especially the major banks, believe that regulation primarily benefits their smaller competitors.

The overt reason for this view is that the larger intermediaries are inherently likely to be better diversified and to have more capital to ride out idiosyncratic shocks, such as fraudulent traders (Sumitomo survived; Barings fell). So the largest institutions have less need for external regulation and supervision, whereas the costs of such regulation are, almost invariably, applied pro rata to the deposit base. Complaint is loudest when banks are asked to finance their own deposit insurance scheme. The largest banks will claim that pro rata financing implies cross-subsidisation of smaller banks. It is, however, not necessarily the case that larger banks are more stable than smaller banks; the crisis caused by the effective default on LDC loans in 1982 affected the larger banks more severely than the small ones.

The covert reason why large banks feel that regulation benefits them less is because they believe that their size makes them 'too big to fail' in any case. They have precedents on their side. The experience of Continental Illinois in the United States in 1984, the effective guarantee given to all the City Banks in Japan, Crédit Lyonnais in France, etc., all demonstrate that no national authority is prepared to allow the dissolution of any of its major national banks; it will allow a change in ownership, certainly, and, if necessary, public ownership, as in Scandinavia, but not bankruptcy and liquidation. The practical reality of 'too big to fail' provides much of the basis of counterparty credit rating. Financial institutions judge each other on the likelihood of their central banks (Ministries of Finance) allowing them to default on their debts, at least as much as, or more than, on an assessment of their innate balance sheet strength. Like it or not, the doctrine of too big to fail is perceived as a central plank of the current financial system.

This doctrine has shortcomings: a conservatively managed small bank may well be rated a worse credit risk than an aggressive large bank. Medium-sized banks, especially those foreseeing troubled times ahead, have an incentive to expand their balance sheets, in order to join the protected group of behemoths. The largest banks, believing in their own invulnerability, have an incentive to expand risky activities (LDC debt? OTC derivative trading?). As noted previously, a possible remedy is pre-commitment.

(v) Idiosyncratic v. systemic shocks and incentives for herding

Economists also argue that it may be worth making a distinction between those circumstances where the erosion of capital arose because of the idiosyncratic behaviour of the institution's managers and where it came about because of a generally adverse market movement (Dewatripont and Tirole, 1994; Nagarajan and Sealey, 1995). The argument is straightforward. Where the loss has been caused by a manager's individual decision, the manager is considerably to blame, no matter whether the decision was taken due to a lack of effort, lack of skill, or willingness to take on excessive risk. When the loss is caused by a general market movement, it is not really the manager's fault. Since one purpose of the system of capital adequacy requirements is to provide an incentive for good managerial behaviour, it makes sense to penalise more severely a loss caused by managerial failings.

A problem with this argument is that in circumstances when the market as a whole has been falling, there is greater likelihood of systemic failure. A 'credit crunch' initiated by a maintained application of unrelaxed capital adequacy requirements, following market declines, can intensify the downturn. Next, a policy that relaxes prudential requirements in response to general market movements may reinforce the *herding* tendency. If a banker is to be penalised more when a loss occurs just in the banker's own institution than when every bank makes a similar loss, then herding will seem safer and more attractive. External regulation should encourage diversification in behaviour, and it should check the tendency to herding, since herding worsens systemic risk.

In general, the adverse effect of idiosyncratic loss, as contrasted with a general condition of losses to all members of the group, already has severe effects on the reputation, future income, and employment prospects of the individual agent. It is doubtful that much would be gained by loading the scales further towards herding (and away from individual experimentation) by distinguishing in the regulatory framework between idiosyncratic and market losses. Moreover, it would often be difficult for regulators to make this distinction or to give quantitative calibration even if they could.

Obviously, some exogenous shocks to the financial system are so extreme, and/or unpredictable, that no sensible government would refrain from some form of direct assistance. The outbreak of war in August 1914 was one such case; the LDC crisis in 1982 was very likely a second; a major earthquake in a metropolitan centre would be a third. It is not possible both to run an efficient financial system in normal times and to ensure that financial intermediaries have sufficient capital and reserves to survive such extreme outlying events. Moreover, it is impossible to assess the statistical probability of such extreme outliers.

C. Conclusions

This chapter includes suggestions for improving the incentive structure of the regulatory system. Some of the suggestions are speculative and controversial, while others are already generally accepted. The suggestions/proposals are:

1 Differentiate between the restrictiveness and the degree of intrusion of regulations and supervision according to the relative portfolio risk and internal control mechanisms of financial institutions (menu approach).

2 Ensure that appropriate sanctions are applied to internal management which allows failures of control to occur.

3 Require large financial institutions to establish an internal audit system.

4 Require the internal audit committee of such financial institutions to

signify that it has considered the implications of the risk preferences of key personnel and their pay structures.

5 Establish an analogous internal audit committee for the supervisors themselves. The supervisors should report regularly to the committee, and their reports should be published.

6 Establish a pre-committed graduated series of responses in the face of capital erosion. The responses could be overridden by the authorities, but the override would need to be specifically justified in the report to the independent audit body, and that report would be published.

7 In the graduated response, do *not* try to distinguish between losses caused by idiosyncratic developments and losses caused by general market developments.

8 Decide what market movements are so extreme as to merit government support to withstand them. Require banks to hold sufficient capital to meet shocks up to this limit in stress tests of proprietary models.

4 Proportionality

A. A tendency towards overregulation?

In Chapter 3 we discussed how regulation generates incentives for agents to act in different ways. In this chapter we discuss how the manner in which regulation is applied, by administrative fiat rather than through market pricing mechanisms, influences the various agents, the public, their government representatives, the regulators, and the regulated to demand and to supply regulatory services.

Regulation is not usually supplied through a market mechanism; therefore, the consumer is unable either to signal what is required or to indicate how much he or she is prepared to pay for the benefits of regulation. This is the first hazard of the absence of a market in regulatory services: a major loss of information both about what extent of regulation the consumer demands and about how much the consumer is prepared to pay. The second hazard is that the impression is created that regulation is a free good, and the latter hazard is likely to give rise to excessive regulation, especially if the regulator's own self-interest and reputation are at stake.

This non-price administrative mechanism and its attendant tendency to result in excessive regulation make the burden (costs at the margin) of regulatory compliance exceed the benefits. Generally, when the regulated review the impact of regulation, their perception of disproportionate cost in relation to the likely benefits of regulation is the heart of their concern.

The main problem, however, in trying to move towards better proportionality between costs and benefits is that it is very difficult to measure either, but especially benefits. (We discuss this in Section B below.) In particular, cases of successful forestalment of financial fragility (a benefit of regulation) often cannot be publicised because of the need for continuing confidentiality. Critics contend, however, that confidentiality is used to hide incompetence, or worse. How, then, in a field where confidentiality and discretion are (regarded by most as) so important, can the proper accountability of regulators still be maintained? (This is the subject of Section C.)

As noted here, efficiency and accountability in the provision of most goods and services is brought about through the operation of market forces.

Although the structure and form of regulation generally preclude the use of the pricing mechanism, might it be possible to make more use of ersatz or quasi-pricing mechanisms? (This is the subject of Section D.)

(i) Is regulation treated as a free good?

Within the private sector, normal market mechanisms generally induce efficient behaviour. Under most circumstances, production will expand only to the point where marginal revenues are greater than or equal to marginal cost, and not beyond. So long as private costs equal social costs (i.e. there are few externalities) and there is sufficient competition (and symmetric information), then the private market mechanism should lead to efficient outcomes.

The same tendency does *not* hold when actions are driven by non-market forces, and especially when the agency supplying a good or service itself has its own interests to consider. So, even when externalities, monopoly, asymmetric information, etc., cause some extent of market failure, it needs to be balanced against the inefficiencies that direct (public sector) intervention into market processes is likely to engender. Whether such costs of 'regulatory inefficiencies' exceed the costs of the market failures that regulation is designed to alleviate is moot. In this area, ignorance abounds, since: (1) it is difficult to quantify the costs of the original market failure; (2) we do not know enough about the impact of regulation and how its benefits can be measured; and (3) the costs of regulatory inefficiencies need to be incorporated into the overall calculations.

Financial regulation and supervision are prone to such inefficiencies. In particular, the public are generally unaware of the costs of the regulatory system. Large movements in the costs of borrowing (and returns on saving) are generally due to highly visible macroeconomic events (e.g. administered changes in base interest rates). By contrast, the actual cost of intermediation itself, i.e. as measured by the spread between depositing and borrowing rates, usually varies little over time and is often treated as an institutional (and historically determined) markup. Within that spread, the cost of compliance with regulation and supervision amounts to no more than a few basis points, widely diffused over all customers of financial intermediaries. In the absence of much, or any, direct information on the small, and quite stable, costs thereby falling on them, customers are usually unaware that the regulatory regime imposes any costs at all.

So, for the majority of clients of financial intermediaries, financial regulation appears to be a free good. It provides benefits both directly, by preventing losses, and indirectly, by eliminating the need for diligence in checking out the reputation and solvency of the regulated firms. Customers' perception is that it is impossible to have too much of a free good, and the free good has obviously been insufficiently provided if they lose money owing to the misbehaviour of intermediaries (in contrast to losing money as a result of market developments whose effects on the customers' funds were specified and understood in advance). Inevitably, under such circumstances, the injured clients call for more and improved regulation and supervision; and such public pressure is naturally transmitted to government representatives (viz. the Treasury Committee 1996 Report on Barings[1]). After all, the potential benefits of extra regulation/supervision are patent, and the costs are nearly indiscernible.

Of course, consumers do not demand regulation only because it appears to be a free good, but they demand more regulation than they would if they appreciated its true costs, and, without market pricing, we cannot know how much they would scale back their demand. There is, therefore, a potential for regulation to be overdemanded and oversupplied.

Under the influence of public pressure, regulators and supervisors have a clear incentive to try to avoid, or to avoid taking responsibility for, market failures, while at the same time trying to ensure that the costs of additional regulation/supervision are fully met by others, usually the private sector. The effect of any major bankruptcy, wherever any misbehaviour on the part of the failing institution itself can be demonstrated, is vilification of the supervisors involved.[2] Inevitably, there will be a twin tendency towards both excessive regulation/supervision (the buck may stop here, but the costs fall elsewhere) and forbearance (i.e. a delay in grasping the nettle of resolving dangerous situations by an action that will crystallise current losses – as is described in Chapter 3). Even if the expected present value of future losses may well be raised by forbearance, those costs may fall on the heads of others; and, if not, one might as well be hanged for a sheep as for a lamb. The incentive to gamble on resurrection may infect supervisors as well as supervised when their (reputational) capital erodes. As noted previously, supervisors are at constant risk of obloquy, but the risk is rarely compensated for in their pay packets, and there is little incentive for the most-qualified people to take on the job.

Of all the players in the regulatory arena, those who feel the costs and burdens of intervention most keenly are the financial intermediaries. They must complete the forms, change their business practices and submit the reports, and they have to find and hire the (skilled) personnel to do so.[3] The practitioners are the main source of complaint about excessive intervention, and the main pressure group for the attempt to establish reasonable proportionality between costs and benefits.[4]

(ii) Regulatory arbitrage as a counterbalance

Of course, financial intermediaries will pass on most of the costs of intervention in the form of higher spreads. (Economic analysis of the determinants of how much can be passed on to customers, in contrast to being absorbed in lower profits, is outside our scope here.) Because all intermediaries face similar regulatory costs, their comparative competitive positions are not adversely affected. So, the greatest complaints about the financial burden of intervention occur when institutions face competition from others under a lighter, less burdensome regulatory regime. This is particularly marked in international competition, but it also happens when separately regulated intermediaries compete in overlapping market segments within countries.

Even if there is competitive neutrality between institutions, however, regulated institutions may still lose business to the capital market. Put another way, regulation of financial intermediaries may be seen as an implicit subsidy to primary capital markets. This is not necessarily unwarranted; indeed, it is justified if the regulation is efficient. It is of no concern if banks lose business to markets because regulation forced them to pay the full costs of their activity, including potential externalities like systemic costs. An analogy is a steel company complaining that anti-pollution regulation is likely to put it out of business because it cannot afford to change its production techniques.

Such competition in regulatory regimes does cause problems both for regulators and for legislators, who otherwise normally treat regulation as a free good. If authorities lose market share, and financial institutions emigrate to another jurisdiction, regulators' potential tax base, as well as their power base, will shrink. So, the natural tendency to overregulate is held in check by fears of losing market share. Regulators naturally deplore the potential erosion of their power, and denigrate it with the phrase 'the rush to the bottom', implying that the result of such competition will be grossly insufficient public regulation. It is, however, rarely demonstrated that an informed public and practitioners prefer to operate in an insufficiently regulated milieu; competition between regimes does not necessarily result in a complete absence of regulation. Indeed, if there is consumer demand for regulation, then it is likely that less-regulated centres will lose business, resulting in an industry demand for tighter regulation. As Coase (1988), has shown, minimisation of transactions costs generally requires considerable self-regulation, and the public sector can play a useful role as an impartial arbiter of conflicting interests and a provider of credible and equitable sanctions.

Some academic liberals have seen such regulatory arbitrage as intrinsically beneficial, since they tend to believe that no regulation is the best regulation (see Dowd, 1996b; Benston and Kaufman, 1996; Kane, 1997[5]). For a well-balanced assessment, see Herring (1997) and Herring and Litan (1995). This position implicitly, or explicitly, denies that externalities, and/or other sources of market failure, can be so serious as to match such inefficiencies as are caused by public regulatory intervention. Of course, this position is often asserted, rather than demonstrated. Moreover, it is a position that is usually rejected by the public, at least in the aftermath of crises, even when, or perhaps especially when, supervisory failings have been (partially) to blame. This may be, as noted above, because the public treat regulation, mistakenly, as a free good, and if it is the case, then the free-market liberals must first educate the public and their politicians about the relative costs and benefits of regulation.[6]

B. Cost–benefit analysis?

How can a proper proportionality between the benefits and the costs of financial regulation be achieved? Theoretically, the answer lies within cost–benefit analysis, which is notoriously difficult to complete successfully in practice, not least in the financial sector.[7] This is true primarily because it is difficult to quantify the *benefits* of regulation and supervision.

At least the costs are fairly concrete. Given that the potential distortions of financial regulation are due mostly to the widespread view of its being a free good, one might have expected more (commissioned) studies of the costs of financial regulation and supervision. In fact, there are relatively few such studies, among which are Franks and Schaefer (1993)[8] and Lomax (1987). Most countries have reasonably good data on the direct costs of the regulatory bodies themselves, but few data on the, probably much larger, secondary costs of the extra burden that regulation imposes on the regulated financial intermediaries. A major difficulty in the latter calculations is distinguishing between the activities that financial intermediaries would have undertaken anyway for their own risk control and internal governance, and the *additional* work that the regulatory regime imposes (above and beyond what they would have done for themselves). There is no good objective way to estimate the additional work, and financial intermediaries may have a tendency, and possibly an incentive, to exaggerate it. In any case, what firms will do for their own internal risk control and governance is greatly influenced by the prevailing views about proper behaviour, which will also have shaped the regulatory regime. Hence any estimate of the additional cost of public sector regulatory intervention to financial intermediaries (and to the economy in general) will have wide margins of error.

Indeed, a broader definition of costs would include distortions to portfolios and to behaviour (e.g. as caused by mispricing deposit insurance) by (ill-designed) regulation itself. This broader definition suggests the possibility of considerably larger costs, but their estimation remains controversial, as was indicated in the discussion of the cost of forbearance for S&Ls.

That said, much more could be done, and needs to be done, to identify and to quantify costs. How do they relate to the average spread? If costs are translated into basis points, how much is the average user of financial services paying for the regulatory regime? Currently there is no appreciation that the regime entails costs for the user of such services, or for the equity owners in such intermediaries, or for the taxpayers. Legislators and supervisors press ahead with proposals while ignoring what they may cost. Some commissioned studies, at both the national and the international level, of the (true) costs of regulatory regimes would be most welcome.

The same considerations apply to compensation when something goes wrong. To the consumer, compensation is likely to appear costless, as if there were a pot of gold outside the industry from which compensation payments are made. It is usually the case that the industry pays compensation (in the

UK, the Deposit Protection and the Investors Compensation Scheme are financed by the industry) and the costs are, at least to some extent, passed on to consumers in the form of higher prices. Thus the price of some financial services implicitly includes the cost of compensation payments. This could be viewed as investors in effect paying an insurance premium to cover future compensation payments made by the firm.

Although the consumer may not be aware that the price of a product includes an implicit insurance premium, this may nevertheless be a rational outcome. If consumers appreciate that there is a greater than zero probability that they may encounter circumstances where they legitimately demand compensation, they may be willing to pay what amounts to an insurance premium incorporated into the price of the financial product being purchased. Of course, as with all insurance, some consumers may end up paying for the compensation of others. This is especially true when the industry as a whole is required to finance the compensation liabilities of firms that have become insolvent. However, this does not make implicit premium payments irrational if consumers are prepared to pay for the comfort of a compensation scheme.

If an accurate measure of the costs of the regulatory regime is difficult, estimation of the benefits is almost impossible. Given the fundamental distinction in conduct of business regulation (i.e. how firms conduct business with their customers) between wholesale and retail business in the financial services industry, the benefits of conduct of business regulation may be easier to identify in the retail sector, even if they are hard to quantify precisely. This type of regulation is designed to enhance the benefits consumers receive through purchasing financial products and services by correcting for market imperfections and failures, by setting appropriate standards of conduct, and by providing necessary monitoring services. In particular, the benefits to consumers include: reinforcement of high standards of integrity, fair dealing and competence; establishment and monitoring of training and competency standards; facilitation of consumers' protecting their own interests through information disclosure; and provision of effective mechanisms for handling investor complaints and for securing redress. These issues are addressed, for example, by the Personal Investment Authority (PIA) in the UK, which is the agency responsible for regulating the marketing of retail investment products and services, although this will change when the UK's new regulatory structure comes into force (see Chapter 8).

In the final analysis, there should be consumer welfare gains if regulation corrects for market imperfections and failures. Regulation can also enhance competition and make it more effective in the marketplace. Competition (particularly price competition) can be enhanced by requiring disclosure of relevant information to consumers (such as the full costs of products and their risk characteristics). Overall, information disclosure is a major route for achieving the benefits of regulation. While the benefits may be difficult to quantify, they are nevertheless real. In fact, however, in the UK, an attempt has been made to measure the benefits of disclosure. The Securities and

Investments Board (SIB) commissioned National Economic Research Associates (NERA) to measure the potential benefits of the disclosure regime being considered for the life assurance industry, and NERA (1994) suggested an estimate of around £1 billion per annum.

Effective competition ensures consumer protection through good products and services at competitive prices. The purpose of regulation is not to replace or to impede competition, but to enhance it and to make it more effective by offsetting market imperfections that potentially compromise consumer welfare. To the extent that regulation enhances competition and, through this, efficiency in the industry, it creates a set of markets that work more efficiently and through which consumers can gain.

Financial firms, because of the nature of their business and the relationship they have with consumers, must be monitored and supervised. This is not practical for individual consumers, and there clearly are economies of scale to be achieved through collective monitoring, which eliminates the substantial social costs incurred by duplicated monitoring by consumers.

The potential benefits of efficient regulation do not accrue only to consumers. The suppliers of financial services may also gain, in three ways in particular. First, if consumer confidence in the industry is enhanced through regulation, consumers' increased demand for the industry's services benefits suppliers. Second, to the extent that authorisation (fit and proper standards) excludes the less scrupulous from the industry, the overall reputation of the industry is enhanced, to the benefit of the scrupulous. Third, financial firms' own counterparty risks should be somewhat reduced.

While the identification of potential benefits is possible, their measurement is a different matter, in particular in the wholesale sector and on the systemic risk side. The main purpose of regulating these areas is to prevent adverse events, such as systemic collapses or opportunistic mistreatment of clients. So, successful regulation here involves the *absence* of adverse effects. But, of course, a lack of disasters may be due to a fortuitous conjuncture, rather than to the efforts of the supervisors. Moreover, even where the supervisors have managed to defuse a potentially dangerous situation, there will usually be constraints on their ability and willingness to reveal their successes publicly. Publicity might damage the reputation of the (rescued) institutions involved, and might reduce confidence in the financial system more generally. It could also induce moral hazard, if others saw this as a precedent.

What are widely known are *failures* of the regime; for example, failures of financial intermediaries, the number of complaints to the ombudsman, the number and amount of payouts from deposit insurance, etc. Even measures of regulatory *process* (e.g. the number of banks visited, the number of hours of conferences with senior managers, the number of forms scrutinised) are measures of the ongoing costs of regulation, not of its benefits, although, absent any better measure, numeration of process is frequently used as a measure of the role and functions of supervisory bodies in practice.

How are the benefits of regulation measured? Since regulation is a form of insurance against systemic risk, against the rip-off of uninformed investors, the standard answer within the private sector would be simply that the benefits of regulation are measured by how much agents are prepared to *pay* for such insurance. But that measuring stick is generally not available for public sector intervention, and the inability to point to a quantifiable benefit is hardly an advantage to supervisors. Because their successes are generally unpublicised and/or unquantifiable, while their failures are widely manifest, their position is uncomfortable, and this alone may create a tendency towards overregulation. The best supervisors can expect is to be unnoticed; any news of them is bad news. In the attempt to achieve public support and recognition for their efforts, they fight with one arm held behind their back.

Moreover, outsiders may feel that the cloak of confidentiality hides incompetence and inefficiency (Kane, 1997: 17, provides a somewhat extreme example[9]). Not only is there no market mechanism to stimulate efficiency, but there is little transparency either. Maybe there are ways whereby transparency can be enhanced, if only a little. The appointment of an independent body, like the Bank of England's Board of Banking Supervisors, to whom the supervisors must report fully and openly may be a useful mechanism.[10] Nevertheless, the question remains of how the benefits of the regulatory regime can be assessed, even for internal purposes, and how that assessment can be made public, to be presented transparently for criticism and possible refutation.

C. Accountability

Regulators have considerable power in two respects: they affect the outcomes for financial firms, and they can have a significant impact (positive and negative) on consumer welfare. So their accountability is important. To whom are the regulators to be made accountable, and how is accountability to be achieved? In other words, who regulates the regulators? Regulators should be accountable for the way they set their objectives, for how they go about achieving these objectives through specific aspects of regulation, and for the efficiency of their operation. Regulation is not a free good, and accountability for the use of resources is necessary. To what extent, and to whom, should regulatory agencies be required to explain and to justify their policies and be made accountable for their decisions?

Some foresee the hazard of regulation becoming too politicised. For instance, Lastra (1996: 153) has argued as follows about the United States: 'The US Savings & Loans debacle might have been prevented, or at least mitigated, had non-political considerations more firmly prevailed in their supervision'. Referring to the independence of central banks, and not specifically to their supervisory role in the banking system, Lastra also warns that: 'Too much independence may lead to the creation of a state within a state, [while] too much accountability threatens the effectiveness of independence . . . An optimal trade-off between independence and accountability must be attained' (pp. 58–9). Similar considerations could apply to regulation more generally. In the UK, for instance, in 1993 a government department (the Treasury) forced information disclosure on self-regulatory organisations – in the face of some hesitancy on their part.

In democratic societies regulatory accountability takes four (*not* mutually exclusive) forms: (1) accountability to the marketplace; (2) accountability to the industry itself; (3) accountability to political authorities, most especially when power is delegated by political authorities to regulators; and/or (4) accountability to the judiciary for the legality of actions and decisions. The prevalent form of accountability is to the marketplace (as is the case for most economic activity). In essence, accountability is to the consumer through the marketplace. If the supplier of a service is not supplying what the consumer demands and is prepared to pay for, this inefficiency is immediately signalled in the market. The problem with financial regulation is that it is not in practice supplied through a market: consumers do not have an ability to express what type of regulation they are prepared to pay for, and what price they are prepared to pay, in a marketplace. In effect, the consumer has no choice but to accept the type of regulation chosen by the regulatory authorities. An alternative is for the regulatory authority to be accountable to the industry itself: this is an extreme form of self-regulation. There are merits to elements of self-regulation in finance, although they also have hazards (Llewellyn, 1986). In practice, self-regulation is not the most tenable structure in finance (and in the UK its residual role under the Financial Services Act, via the SROs, will be removed by measures to be enacted by the new Labour government). In this area, finance contrasts sharply with professions like medicine or architecture.

If accountability is to political authorities, the issues are what degree of accountability the regulators have to political authorities and what structure of accountability is to be put in place. In particular, are front-line regulators (i.e. those immediately responsible for regulating and supervising parts of the financial sector) to be made accountable directly to a government department (Minister) or Parliament, or is accountability to these organisations to be via an intermediary? In the UK, front-line regulators like the PIA, IMRO and SFA are accountable not directly to the Treasury or Parliament, but via the SIB, which in turn is responsible to the Treasury.[11] In effect, the issue is how close political entities are to be to the actual operation of the regulatory authorities.[12] McDonald (1996) notes that questions of accountability are even more complex in countries where different regulatory agencies are responsible to different layers of government (e.g. national and regional) or different bodies within governments (e.g. executive, legislative, judiciary) that may not always have the same objectives. These are complex issues that raise difficult questions, which can only be settled within the context of the political structure of the particular country concerned.

D. Quasi-market mechanisms?

An approach that is commonly used to assess the perceived value of non-market services like regulation is the survey technique (e.g. surveys are widely used to ascertain the value that students attach to their courses in higher education). Of course, the insurance nature of regulatory services makes it difficult for anyone to assess its value. Thus, *after* a crash of some kind, the *ex post* value attached to a strong regulatory regime may well be a multiple of the previous *ex ante* value. Even so, there may be a case for surveying clients of financial intermediaries to ascertain how serious they think the probability of financial loss from preventable failures is,[13] and how much they would be prepared to pay to avoid possible losses.

Currently, our knowledge of client perceptions of the value of the regulatory regime put in place for their protection is remarkably slight. Apart from the sharp cries of pain and fury emanating from those who have suffered from a (regulatory) failing – and who hardly amount to a representative sample – we have very few indicators of whether the financial customer would prefer to pay more, or less, for protection (given that he or she is also unaware of what he or she does pay).

Therefore, in view of the customers' ignorance of either the costs or the potential benefits of reducing the probability of market failure, surveys of clients are unlikely to be very informative (but might at least be cheap). Practitioners, however, have a much more informed understanding of the costs and benefits to themselves of the regulatory regime. Yet even their responses to a survey will be an incomplete assessment, since the social benefits of preventing systemic collapses are likely to exceed the private benefits considerably. Even so, a relative ranking by practitioners of which aspects of the regulatory regime are perceived as better value, relative to their cost, and which worse, could be helpful. Although surveys of practitioner opinion in this area have been conducted (e.g. in the G-30 surveys), more could be done in a structured, regular way. All surveys have their limitations, but given the paucity of information on the cost–benefit balance and the relative inexpensiveness of surveys, more could usefully be done.

A more ambitious approach is to give the client of financial services a *choice* between institutions subject to more regulation and those subject to less. An example is the 'narrow bank' proposal. Under this scheme, a bank, or even separate parts of the same bank, can elect to be made 'safe' by holding only a limited set of highly liquid, almost capital-certain assets, as asset counterparts to the deposits. This 'safe' (part of the) bank could be given 100 per cent deposit insurance. One could then have a gradation of (parts of) banks, depending on the characteristics of their allowable counterpart assets (collateral), all the way from totally safe to highly risky. Deposit insurance could similarly be arranged from 100 per cent down to zero, and the extent of regulatory intervention/oversight would also reflect the gradations. The safe (part of the) bank would, normally, have a lower rate of return than the risky bank; usually, there would be an inverse relationship between risk and return, but consumers could make a choice. The risk-averse consumer could choose the safe narrow bank, and the risk-neutral client, the riskier bank. Consumer choice, and hence some role for market mechanisms, would be restored. Not surprisingly, this approach has been supported, from time to time, by many eminent economists (e.g. Friedman and Tobin, although Litan is perhaps the best known exponent).[14]

The problems with this approach are, first, that it does not deal fully with the information asymmetry problem. One may think that the division between safe/low-return and risky/high-return institutions would be clear to everyone, and that those who invested in risky banks should remember *caveat emptor*. But experience suggests that the vulnerable, old, sick and stupid are particularly prone to Ponzi games, and will indulge in ruinous financial gambles that the informed would shun. (Recall the wide support of Ponzi/pyramid games in Russia, Romania and now Albania. Also, BCCI was known to be dodgy, but it had a large following of credulous clients.) It is simply not politically possible, in the aftermath of financial disasters, to leave the vulnerable/old/ignorant/stupid clients at the mercy of their choice to invest in risky activities. Thus it may be possible for the authorities to employ graduated regulation, but it is doubtful whether they can withdraw altogether from riskier areas.

The next problem with this approach is that the division of banks (and maybe of other intermediaries) into low-risk/low-return and higher-risk/higher-return entities may have the undesired side-effect of exacerbating macroeconomic volatility. During booms, when confidence is high and the prospects of failure are correspondingly low, investors are likely to shift to the higher-risk/higher-return entities, thereby driving the relative price of (cost of) risky assets up (down) and further reinforcing the boom. When the boom breaks, there will be an equivalent flood back to safe entities. The flow of funds from riskier to safer entities will then force the risky banks to liquidate their (risky) assets, thereby reinforcing the severity of the slump. While there is inevitably some tendency for funds to move towards safe havens during slumps, reinforcing this tendency by an overt distinction between safer and riskier entities seems ill-advised.

Nevertheless, division into higher-risk/less-regulated, lower-risk/more-regulated entities may be happening willy-nilly as a result of market developments. The growth of equity mutual funds, with some payment facilities, especially in the United States, may be leading to shifts of funds between mutual funds and banks, over the cycle, that could exacerbate volatility in asset prices. But the structure of such equity mutual funds, with market-valued liabilities, at least should make them immune to failure should funds flow out during downturns in equity prices. Moreover, if banks lose (gain) market share during booms (slumps), it might lead to some offset to the credit cycle.

There may also be a stronger case for introducing 'narrow' (safe) banks in developing countries, as opposed to their industrialised counterparts. Ensuring that narrow banks hold only a restricted set of liquid assets, while giving less oversight to the remaining risky banks, could help economise on scarce resources of skilled labour among the regulatory agencies in these countries. It may well be that the riskiest banks in some emerging and transitional countries are those with the strongest political and industrial group support (e.g. Banespa in Brazil). There would be more external pressure for public sector support of such banks, unless the responsibility of the regulatory authorities was more narrowly defined. Given the more extreme economic fluctuations evident in such countries, the maintenance of at least a safe core of narrow banks that can maintain the payments system and the real value of savings for the risk averse under almost any circumstances would seem to be a useful objective. So some version of a narrow bank scheme might be better suited to emerging economies than to industrialised countries (see Chapter 6).

5 The new techniques for risk management

In addition to investor protection, financial regulation is concerned with the control of systemic risk (Chapter 1), which is dependent on the probability of the failure of individual institutions. There are basically two determinants of systemic stability, the first being the market infrastructure – such as payments systems, clearing houses, etc. – which channels the exposures of financial institutions to each other, and the second being individual banks' risk taking within that infrastructure. We focus on the latter in this chapter.[1]

More precisely, we review some of the newly developed risk management techniques and their implications for the form and the incentive structures of financial regulation. Section A looks at value-at-risk (VaR) models for the management of market risks and their application as set out in the recent amendment to the Basle Capital Accord (Basle Committee, 1996a,1996b). We evaluate both their precision in measuring market risks and their usefulness as regulatory tools. Section B then presents the pre-commitment approach to market risk regulation (Kupiec and O'Brien, 1995a; 1997b), which addresses some shortcomings of the Basle internal models approach from the perspective of incentive theory, as outlined in Chapter 3. Finally, Section C covers the revival of interest in credit risk management. We describe the emergence, main types and further evolution of credit derivatives and ask whether a revision of the 1988 Basle capital rules might involve some consideration of quantitative credit risk management models, such as JP Morgan's (1997) recent CreditMetrics release.

Market risk refers to the variability of portfolio values due to changes in market prices of the portfolio components (or even due to changes in the changes). For example, a general increase in interest rates usually depresses bond prices, or depreciation of a foreign currency reduces the value of instruments denominated in that currency within a domestic portfolio. *Credit risk* relates to the occurrence of defaults or to changes in the likelihood of such defaults in the future. For example, if a commercial borrower's business profits decline, or turn into losses, a bank will perceive an increased likelihood that this lender might (partially or completely) default on the payment obligations and that the bank might recover only a fraction of its original claim, reducing the expected value of its total portfolio. Thus, if they are defined in this simple way, there is substantial overlap between credit and market risk. For example, when a credit-rating agency downgrades its rating of some emerging country's public debt, then the market prices of its bonds will fall.

This latter part of market risk is often referred to as *specific risk*, to distinguish it from *general market risk*, which is not related directly to any default or other credit event. However, a large share of bank assets do not have publicly observable market prices, and their specific risk has to be determined differently. As is illustrated in Section C, this does not mean that the assets are not affected by market risk. Nevertheless, until now practically all bank regulations have treated general market and specific (or credit) risk separately.

Traditional capital adequacy regulations for market or credit risk have imposed the same simple rules on all banks, or on all securities firms, to determine their regulatory minimum capital (or maximum exposure, given the amount of capital).[2] Examples of simple minimum capital rules are the Cooke ratio for credit risk in the 1988 Basle Capital Accord (Basle Committee, 1988), the building-block approach still figuring as an option in its recent market risk amendment (Basle Committee, 1996a), and the SEC comprehensive approach for US securities firms (Dimson and Marsh, 1994).

What all traditional approaches have in common is that the same basic formula for determining minimum regulatory capital is applied to all financial institutions, independent of differences in their risk management techniques and capabilities, their actual portfolios, or their attitudes towards risk taking. This has provoked a series of objections from the more competitive financial institutions, as well as from many academics, that:

1 Traditional approaches do not generally reward risk-reducing diversification with lower capital charges. For example, the position risk measure for corporate loans in the 1988 credit risk accord is strictly additive over different regions and industries.
2 They attach higher (lower) capital requirements to riskier (less risky) activities incoherently, thereby implying perverse incentives for portfolio recomposition.[3] For example, Grenadier and Hall (1996) found that home mortgages, which got a 50 per cent risk weight in the Basle Accord, have about the same default history in the United States as mortgage-backed securities, which received a 20 per cent weight, which amounts to an implicit tax on direct mortgage lending as opposed to securitised lending. Similarly, all corporate bonds received the same 100 per cent risk weight, no matter whether their issuer's credit rating was AA or B.
3 Traditional capital adequacy requirements are not designed to cover non-linear risks, as incorporated in derivatives instruments (see below). In short, they measure actual portfolio risks very imprecisely (Dimson and Marsh, 1995).

In response to these apparent imprecisions, regulators have made capital adequacy requirements quite conservative, possibly thereby inducing evasive behaviour.[4]

However, there is no simple general position measure that does justice to the risk management capabilities of the leading players while at the same time providing a simple rule for all other institutions. Also, as pointed out in Chapter 2, rapid changes in financial markets, institutions and their risk management techniques require flexible approaches to regulation. We now turn to these new risk management techniques and their implications for more flexible and focused (menu-type) market and credit risk regulation.

A. Value-at-risk models for market risk

Quantitative market risk management models emerged at the end of the 1980s. Their spread has been accelerated by discussion of the possible amendment of the Basle Capital Accord for market risk beginning in the early 1990s. Partly in response to the first proposal from the Basle Committee for this amendment in April 1993, JP Morgan launched its RiskMetrics data set and VaR model and put it in the public domain. After two proposals and two rounds of industry consultations, G-10 regulators finally agreed on the way to incorporate market risk in the Basle Accord.[5] The two outstanding points in the agreement were, first, endorsement of the use of banks' in-house models (such as Bankers Trust's Raroc 2020, Chase Manhattan's Charisma, CS First Boston's Prime Risk, Deutsche Bank's db-Analyst, JP Morgan's RiskMetrics, etc.) to determine the minimum regulatory capital against market risk and, second, allowing the banks to consider correlations between the four basic market risk categories (Basle Committee, 1996a).[6] A standardised and more traditional methodology, without the option of considering such correlations, is provided for less sophisticated players. European Union governments have recently agreed on the inclusion of a similar internal models approach in EU capital adequacy regulations (Commission Européenne, 1997).

(i) The basic techniques

Market value-at-risk (VaR) models are designed to estimate potential losses on given portfolios through fluctuations in interest rates (at different maturities), exchange rates, equity and commodity prices. The value of any instrument in a portfolio will be influenced by one or more of these *risk factors*. For example, the value of a French bank's long position in US government bonds changes with the franc/dollar exchange rate and US interest rates; the value of a call option on such bonds not only changes with the level of US interest rates but also with their volatility (and some other risk factors), and so on.

Jorion (1997) defines VaR as the 'expected maximum loss (or worst loss) over a target horizon within a given confidence interval'. Therefore, at the outset two parameters have to be decided: the holding period (or target horizon) and the confidence interval. Figure 5.1 illustrates the derivation of VaR from the frequency distribution of portfolio returns.

The *holding period* chosen should depend on the frequency of portfolio

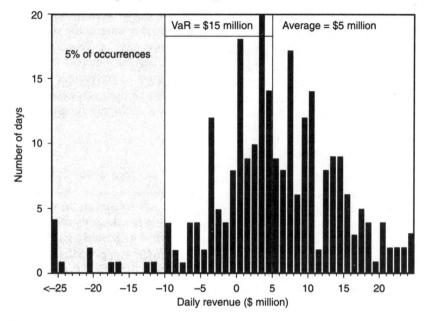

Figure 5.1 Deriving value at risk

The figure shows how value at risk (VaR) can be derived from a frequency distribution. The particular example refers to JP Morgan's revenues during the year 1994. The target horizon is chosen to be one day and the confidence interval 95 per cent. The shaded area shows the 5 per cent smallest daily revenues over this year. The VaR is the cutoff point of this region (US$10m) as compared with the average daily revenue (US$5m), i.e. US$10m + US$5m = US$15m = VaR
Source: Jorion (1997: 89)

adjustments and the potential speed with which the respective financial institution may liquidate its position. For example, many commercial and investment banks with trading positions in relatively liquid markets use daily returns and VaRs. Institutions that usually adjust their portfolios at a slower pace, such as pension and other investment funds, may instead target a monthly horizon. The G-10 banking regulators from the Basle Committee have taken a relatively conservative stance, choosing a two-week (ten business days) holding period.

On the issue of the *confidence interval*, the second model parameter, bank practice is more diverse, varying at least from 95 per cent intervals to 99 per cent intervals.[7] On the one hand, its choice of interval may indicate the institution's attitude towards risk taking, since the selection of a wider confidence interval (e.g. 99 per cent instead of 95 per cent) reduces the likelihood that a model will fail to predict extreme events. In this respect, as might have been expected, the Basle Committee required a 99 per cent interval. On the other hand, as the confidence interval widens, the number of historical data in the sample to determine the cutoff point becomes smaller and smaller. Therefore, the more closely one focuses on the probability of really large losses (which are, of course, the main concern of the regulators), the more imprecise the VaR estimate also becomes (Kupiec, 1995; Jorion, 1996).

Perhaps the most important and also the most difficult element in VaR estimations is the way that the frequency distribution of predicted portfolio returns (as plotted in Figure 5.1) is obtained. Table 5.1 explains the basic functioning of the main techniques. The *historical simulation* method on the left uses past realisations of risk-factor returns as the main input (non-parametric method), while the *variance–covariance* approach (such as RiskMetrics, sometimes also called – for reasons explained below – the delta-normal approach) on the right presumes that risk-factor returns follow a particular parametric distribution, almost always the (multivariate) normal distribution. In the former case the VaR is derived from the historical port-folio return frequency distribution by finding the cutoff return level, so that only 1 per cent (or 5 per cent) of all simulated portfolio losses exceed that level. The portfolio return distribution itself is found by expressing the mark-to-market value of each instrument in the portfolio as a function of the underlying risk factors and applying the historical risk-factor returns directly to these formulae.

In the delta-normal approach, the VaR can be calculated from the historical variances and covariances of all risk factors by applying the following simple formula (which holds as a consequence of the normality assumption):

$$\text{VaR}_\alpha = \kappa\,(\alpha)\,\sigma = \kappa\,(\alpha) = \sqrt{\sum_{i=1}^{I} \sum_{j=1}^{I} x_i\, x_j\, \rho_{ij}\, \sigma_i\, \sigma_j}$$

σ is the standard deviation of portfolio returns, which is the square root of a simple weighted sum of the variances (σ) and covariances ($\rho_{ij}\sigma_i\sigma_j$) of the individual risk factors $i=1, \ldots ,I$. The weights x_i measure the (linear) sensitivities of the total portfolio return to the variability of the risk factors, sometimes called deltas. Under normality, each x_i is a sum of the deltas of each instrument with respect to risk factor i. Therefore, in contrast to historical simulation, all instruments (that depend on more than one risk factor) in the portfolio have to be decomposed into a number of standardised positions, with each of the positions depending only on a single risk factor (risk mapping). α is the confidence interval chosen. Again as a consequence of the normality assumption on the return distribution, $\kappa(95$ per cent$) = 1.645$ or $\kappa(99$ per cent$) = 2.326$.

From the above it can be seen that there is a third parameter that has to be determined before applying the two most widely used VaR models, i.e. the *data window* (the period for which the historical distribution is sampled or for which variances and covariances of risk-factor returns are computed). Long data windows of several years have the advantage that a larger number of observations lead to more precise coverage of the actual return distribution,

Table 5.1 Comparison of value-at-risk techniques

Steps	Historical simulation (full valuation, non-parametric)	Monte Carlo simulation (full valuation, 'bootstrapped' or parametric)	Variance–covariance approach (parametric, local valuation)
1 Identification of positions	Find all positions in financial instruments affected by market risk		
2 Choice of risk factors (RFs)	Identify risk factors influencing financial instruments in the portfolio		
3 Obtain return distribution of RFs assuming holding period (x days)	Compute historical frequency distribution over last y years	Random generated assuming particular param. distribution or 'bootstrapped' from hist. data	Compute historical standard deviations and correlations of risk factors over last y years
4 Link RF returns and instrument positions	Express mark-to-market value of positions as a function of RFs		Decompose positions in RFs ('risk mapping')
5 Compute portfolio variability	Simulate portfolio return frequency distribution from results in steps 3 and 4		Compute portfolio standard deviation assuming multivariate normal distribution of RFs
6 Deduce VaR assuming one-sided confidence interval of 99 per cent or 95 per cent (or other)	Order portfolio losses and select the loss that is equalled or exceeded in 1% or 5% of the cases		Multiply portfolio standard deviation by 2.33 (1%) or 1.65 (5%)

in particular for historical simulation. However, long data sets might be available for only a limited number of standard risk factors in industrial countries. In addition, longer data windows increase the likelihood that the return distribution has changed over the sample period, potentially introducing biases in VaR estimates. The Basle Committee fixed on a data window of one year, which reflects these trade-offs.

An important distinction between historical simulation and the variance–covariance approach is that the former is a *full-valuation* model, while the latter is a *partial valuation* model. The historical simulation method can account for *all* types of dependencies between portfolio value and risk factors, whether they are linear or non-linear. However, the variance–covariance approach can account for only linear dependencies (deltas), neglecting non-linear factors, such as option gammas or bond convexities (see below).[8]

The third VaR approach, which is more complex than the first two, is called *Monte Carlo simulation*. This technique uses randomly generated risk-factor returns, which can be obtained by either *assuming* any type of parametric distribution (again usually the normal) or by *bootstrapping* them from the historical distribution.[9] Hence, Monte Carlo simulations can be both parametric and non-parametric, but in contrast to the historical simulation or the variance–covariance approach, a Monte Carlo simulation can generate a much larger number of portfolio return realisations from which to derive the VaR estimates. Monte Carlo simulation is a full-valuation technique, like historical simulation. Because of the high computational costs of Monte Carlo simulations, so far most research has focused on the relative merits and disadvantages of historical simulation versus the variance–covariance approach. Thus, in what follows we mainly compare these two techniques.[10]

(ii) A critical evaluation

It has been observed that the three basic VaR approaches above can lead to substantially different risk estimates, as do variations in the three major model parameters (i.e. holding period, confidence interval, data window) for a given model type (Beder, 1995). The former problem, generally known as model risk, highlights the importance of model verification, or back-testing.[11] Back-testing procedures compare the actual realisation of losses with those predicted by the VaR model.[12] For example, the Basle market risk amendment defines a green zone, a yellow zone and a red zone, depending on the number of occasions over the monitoring horizon of one year (250 business days) that realised losses exceed the daily VaR estimate (Basle Committee, 1996b). Notice that, at a 99 per cent confidence interval, two or three violations would be compatible with the assumption (250×1 per cent = 2.5). In the green zone (zero to four violations) the model is presumed to be precise. In the yellow zone (five to nine violations) the VaR estimates from the bank's model have to be multiplied by an increasing add-on factor. In the red zone (ten violations and more) the regulator can require the bank to adjust the model or can even suspend approval of the model.

However, many back-testing procedures have a fundamental problem. As pointed out by Kupiec (1995), for limited monitoring horizons, such as the minimum of one year specified in the Basle market risk amendment, they have little statistical power to distinguish good and bad models. This is true basically for the same reason that the standard errors of VaR estimates are so large. Since VaR is fundamentally concerned with the extreme tails of portfolio return distributions, only a limited number of violations will determine whether to reject or not. For short monitoring horizons, there is considerable likelihood of erroneously accepting a relatively imprecise model. Naturally, this problem troubles regulators as well as bank risk managers.[13]

Nevertheless, historical simulation has two basic advantages over variance–covariance analysis. First, it is now well known that financial market returns are only imperfectly described by the normal distribution. In particular, the empirically observed frequency distributions have fat tails, i.e. large market movements occur more often than predicted by the normal (Figure 5.2). Empirical research by Jackson *et al.* (1997) confirms that historical simulation can account for this reasonably well, while variance–covariance analysis cannot.

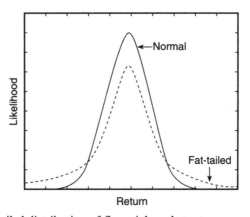

Figure 5.2 Fat-tailed distribution of financial market returns

The figure shows how a fat-tailed distribution (dashed line) differs from the normal distribution (solid line). The frequency distributions of financial market returns typically have fat tails. The normal distribution attributes a higher likelihood to returns close to the mean (usually 0) and a lower likelihood to large negative or positive returns, i.e. when one assumes normally distributed returns, one tends to underestimate value at risk for large confidence intervals.
Source: Duffie and Pan (1997: 7–49)

Another advantage of non-parametric simulation approaches is their ability to trace non-linear relationships between portfolio returns and risk-factor returns, which are most apparent in derivatives positions, such as options. For example, the market value p of a financial instrument might depend on a risk factor r in the following way:

$$dp = \Delta dr + \frac{1}{2}\Gamma(dr)^2 + R$$

where dp and dr are the price changes (returns) of the instrument and the risk factor, respectively. The Δ-term measures the linear relationship, while the Γ-term measures the quadratic (non-linear) relationship between p and r. R captures higher-order terms (e.g. cubic) or other risk factors. In particular, for longer holding periods, such as the regulatory compromise of ten days, risk-factor returns (dr) can be quite large (they can 'jump'), which enhances the impact of the Γ-term, easily tripling potential losses or gains. In Figure 5.3 we illustrate the consequences of non-linearities using the example of the 'Leeson straddle', the option trading position established by Barings' Singapore derivatives trader that finally led to the bank's default.

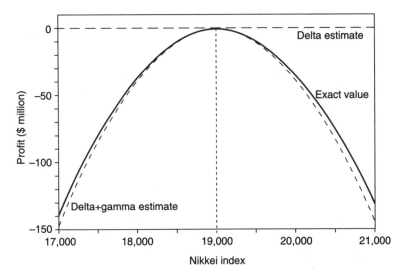

Figure 5.3 Non-linear risk and delta-normal VaR – the 'Leeson straddle'

The figure shows the pay-offs of Barings trader Nick Leeson's option portfolio in February 1995, a *short straddle*. A short straddle is a combination of call and put options with the same strike price and maturity (all sold). In his case, they were options on Nikkei index futures. The horizontal axis therefore measures changes in the Nikkei stock index (risk factor). The solid line shows the exact value changes of his straddle, while the dashed horizontal line shows only the linear dependency (delta approximation) when the Nikkei stands at 19,000. (The parabolic dashed line shows the quadratic dependency (delta and gamma approximation), which appears to track the actual pay-offs quite well.) It turns out that with the Nikkei close to 19,000 Leeson's straddle is 'delta neutral', i.e. ('locally') the pay-off does depend on the underlying Nikkei index in a linear fashion. However, there is a non-linear dependency. Whether the Japanese stock market goes up or down, in both cases considerable losses can occur. (In Leeson's case the Kobe earthquake depressed the stock market.) The delta-normal VaR model will always underestimate this loss potential and cannot detect it at all when the Nikkei stands close to 19,000.
Source: Jorion (1997: 145)

The disadvantage of historical simulation is that it is relatively sensitive to the sampling period (Danielsson and de Vries, 1997). Relatively few observations at the lower extreme tail determine the cutoff point, making the portfolio return distribution discrete in that area, and they can change considerably from one sample to another. In simpler terms, whether October 1987 is inside or outside the sample period makes an enormous difference for portfolios including equities. Also, historical simulation attaches zero probability to any return in excess of the largest one in the current sample, implying that future extreme returns will not exceed historical extreme returns.

This points to another fundamental issue for VaR models in general. In most cases they rely on historical data. However, past returns might not always be a good indicator of future returns. Implied volatilities from option prices, which can be incorporated in variance–covariance analysis quite easily, but not in historical simulation approaches, can cope with this problem only partly. Currently, the Basle Committee has not endorsed their use in its internal models approach for market risk capital requirements.

The most widely debated feature of the Basle internal models approach has probably been the fixed factor of 3 (which can even increase up to 4 when too many VaR violations occur during the back-testing procedure) by which a firm's VaR estimate has to be multiplied in order to determine the minimum capital requirement for market risk. Representatives of large banks and their industry bodies argue that 3 is much too conservative, discouraging the use of models. The Basle Committee points to the failure of standard VaR techniques to capture the likelihood of extreme market movements sufficiently, as discussed above. Moreover, an additional buffer might be justified by the historical data problem.

Stahl (1997) has provided a theoretical justification of the 3-factor, based on a fundamental statistical relationship known as Chebyshev's inequality. This inequality implies upper boundaries for the distances of extreme percentiles from the mean that are valid for *any* type of distribution. Applying Chebyshev's inequality to various potential mis-specifications in variance–covariance analysis and historical simulation, Stahl finds that scaling factors between 3 and 4 can compensate for the potential bias. The obvious counterargument is the crude nature of the inequality. By ignoring the properties of financial market return distributions, it necessarily leads to very conservative multiplication factors.

Jackson *et al.* (1997) address the size of the multiplication factor empirically. They analyse some typical portfolios for a single, relatively well-diversified bank, excluding derivatives and commodity positions. When standard parametric VaRs were tested with a *ten-day* holding period, no losses exceeding the minimum capital requirement occurred for multiplication factors of 2.5 or 3, while single marginal outliers occurred for some portfolios with a factor of 2. Moreover, Jackson *et al.* show that, with *daily* VaRs, the predicted bounds are violated more frequently, thereby increasing the add-on.

Danielsson and de Vries (1997) show, with a random-portfolio approach, that historical simulation usually leads to substantially higher VaR estimates, making the number 3 look even more conservative. However, as yet no study has been published dealing with that issue for a wider, more representative range of real bank portfolios. One way of reducing the risk of adverse incentive effects (discouraging model use or favouring simpler models over more precise models) would be to lower the *fixed* part of the factor from 3 to, say, 2, and at the same time to increase the range of the *variable* (back-testing) add-on from [0,1] to [0,3], for example. Another, more far-reaching, step would be to switch to a pre-commitment approach (see below), which implies a fully endogenous multiplication factor.

Some banks also find fault with the ten-day holding period, which makes the minimum capital requirements more conservative than with a shorter holding period. A standard procedure, endorsed by the Basle Committee, is to multiply the daily VaR by the square root of 10.[14] The banks argue that portfolios are adjusted dynamically, depending on market conditions. For instance, they could trade out of positions before realising excessively large losses. The proponents of the Basle approach counter that this might not be possible for all instruments and market conditions. In times of crisis, market liquidity usually dries up. In reality, there is no simple multiplicative procedure that can allow one to pass from banks' use of daily VaRs to the regulatory ten-day VaRs. In particular, when non-linear claims, such as options and other derivatives, are important, or when return volatilities are not independent over time, as documented by studies finding 'conditional heteroscedasticity' (ARCH or GARCH effects; Bollerslev *et al.*, 1992), then adding up the daily VaRs can lead to considerable under- or overestimations of the actual risks involved (Kupiec and O'Brien, 1995b).[15]

Problems with the technical details of VaR estimations, however, should not be interpreted as an argument against using quantitative risk management models. The list of pitfalls in VaR applications should not obscure the fact that they are still much more precise than the older risk management techniques, such as asset-liability management, or the standardised methodology for regulatory capital requirements, which are still contained in the Basle market risk amendment for less sophisticated banks. However, risk managers must be aware of these pitfalls. Ultimately, the abilities of the people handling the models and their capacity to understand the models' working are essential for the successful introduction of new risk management techniques.

B. Pre-commitment in market risk regulation

When the Basle Committee for Banking Supervision decided to incorporate recent advances in market risk management techniques into G-10 regulations, it gave national authorities the responsibility for endorsing or rejecting a bank's internal model. This puts regulators in a difficult position, since assessing the precision and merits of models is not easy, as is discussed above.

A new approach, recently advanced by research economists of the US Federal Reserve, would shift the responsibility back to the banks themselves (Kupiec and O'Brien, 1995a; 1997a, 1997b).

(i) Incentives for banks

The new approach is particularly designed for trading risks and is directly related to the development of quantitative market risk measurement models by the financial industry. It stipulates that a bank or trading company has to pre-commit to its regulator not to exceed a maximum ten-day cumulative portfolio loss (value at risk) for the quarter or half-year to come. This pre-committed amount, which will usually be determined using the institution's own internal VaR model as a major tool, is at the same time its regulatory market risk minimum capital requirement. If it violates this commitment some time during a quarter, then it has to face a regulatory penalty, which could be either monetary or non-monetary.

This scheme can be interpreted as an incentive contract between the regulators and the regulated, as defined in Chapter 3. Why should a bank tell the regulator its best estimate of future maximum loss (so that no adverse selection occurs)? If it undercommits, it risks being penalised relatively frequently, which is costly and interferes with its business. Overcommitment is made unattractive by the higher capital charge implied; hence the incentive compatibility of the contract. An additional requirement for (delayed) public disclosure of banks' pre-commitments (and possibly subsequently realised trading losses) could reinforce incentives against under- or overcommitment.[16]

In contrast to the Basle internal models approach, in this approach regulators withdraw from the endorsement of particular model types. By focusing on the *outcomes* rather than on the *process* whereby the outcomes are achieved, this approach leaves the tricky issue of model choice to the market and to competition. Such a result-oriented approach has two further important incentive effects: it is in the banks' own interest to improve internal models and to add any safety buffer (multiplication factor) necessary against remaining model risk.

In the pre-commitment regime, banks also have to assess their own ability to undertake nimble portfolio adjustments in their loss estimates for the regulatory holding period of ten days (requiring them to evaluate possible market illiquidity). The Basle internal models approach is basically static, ignoring dynamic portfolio strategies. Operational risk is particularly relevant for large sophisticated banks, which can usually be expected to have very good models running in the different areas of their trading business, while the complexity of their organisation involves many sources of error in the co-ordination and aggregation of firm-wide VaR estimates, besides problems of fraud and failure to control incorrect inputting of data.

Until now, pre-commitment has only been debated as an approach for market risks in trading books. However, as we pointed out at the beginning of this chapter, market and credit risk are related and, as we discuss at greater length in Section C, the distinction between banking and trading books will erode in the future, if new credit risk management techniques (such as credit derivatives and credit VaR models) are developed. This raises the issue of extending pre-commitment to the banking book and counterparty risk. Since pre-commitment would probably lead to lower capital requirements for market risks than with the Basle internal models approach (let alone the standardised approach), banks could be induced to engage further in trading activities and to reduce traditional lending, if their credit risk capital requirements (still determined by the 1988 Basle Capital Accord) stayed the same.[17]

Of course, how penalties are imposed is of great importance to the incentive compatibility of the scheme. Under pre-commitment, the penalties are the means of closing the gap between private and social costs of financial distress. In this sense, it is *not* purely market based, but still a form of public external regulation, although it allows market forces to act in many more respects than traditional regulatory approaches or the Basle market risk amendment.

Monetary penalties can be specified in an exact and verifiable way. For example, fines can be determined as a proportion of the trading loss in excess of the pre-committed amount. Alternatively, additional minimum capital could be required for a limited period after pre-commitment violations (Kupiec and O'Brien, 1995a). In order for *ex ante* incentives against under-commitment or excessive risk taking (adverse selection) to work effectively, it is essential that banks perceive the (*ex post*) imposition of penalties to be credible (see Section (ii) below).

As it turned out from the Fed's industry consultation in June 1995, monetary penalties are unpopular among financial institutions, although a majority of banks were generally in favour of the pre-commitment approach. The main argument is that monetary penalties hit banks when they are already down. Non-monetary penalties, such as potential restrictions on trading activities or demands to improve risk management techniques (with a subsequent review), would also be more familiar to the regulators.

There is also debate about the size of monetary fines. Prescott (1997) argues that fines that are imposed only for the low-probability events of pre-commitment violations (extreme portfolio fluctuations) would have to be large, in order to offset the high-probability benefits of lower capital for banks. Marshall and Venkataraman (1997) simulate optimal fines within a specific theoretical framework. Their finding is that fines might not have to be much larger than 30 per cent of the pre-commitment violation. Moreover, in their framework, pre-commitment dominates more intrusive forms of capital adequacy regulations, because it achieves the same regulatory objectives with a lower total amount of capital in the economy.

Pre-commitment – like other capital adequacy approaches – cannot prevent banks whose franchise value has been eroded from 'gambling on resurrection' (moral hazard), especially if they conceal their actual trading losses. In order to avoid adverse selection of banks that have strong 'go-for-broke' incentives in the pre-commitment regime, Kupiec and O'Brien (1997a) propose a maximum leverage ratio as an additional fail-safe mechanism. Bliss (1995) suggests that more frequent reporting and fining should reduce the per-period costs of regulatory sanctions and, therefore, would also reduce the temptation for banks to defer or to hide the realisation of losses.

(ii) Incentives for the regulators

As discussed in Section B of Chapter 3, financial regulation can gain credibility when strengthened through a 'contract' aimed at avoiding costly (to the taxpayer) forbearance. Pre-commitment is particularly well designed to be used as such a rule-based regulation, because regulatory action can be related *ex ante* to the discrepancy between pre-committed amounts and actual trading outcomes relatively objectively (particularly with fines). Both are *ex post* verifiable, which can give a regulator bound (by law) to a *predetermined graduated ladder of responses* a high degree of credibility.[18] It is much easier for the courts (or agents acting on behalf of the public) to verify that a trading outcome in excess of the pre-commitment was not penalised than it is to determine that the regulators did not apply sufficient care when testing a bank's VaR model.

However, as is also pointed out in Chapter 3, an 'escape clause' is necessary for special circumstances. For example, in a major systemic crisis, monetary fines cannot be imposed, because they would render the problem more severe. The option for overriding the general rule also leaves some space for 'constructive ambiguity'. Whether loss of regulatory credibility due to such a waiver actually materialises may depend on the existence and independence of the body watching over its use.

While pre-commitment is currently being tested in the United States in a pilot study sponsored by the New York Clearing House, the time might not yet be ripe for adopting it. The switch to the Basle internal models approach will not be finalised before January 1998, and some EU countries are still struggling with the transformation of the first Capital Adequacy Directive (CAD) into national laws (Conseil des Communautés Européennes, 1993; Hartmann, 1997a). The European Commission has made a proposal for a new Directive (CAD II), considering a Basle-like internal models approach for EU regulations as well. At the time that this monograph went to print, it could not be predicted when CAD II would become effective in the EU.[19]

A rapid shift to pre-commitment in G-10 countries is not very likely under these circumstances. Moreover, the theoretical discussion of penalty schemes that impose the right incentives on banks has only begun. More research is definitely advisable before the full implementation of a pre-commitment regime. Nonetheless, this proposal has greatly enriched the discussion of regulatory reform and points the way to more incentive-compatible financial regulation.

C. Credit derivatives and recent advances in credit risk management

Credit risk management issues have recently been revived in the public debate on prudential regulation for the following reasons. First, in spite of the growing involvement of banks in trading activities, credit risk remains the single most important component of the total risk exposure of banks, and bad loan problems remain the primary source of bank failures (Beattie *et al.*, 1995; Lindgren *et al.*, 1996). There is concern that the general reduction in credit spreads currently observed – the markup different borrowers have to pay on top of (low-risk) government bond yields – may be thoughtlessly perceived as an indication of less credit risk in the international financial system.

Second, the emergence of loan securitisation and credit derivatives, as well as their growth in the last couple of years, has made part of the credit risk exposure tradable and therefore subject to more active and competitive portfolio management. If these markets continue to evolve rapidly, the differential treatment of banking and trading books in regulations may have to be removed. Third, the rapid evolution of market VaR models has improved the risk management technologies of many banks, and enabled them to tackle the more difficult task of quantitative credit risk management. And, related to that, the adoption of a model-based approach for market risk capital adequacy requirements by the Basle Committee (1996a) has increased the awareness of imprecise and partly incoherent risk weightings in the original part of the Basle Accord (Basle Committee, 1988) covering credit risk. Credit risk management and trading will be a major, perhaps the main, concern of bank risk managers and financial supervisors in the next decade.

(i) The special features of credit risk and its management

There are several important differences between credit risk and market risk. First, the shape of many credit events is not as smooth as market price changes. If an unsecured loan defaults (which has a low but positive likelihood), then the loss is often large for a bank. If it does not (no loss, with high likelihood), the gain, in terms of earned net interest income, is more moderate. This asymmetry results in a distribution of returns of items due to credit risk that is skewed 'to the left' (Figure 5.4). The left tail of the frequency distribution of, for example, loan losses is 'fat', and the expected value of losses is to the left of the highest-probability loss.[20] Although this feature of credit risk can become less pronounced in a large and highly diversified loan portfolio, it will not disappear altogether (Oda and Muranaga, 1997). In contrast, market risk distributions are more symmetric; gains or losses of some size have about the same probability.[21] Other credit events, such as changes in bond credit ratings (e.g. from BBB to A), reflecting changes in the likelihood of debtors' defaulting in the future, are also smoother than the 1–0 events of default/no default.

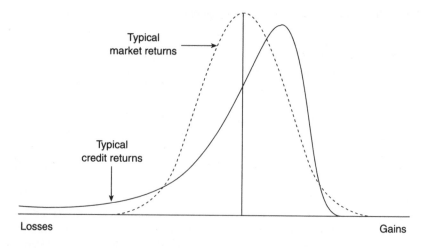

Figure 5.4 Comparing credit return and market return distributions

The figure shows that market returns are usually symmetric around 0, while credit returns tend to be 'skewed to the left'. The default of a borrower has usually a low probability compared with the likelihood of proper reimbursement, but when default occurs the loss for the lending bank is often severe. However, the total interest income in the case of full reimbursement is usually more modest than the credit loss potential or than large positive market returns.
Source: JP Morgan (1997: 7)

A second major difference between market and credit risk is that changes in counterparties' creditworthiness are generally not directly observable in the way that changes in most market prices are. For example, while the bond ratings of large borrowers may be publicly available, information on many corporate and consumer loans is not. This feature is probably the most important obstacle to the application of VaR-type quantitative credit risk management models. A related issue is the difficulty of calculating correlations between various debtors', or groups of debtors', changes in creditworthiness (JP Morgan, 1997).

Third, the presence of credit-enhancement facilities, such as collateral or guarantees, together with the legal uncertainties affecting recovery rates of defaulted assets, make the precise evaluation of credit risk exposure more complex. This complexity has a market risk and a legal dimension. Take the example of real estate or equity pledged as collateral. As land or equity prices fluctuate, so do the potential net losses on loans collateralised by such assets. This illustrates one reason why one cannot dissociate credit and market risk for certain types of secured assets. The legal risk in recovery rates relates, for example, to uncertainties about the relative seniority of different claims on a corporation in receivership and about the precise ownership of the asset. In some countries foreigners may find it hard to get domestic courts to transfer such assets to them.

Another, more 'famous', feature has become known as the *credit paradox*. This phenomenon stems from two observations. First, there are (or have been for a long time) few hedging instruments available for credit risk. Second, many bank loan portfolios have a low degree of diversification. On the surface these two observations seem contradictory; in the absence of direct hedging instruments, such as 'credit options' or 'credit forwards', important gains could be derived from diversification. Part of the explanation of the paradox lies in the formidable information problems in credit risk evaluations of non-credit-rated corporate borrowers, which could be overcome by long-term lending relationships with a few customers ('relationship banking').[22] In any case, the credit paradox may become less relevant with the further growth of loan securitisation and credit derivatives markets (see Section (iii) below).

The final difference between market and credit risk is related to the notion of the risk evaluation period or the period over which returns are defined. While equities, government bonds or foreign exchange instruments can be traded and liquidated quickly, many credit relationships are founded on a more long-term basis. Instead of market value changes over a 'holding period' of one or several days, risk evaluation over the time to maturity (several months or even much longer) will be relevant. Therefore, value changes have to be simulated on the basis of the sum of future cash flows until maturity discounted to the present.

(ii) Credit scoring and the 'post-millennium project'

Given the greater complexity of credit risk management as compared with market risk management, is there scope for more precise, quantitative techniques? Can credit VaRs be accepted by prudential regulators in the near future? For example, can they be incorporated in a revision of the Basle counterparty risk capital adequacy regulations? JP Morgan's (1997) recent CreditMetrics release, which has found support among many other major players in the industry, illustrates that credit VaR models have to be more complex than market VaR models. However, statistical means are available for dealing with skewed, non-normal credit return distributions over longer evaluation periods, and the price dynamics of collateral can be integrated with the help of the available market risk techniques.

Evaluation of changes in the risk exposure to credit-rated companies (although imperfect) is possible with data from credit-rating agencies, such as Moody's, Standard and Poors, or IBCA. Moreover, credit spreads of traded debt contain *implied default probabilities*, which can be extracted. CreditMetrics uses a third approach: default probabilities are derived from a firm valuation model, combining accounting data with information contained in firms' share prices.[23]

However, for many credit items, information on default probabilities is not publicly available. The pricing and risk assessment of these non-traded, non-credit-rated loans is the classical problem of the banker. A distinction is usually made between standardised retail products, such as consumer loans or mortgages, and larger, more tailor-made corporate loans. For the former, *credit-scoring* techniques have proven relatively successful, while for the latter, a more subjective *loan-grading* system is often used (Nelson, 1997).

Credit-scoring techniques, such as the *Z*-score or ZETA analysis, were pioneered by Altman (1968, 1983) and their refinements have become widely used banking instruments. The basic procedure is roughly as follows. Banks group their historical information on lenders (e.g. into those who defaulted and those who did not default). Then they select a number of potential indicators ($X_1, X_2, \ldots, X_N$) of the financial healthiness of the borrowers and test by simple regression or discrimination analysis which weighting ($\alpha_1, \alpha_2, \ldots, \alpha_N$) of these indicators provides an index Z (*Z*-score) predicting defaults and non-defaults:

$$Z = \alpha_0 + \alpha_1 X_1 + \alpha_2 X_2 + \ldots + \alpha_N X_N$$

The selection of indicators and weightings that perform best in predicting group membership (default or not) in the future is maintained as a credit risk prediction index for borrowers. Of course, the *Z*-score can also be used for more than two groups (e.g. reflecting different probabilities of future defaults). Many banks employ a loan-grading system with ten risk categories.

Once banks receive a request for a new loan, they collect the information on the indicators from the potential borrower, derive its *Z*-score, and assign the borrower to a risk group, in order to price the credit risk into the loan conditions (interest rates, etc.). If the borrower is obliged to continue reporting the indicators, banks can also make ongoing evaluation of changes in their credit risk exposure. A time series on borrowers' changes of risk group can be used to derive 'transition matrices', giving the historical likelihoods that a borrower in a certain risk group switches from this group to either a higher default probability or to a lower default probability. With this information, the potential evolution of credit risk losses can be simulated to get a picture of the dynamics of credit risk over time.[24]

Of course, this same time-series 'state-switching' model can be applied to changes in public credit ratings or quoted credit spreads, except that in this case the data gathering on default probabilities is much easier. Whether the fundamental data problems can be overcome for banks' corporate loan books, where loan gradings are evaluated on the basis of a much smaller number of borrowers, and therefore are more subjective, is currently an open question. Credit-scoring techniques improve the data situation a bit, in particular for standardised retail loans. Nevertheless, a single bank's own loan default experience will in most cases be only a small snapshot of actual credit risks.[25] For this reason, initiatives to pool the loan default experiences of a large number of banks can only be welcomed.

A similar qualification of data quality applies to the determination of recovery rates for bad loans. The CreditMetrics data set contains relatively detailed information on recovery rates in the United States, but – given substantial international differences in legal systems – these data may be a poor predictor of recovery rates for other countries. As shown by Oda and Muranaga (1997), different *ad hoc* assumptions about recovery rates can have a substantial impact on the outcomes of credit VaR models.

What do these considerations mean for the role of quantitative credit risk management models in prudential supervision? Clifford Smout (1997), the head of the Bank of England's Regulatory and Supervisory Policy Division (as it was then), describes the potential adoption of an internal models approach for credit risk capital requirements, somewhat provocatively, as the 'post-millennium project'. Many banks have only begun to develop credit VaR models, and research is still at a very early stage. As with market risk, risk management leaders have taken the first step, proposing the CreditMetrics approach to the market. However, little information on the working of this and other approaches is currently available. It will probably be several years before these models are ready to be considered by the Basle Committee for an internal models approach to credit risk capital requirements, although many, including Smout, agree that preparatory work should start now.

This implies that the established, but unfortunate, difference between the regulatory treatment of counterparty and that of (general) market risk – the former with simple and imprecise risk weighting, the latter with sophisticated VaR models – will prevail for some time in G-10 countries. However, regulators will be well advised to encourage the further development of models and to follow the banks' efforts closely to determine when the time is ripe for another 'great leap forward' in capital adequacy regulations.

(iii) Credit derivatives – a new beast to be tamed?

Credit derivatives may turn out to be the most significant financial innovation of the 1990s. They are instruments that allow banks to trade out of their current credit exposure, or to take on new credit exposures, without terminating the underlying customer credit relationship or entering a new relationship. By separating the underlying lending relationship from the actual credit exposure, credit derivatives may resolve the *credit paradox* through the availability of a new hedging instrument. However, like other derivatives, such as forwards, swaps and options on interest rates or exchange rates, they could be used in the opposite, more speculative way, increasing credit risk exposure and concentration. In what follows we sketch the emergence and functioning of the main credit derivatives instruments and analyse their implications for risk management and prudential regulations.

Credit derivatives are not, of course, the only credit-related off-balance-sheet item. Traditional instruments, such as guarantees or credit lines, contain similar elements. At the time that such agreements are reached, banks can face uncertainty about whether, or at what time, or in what amount, a claim will be made or a credit line drawn. Similarly, credit derivatives make the payment of cash flows dependent on the occurrence of uncertain *credit events*, such as the downgrading of emerging-market sovereign debt or default on a corporate bond. One important difference between the traditional instruments and the new credit derivatives is that the latter can sometimes be traded to other financial or non-financial institutions, so that the related credit exposures can accumulate or diminish at one firm relatively quickly.

Contemporaneous *loan securitisation* techniques also have elements with the characteristics of contingent liabilities. Banks frequently bundle a large number of loans under the management of a *special-purpose vehicle* (SPV) or securitisation conduit. The SPV issues various classes of securities backed by the loan portfolio. In order to be able to place most of the securities with the general public, the SPV needs a high credit rating, usually AAA or AA, which it achieves through credit enhancements, such as buy-backs of the most junior securities or standby letters of credit, from its bank sponsor. These credit enhancements also have contingent characteristics, similar to classic guarantees. However, they are smaller (more concentrated) but riskier than the whole securitised loan portfolio, and therefore lead to a concentration of credit risk on the sponsoring bank's accounts (Yellen, 1996).

a. Emergence and main instruments

This new class of derivatives developed mainly among the major investment banks active in the New York swap market in 1992–3. Since only a limited number of 'swap houses' dominated the market, they developed large credit risk exposures to each other and to a number of large corporate customers. In order to respect their internal credit exposure limits, they felt the need to develop instruments for trading part of their large exposures to outside investors. Because of the size of international debt markets as well as the advantageous regulatory environment, most of the activity in credit derivatives trading has subsequently migrated to London.

The basic instrument and in a sense the prototype of a credit derivative is the *credit default swap*. In this transaction, one party (A) sells the potential loss from a reference credit to a potentially defaulting counterparty (C) to a third party (B) against the payment of a periodic and fixed fee. If the credit event (default of C) occurs, B has to pay A the full amount or a fraction of the notional value of the underlying reference credit and receives the asset in exchange. Of course, the credit risk and any liquidity risk should be priced into the fee. According to a recent survey by the British Bankers' Association (British Bankers' Association, 1996), credit default swaps (and options together) are still the most widely used credit derivative and are likely to remain so for the coming years.

Another credit derivative, similar to the default swap, is the *total return swap*. Here A has to pay all capital gains and coupons earned from the underlying reference credit to B and receives from B reimbursements for any capital losses incurred. B pays to A a reference interest rate, such as LIBOR or US

Treasury bond yields, plus or minus a margin. The main difference from the default swap is that the total return swap hedges credit *and* all market risk, while the default swap only hedges credit risk.

Until now, *credit spread options and forwards* (second-generation products) have been less important than default and return swaps according to the BBA survey. However, London credit-derivative-market participants consider that credit spread options and forwards have the highest growth potential among the different products. The credit spread is defined as the difference between the underlying yield and a benchmark yield (LIBOR, US Treasuries). For example, a spread put (written by B) can be used to hedge party A against a credit downgrading of a corporate floating rate note (FRN) by issuer C, resulting in a fall in its market price. (A put option in general gives the buyer of the option the right to sell an underlying asset at a predetermined strike price. The price of this option is the put premium. The buyer has an interest in exercising the option if the actual market price falls below the strike price the buyer gets when selling.) In credit spread options, the underlying asset is the FRN and the strike price is a certain credit spread of that note. A has an interest in exercising the put if the spread increases *above* the strike spread.

Apart from these major manifestations, credit derivatives can also take many exotic and hybrid forms already known from standard derivative instruments.[26] Those that are contingent on credit events in a *bundle* of loans (potentially written by an SPV) resemble the securitisation techniques discussed above and are called *structured notes*.

The special characteristics of credit derivatives, in particular credit default products, pose major difficulties for fitting them into the traditional regulatory framework for capital adequacy requirements. For example, on the surface, a credit default swap resembles a classic banking book guarantee or letter of credit. However, banks often use them to hedge trading book exposure. If there is a liquid market for the underlying asset, they can be marked-to-market and also actively traded. Whether default swaps are held in the banking or in the trading book can have substantial consequences for the regulatory minimum capital (Bank of England, 1996). Both the Bank of England and the Federal Reserve have recently taken the view that not only total return swaps but also credit default products *can* qualify for the trading book, adopting a case-by-case approach, where the characteristics of single transactions are taken into account (*Risk Magazine*, 1997: 15).

b. Opportunities and pitfalls

From a management perspective, the separation of credit risk exposure from lending relationships is probably the most important advantage of credit derivatives. Traditional syndication or the sale of a loan can disrupt a long-term customer relationship, while credit derivatives – which do not imply an automatic ownership transfer in the underlying asset – change the exposure 'silently'. Also, by trading out of some old exposures, internal credit lines can be freed for new, more profitable business. Similarly, derivatives allow for the acquisition of new exposures without entering a new lending relationship.

Another essential aspect of credit derivatives is that they enable risk managers to divide their credit exposure into pure default risk (specific risk) and general market risk and to manage them separately, if necessary. For example, the purchase of a default swap can be used to take on the counterparty risk of a corporate bond but not the general market interest rate risk. Some of these new derivatives instruments may be tradable, so that adjustments of credit risk exposures can be quicker and more flexible than before.

In sum, credit derivatives offer a means for more active and, potentially, more successful portfolio management of banks' credit risk exposure by adding formerly unavailable hedging instruments for particular counterparty risks as well as considerably extending the possibilities of geographical and sectoral diversification.

Financial institutions also like credit derivatives, because in times of relatively stagnant foreign exchange revenues, they can provide a new source of trading income. Moreover, some of their popularity results from legal and tax reasons. For example, Irving (1996) reports that default swaps played an important role in deriving arbitrage benefits from the withholding tax on Italian government bonds (Buoni del Tesoro Poliennali, 'BTPs').

A disadvantage, from a business perspective, is the difficulties involved in pricing credit derivatives. As is argued above, the evaluation of credit risk is more complicated than the evaluation of market risk. For example, data limitations on default probabilities and recovery rates affect derivative pricing in the same way that they affect, for example, the precision of credit VaR models. However, as Paul Varotsis writes in a recent BBA volume on credit derivatives, 'the lack of a scientific pricing method has never been a deterrent to trading' (British Bankers' Association, 1997).

The business advantages for companies actively using credit derivatives do not necessarily lead to welfare gains overall. In principle, adding this new credit risk management tool should make the global allocation of risk more efficient through the improvements described above. Moreover, arbitrage possibilities between different credit market segments, such as bond and syndicated loan markets, should disappear more quickly. The new instruments make *credit markets more complete*. However, Duffee and Zhou (1996) warn that financial innovations might also result in the breakdown of other markets, so that the welfare effect of their introduction can sometimes be ambiguous. For example, if the emergence of credit derivatives leads to the disappearance of other loan risk-sharing markets, such as loan securitisation markets, then – in an extreme case – the overall risk allocation might even deteriorate. Whether such a situation will actually materialise has to be left to future experience.

Other problems might arise from interactions between these financial innovations and the current regulatory environment. If regulators make all credit derivatives fully eligible for the trading book, the threat of potentially risk-enhancing *regulatory arbitrage* between the banking and the trading book emerges.[27] Since (at least for non-EU banks) trading book activities can be run at lower capital requirements, more sophisticated banks might try to shift part of their credit business to the trading book. However, active credit derivative markets will mainly develop for investment-grade names. Hence, the remaining total banking book business may have lower credit quality, while – with the current Basle Accord arrangements – the capital requirements will not change, potentially implying increased risks.

Therefore, in the way that the complexity and speed of portfolio adjustments resulting from interest and exchange rate derivatives have reduced the ability of authorities either to impose appropriate (one-size-fits-all) external regulatory ratios or to monitor them through occasional balance sheet snapshots in market risk and in the trading book, so the advent of credit derivatives is likely to undermine the traditional mechanisms of credit control (e.g. the standard capital adequacy ratios, large exposure limits, etc.). Instead, depending on advances in abilities to measure credit risk, internal credit risk models will be further developed, and the battery of techniques and metrics already introduced in the analysis and control of market risk will also be applied to the banking book (see Section (ii) above). The somewhat artificial distinction that has been made between the regulatory treatment of the trading and the banking books is unlikely to survive long after the market for credit derivatives has become fully established.

Further regulatory concerns are related to internal controls and the proper handling of the new credit products. While credit derivatives can be used for more efficient risk management, they may also increase *systemic risk* if applied improperly. For example, a bank 'gambling on resurrection' could take on concentrated credit risk positions much more quickly than through the traditional lending process. Second, the credit derivatives markets are currently over-the-counter markets and relatively illiquid compared with other derivatives markets. It is therefore important that banks take the related liquidity risks into account in their control of trading activities.

Third, like other derivatives, credit derivatives can be used by banks to take leveraged positions. If there are improper internal capital allocations, then the writing of credit derivatives among a limited number of banks can lead to a 'cascading' of credit risk among the market participants, with systemic consequences if there is default in this group. Fourth, a potential group of credit derivative *buyers* are the small and medium-sized banks, which have the highest regional and sectoral credit concentrations. It could be argued that these banks might have little understanding of some of the credit risks they are taking on through these new derivatives. Although the smaller banks might not pose systemic threats, they may pose a problem for deposit insurance funds. Fifth, risk managers must be aware that many credit derivatives provide only imperfect hedges for some of their counterparty risk.

Some of the risks previously confined to the banking sector might spread to other economic sectors via credit derivatives, and some commentators worry whether this might be undesirable. We think that it would be an advantage, because non-financial institutions are not a source of systemic risk. If some banking risks can be unloaded onto non-banks, this should decrease systemic risk, rather than increase it. But third parties should be aware of the risks they are taking on; otherwise, among other things, there will be lawsuits, as occurred recently with Bankers Trust in the United States.

Other regulatory concerns with credit derivatives relate to investor protection issues rather than systemic risk – for example, the enhanced potential for *insider dealing*. Banks have an obvious information advantage about the creditworthiness of counterparties in their loan book. Although it is not a viable long-run strategy for market participants, occasional abuses of this superior information could damage the beneficial potential of the new markets. Brown (1997) argues that EU insider-dealing legislation would apply to credit derivatives, while some non-EU anti-insider-dealing laws might not. Of course, this risk is much more severe for exposures to banks' private loan books than for exposures to publicly traded debt items.

On the retail level, investor protection implies an obligation for banks to inform their private customers properly before selling them a credit derivative product, or indeed to discourage any amateur from entering the market at all. However, on the wholesale side, *caveat emptor* should apply.

We conclude that – in the long run – credit derivatives probably offer more advantages than disadvantages for the efficiency of financial markets as well as for the management of systemic risk. However, during the coming years, as these markets evolve, further regulatory reforms will be necessary to avoid adverse regulatory arbitrage, particularly regarding the differential treatment of trading and banking book items. There may also be a risk of some financial upsets, as has been true with ordinary derivatives (e.g. Procter and Gamble, Orange County, and others). As long as the understanding of credit derivatives and their proper use by most market participants has some way to go, regulators will be well advised to ensure that adequate internal controls are in place.

c. The future of credit derivatives

Until very recently, the effective size of the credit derivatives market has been relatively limited. According to the BBA survey, the notional amount of outstanding credit derivatives written by London dealers has been around $20 billion. Hence, the current notional amount globally is likely to be lower than 0.1 per cent of the $47,500 billion outstanding in more conventional OTC derivatives contracts in 1995 (Bank for International Settlements, 1996). However, leading London credit derivative dealers expect the market to grow to about $100 billion by the year 2000 (British Bankers' Association, 1996). This corresponds roughly to a 50 per cent annual growth rate for the near future, a rate comparable with the growth rates of interest rate derivatives during the 1980s, for example.

What will be the main impetus for this growth? First, given the present lack of credit hedging instruments, there is considerable demand potential. As customers become more familiar with the new instruments, their demand for them will increase. Similarly, as the writers of credit derivatives improve their valuation methods and overcome the outstanding accounting and legal issues, the supply will be provided. However, the growth will not be completely balanced. While market size, and therefore liquidity, will substantially increase for derivatives on listed debt securities, such as sovereign bonds or corporate bonds of multinationals, derivatives on small companies' debts will probably remain more limited. This is because the information problems for these unlisted debts are more severe and there is less scope for standardisation of contracts.

There will also be regional differences in the evolution of the OTC credit derivatives markets. An important factor for them is European Monetary Union (EMU). According to the Maastricht Treaty and follow-up agreements, such as the Madrid Communiqué and the Dublin growth and stability pact, a potential maximum of fifteen European countries will give up their national currencies for the euro by 1 January 1999. On the one hand, this will lead to a drop of about 18 per cent in global foreign exchange trading (Hartmann, 1996b), which implies the need for the leading trading houses in intra-European foreign exchange dealing to look for new sources of trading revenues. On the other hand, the removal of currency risks within Europe will lead to an increased focus on differences in credit risks, in particular on national euro debts. Given that London is already the most important credit derivatives trading centre, a lot of the growth potential lies in Europe.

Another source of growth potential for credit derivatives is emerging-market sovereign debt. In these markets, volatility of government credit risk is a major concern for international investors, whose exposure can sometimes be very concentrated. For example, according to *The Economist* (1997b), 70 per cent of total emerging market debt in eurobond markets is owed by only three countries: Argentina, Brazil and Mexico. This signals further demand potential for hedging products. Brady bonds have already played a role in credit derivatives growth in the early 1990s. As the international integration of those countries' capital markets advances farther, this trend should continue.

6 Regulation in developing countries

A. Introduction

A major theme of this monograph is that a combination of geographical and functional diversification, plus information technology and competitive pressures in a more liberalised system, have made financial intermediation more complex and capable of rapid readjustment. Consequently, the previous styles of regulation and supervision are becoming outdated, and new approaches and techniques (e.g. pre-commitment) need urgent consideration.

It might be argued that new approaches are not applicable to developing countries. Instead, with underdeveloped and fragile financial institutions, the need is to make the traditional precepts of financial regulation more effective, to impose effective ratio controls on capital, large exposures and liquidity, to prevent connected lending, and to limit political influence on management decisions;[1] in short, to put the CAMEL[2] through its paces. While this is certainly true, it would be foolhardy for developing countries to believe that the latest concerns about financial regulation in developed countries do not apply to them.

In their paper Folkerts-Landau and Garber (1997) describe how the Mexican banks used carefully designed derivative contracts to borrow dollars (they established a short-dollar, long-peso position) in order to invest in higher-yielding Mexican assets. This was, of course, speculation, relying on the maintenance of the existing dollar/peso exchange rate and on Mexican interest rates continuing to drop towards US levels. Such speculative positions (e.g. the effective net short position in US dollars) were expressly forbidden under Mexican regulations, but the off-balance-sheet derivatives were structured so that the positions were effectively hidden from the authorities. When the peso was devalued in December 1994, the banks with net short positions had to cover their exposures by massive peso sales for dollars. The unexpected flood of peso sales caused by the devaluation itself helped to overwhelm the monetary authorities, and transformed the planned devaluation into a (less controllable) float.

What the Mexican banks could do yesterday, banks almost anywhere can do tomorrow.[3] Not only will foreign banks and foreign bankers teach the locals these new tricks, but the brightest new entrants into the business will have been trained at business, finance and economics schools where such techniques are routinely taught. Moreover, as Folkerts-Landau and Garber emphasise, derivatives have another use beyond hedging or assumption of specific risks: they can be structured to enable banks to circumvent externally imposed balance sheet controls. Since such controls are generally more pervasive in developing countries, it is arguable that the incentives to use derivatives to re-engineer and to conceal the true financial position (from the authorities) will be even greater in developing (than in developed) countries.[4]

In any case, the general analysis of, rationale for, and principles of, financial regulation are not fundamentally different in developing countries. Thus, most of the analysis we have presented is valid for, and relevant to, them as well. It would be a mistake to distinguish the position of developing countries too much.[5]

This position is recognised by the many developing countries who choose to adopt, for instance, the same capital adequacy approach that developed countries use, although they are not formally required to do so by any international agreement, unless they are an international financial centre (Price Waterhouse, 1991). A survey conducted for 129 countries participating in the ninth International Conference of Banking Supervision in Stockholm shows that in 1996 more than 90 per cent of the 129 countries applied Basle-like risk-weighted capital adequacy requirements (Padoa-Schioppa, 1996a). Furthermore, many developing countries are hosts to banks from countries where regulation (on a consolidated basis) is applied according to international standards. If hosts imposed less stringent regulatory requirements on indigenous banks, foreign banks would be at a competitive disadvantage and might not enter, denying the hosts needed banking expertise.

It is also the case that banks from developing countries have offices in developed countries and borrow in national and international markets overseas. Their banks' credit standing would be jeopardised if their regulatory requirements were clearly weaker than the norm, and this point is emphasised by regulators in many developing countries. In brief, there are many reasons why they should adopt requirements in line with the international norm, although there is no formal requirement for them to do so. They also recognise that tremendous experience underlies international requirements and that there is merit in adopting what might be considered 'best practice'. Why spend a lot of energy and human resources reinventing the wheel?

While some of the more technical aspects of financial regulatory issues in the developed world, e.g. whether VaRs properly capture the kurtosis in financial markets and the potential impact of credit derivatives (see Chapter 5), may still seem outside the context of developing countries, they are likely to become relevant to many of those countries in the future. But that is not to suggest that there are no special problems and difficulties with financial regulation in developing countries, and it is to them that we turn next.[6]

B. Some special problems in developing countries

(i) The banking system

As noted before, commercial banks are the heart of the financial system. Indeed, in many developing, emerging and transitional economies they represent virtually the only financial institution.[7] This mirrors the situation of the industrialised countries during their early stages of financial development (Cameron, 1967). Yet the main types of commercial banks present in developing countries generally each have some deficiencies.

A taxonomy for the commercial banks in developing countries would be: (a) transformed state banks, (b) new entrants established by industrial (and sometimes political) groups, (c) foreign banks in countries with a dominant, or large, domestic banking system, (d) international commercial banks that dominate the local banking system, (e) specialised banks, usually of parastatal origin, and (f) co-operatives. Their separate problems are outlined below, by taxonomic group.

a. Transformed state banks[8]

Transformed state banks (TSBs) will previously have made (under the direction of the central planning authorities) loans to favoured state-owned enterprises (SOEs). After the reforms and in the transition, the more decentralised, market system causes the SOEs to become loss making (a common phenomenon, in particular due to the transition from administered to real market prices), so the TSBs become weighed down with the burden of bad debts from existing loans. In some countries the TSBs are rendered effectively insolvent. Just as the (loss-making) SOEs are often difficult, or impossible, to liquidate (or to sell, since they have a negative present discounted value), and are thus effectively on a soft-budget constraint, so too are the TSBs, on which the SOEs are reliant, effectively on a soft-budget constraint.

Before liberalisation, many TSBs were in a quasi-monopolistic position, with much of their loan book and overall asset structure externally imposed (e.g. with large required holdings, often at below-market interest rates, of government debt). That experience, plus their possible ongoing soft-budget status (refinanced by a still politically dependent central bank) and their role as financial milk-cow to the continuing SOEs, tends to weaken their commercial drive and their incentives to seek out and to encourage profit-making borrowing projects, especially among small and medium enterprises (SMEs).[9] The inability to use the price mechanism and interest rates is a metric of soft budgets where the discipline of capitalism is not fully operative.

b. Banks linked with industrial groups

Because both capital and entrepreneurial skills are in relatively short supply in emerging countries, the readiest source of both may be existing industrial groups. The problem, however, is that much of the incentive to establish banks linked with industrial groups is to channel the resultant deposits back into the founding industrial groups. While this process can foster growth, as Gerschenkron (1962) described, connected lending not only causes conflicts of interest but also can become a serious source of weakness during periods of economic difficulty.

In some cases, industrial groups can exert considerable political influence, with patronage going in both directions. This not only can weaken the banks further, since more of their loan book will be determined by non-economic criteria, but also makes it harder for the central bank (and/or any separate regulatory authority) to monitor, control or discipline them, since they may well be under political protection. This has been true in several Latin American countries.

c. Foreign banks in countries with an existing domestic banking sector

The problem with foreign banks essentially is that they are foreign. If they have a large presence, it will be resented (at least politically) on the grounds that the 'commanding heights' of the local economy are in foreign hands. If they have a small presence, their commitment to the welfare of the country will be doubted, and they will be accused of 'cream-skimming' and/or primarily looking after foreign business.

Joint ventures may help with the political perception, but they can easily lead to problems with corporate governance and with assimilating different cultures.

As elsewhere in the economy, the advent of foreign banking institutions can lead to technology transfer and benefits from enhanced competition. Even so, retail banking remains a field that developed countries have protected as an essentially domestic enclave, and there is no reason to expect the emerging countries to behave in a more far-sighted manner.

d. Dominant international banks

In many former colonies, especially in southern Africa, a small number of international commercial banks, often headquartered in the former mother country, continue to dominate financial markets. These institutions are simultaneously regulated by their home base and expected to work within the regulations of the countries where they operate. Achieving satisfactory coordination between local and international supervision is a problem. It is further complicated by the likelihood that the local supervisors will have limited technical capacity, while the international supervisors will have limited local knowledge and/or limited interest in what seems, by their global standards, to be a relatively small enterprise.[10]

e. Specialised, parastatal banks

Specialised banks are usually created directly by governments, and include development banks, export–import banks specially established to finance certain economic (e.g. agriculture) or geographic sectors or certain (under-privileged) groups. They are frequently kept outside the jurisdiction of the supervisors, at least until they become insolvent. In some countries they have become a serious source of instability in financial markets, first because they are under pressure to grant political loans that cannot be recovered, and, second, because of poor management.

A major unresolved question is how supervisors in emerging economies can deal with parastatal financial institutions, or indeed with those private financial institutions in which government has a significant shareholding.[11]

f. Co-operatives

Both TSBs and banks established by industrial groups are likely, for the reasons outlined, to focus their lending on large enterprises. SMEs and agriculture are often badly served, and co-operative banks emerge to fill the void.

Unfortunately, co-operatives are frequently small and undercapitalised, and their managers are short on banking skills. Authorities are often required to encourage the development of a central umbrella institution for the co-operatives, to provide a source of liquidity, banking skills, and in some cases of capital as well.

(ii) The economic infrastructure

Thus, in developing countries not only is the banking system likely to have shortcomings, but also the economic infrastructure in which the banks have to operate is likely to be more difficult. The economy may be dependent on a limited set of (primary) products, and therefore may be subject to greater volatility. Financial markets, where they exist, will be less liquid and more volatile than in developed countries.

Indeed, a hallmark of emerging economies is that they are much more volatile than industrial economies in real economic growth, inflation, nominal and real exchange rates, equity prices (Bekaert and Harvey, 1997), and nominal and real interest rates. In this environment, bank supervisors find themselves reacting to the consequences of the volatility rather than proactively reducing volatility. Sharp fluctuations in any or all of these variables can wreak havoc on the balance sheets of even the most sound banks, let alone those banks whose portfolios can only reflect the undiversified nature of the local economy. For example, sharp appreciation in real exchange rates can force exporters into default, even if a bank maintains a currency-neutral stance on its own balance sheet. Sharp increases in real short-term interest rates can cause even a borrower who has a healthy business to default.

In addition to the volatile economic environment, in many emerging markets, bank supervisors must deal with structural obstacles. Chief among them are a lack of strong and transparent accounting systems[12] and a lack of legal protection for creditors. Lack of transparency in accounting not only hinders bank supervisors in evaluating bank balance sheets, but also makes it difficult for bankers to evaluate borrowers. This naturally creates a tendency to rely on collateral rather than cash flow in evaluating loan customers. However, legal rights to pledged collateral of borrowers in default are highly circumscribed in many markets, making it difficult for banks to rely on collateral. Banks often lack the legal authority to assign loan collection rights to other parties without the consent of the borrower, which constrains their ability to sell assets. As a result, despite the difficilty with the accounting system, banks tend to make short-term signature loans rather than loans collateralised by movable property like inventory.

The difficulties faced by bank supervisors in emerging markets are compounded by the fact that the unstable environment usually means that banks are by far the most important financial intermediaries in these countries, which implies they must take responsibility for the performance of most of the financial system. Investors take into account the unique factors in these financial markets when considering what kinds of financial assets they are willing to hold. They are reluctant to commit long-term funds to emerging markets, preferring instead highly liquid short-term assets that give them the option of withdrawing their capital at the first sign of trouble. These preferences are largely satisfied by banks, because markets for short-term paper issued by private financial institutions are undeveloped or illiquid. Banks are able to issue liquid liabilities because they have access to both interbank funds markets and, in emergencies, central bank funding to ensure that their liabilities remain liquid.

Furthermore, in developing countries the financial experience and sophistication of the general public are weaker, so their problems of asymmetric information are even greater. Although there are credulous candidates everywhere for Ponzi games, it is not accidental that the most notorious recent cases, in Albania, Russia and Romania, have been in countries just beginning to emerge from a planned economy into a market economy. As a result, central banks (and/or the regulatory authority) have an important role to play in requiring the prior authorisation of any institution soliciting deposits from the public. On the other hand, the tendency for the main established banks (especially the TSBs) to ignore SMEs and personal borrowers means that not only will there be a role for a variety of co-operative financial ventures, but also the informal (e.g. curb) market may continue to play a useful role for a considerable time. It is important that the powers of authorisation are not used indiscriminately to prevent the growth of small-scale (and perhaps experimental) co-operatives, despite their weak capitalisation, or to attempt to shut down the informal market.[13]

As already noted, the links between the political hierarchy and the banking system are generally stronger in emerging countries than in developed countries. The TSBs were previously under direct political control, and in some cases the commercial banks remain state owned, as in Brazil and most of the former Communist countries. Links between the 'Grupo' (industrial group) banks and politicians are often close, which makes it harder to monitor and to discipline them. This is particularly true when the regulatory authority is itself under direct political control. The central bank in emerging countries is usually somewhat better placed to distance itself from direct political interference. (In Chapter 8 we conclude that it does not, perhaps, make a great deal of difference whether the regulation and supervision of banks are done within the central bank or by a separately designated regulatory authority, because the two would have to work hand in glove anyway.) To the extent that the central bank in an emerging country can establish independence from political interference, the stronger the case is for entrusting financial regulation to it.[14]

C. The role of the regulator

The above considerations suggest that:

1 the need for regulation is even greater in emerging countries than elsewhere;
2 externally imposed rules and ratios should be relatively *more important* in emerging countries, since less reliance can be placed on internal mechanisms;
3 following from 2, there is a greater need for the relevant authority (preferably the central bank) to monitor and to supervise the banks, and to authorise all new deposit-taking institutions.

At the same time, however, the central bank itself is likely to face the shortages of skilled personnel that we described earlier. Furthermore, the deficiencies of adequate data and (balance sheet) reports on banks make adequate assessment of financial conditions harder to carry out.

Under these circumstances there is considerable advantage in trying to keep the regulations, and thus the need for monitoring, simple and straightforward. For example, there could well be a case for introducing a simple, but higher, capital adequacy ratio, in place of (or, in addition to, for banks with some international exposure) the Basle risk-weighted requirements (Dziobek *et al.*, 1995). As discussed in Chapter 4, there is a stronger case for introducing some variant of the 'narrow bank' proposal in emerging countries, as opposed to developed countries. If, for example, deposit insurance were limited to deposits in banks (or in special bank subsidiaries) holding at least a certain large percentage of 'safe' assets, the moral hazard of an excessively widely spread safety net would be avoided, while at the same time the public would have the opportunity to hold deposits with a guaranteed nominal value.[15] If the narrow bank idea is rejected, then we, in conjunction with

Garcia of the IMF (1996), would strongly oppose the adoption of 100 per cent deposit insurance on all categories of deposit (far too much moral hazard), and would instead advocate that such insurance be restricted in coverage and amount, and, if possible, be financed by the constituent member banks, rather than by the authorities.

Of course, the authorities are almost certain to provide a considerable degree of implicit insurance, either against a systemic crisis or even against the failure of one of the larger commercial banks (the 'too big to fail' syndrome persists in developed countries, viz. Crédit Lyonnais, so we should not expect a different condition in emerging countries).[16] The correct response to crises, should they occur, as they have all too frequently in recent years, is set out in Chapter 7.

Let us return to the possible need for the adoption of simple regulatory requirements. Morris Goldstein (1997: 41–50) has advocated the adoption of a set of standards for, and by, all emerging countries, as a measure to reduce the incidence of banking sector problems that have recently plagued emerging countries. The standards would cover: (1) the content and frequency of bank reporting (i.e. disclosure), (2) improvements to the accounting and legal framework, (3) procedures for internal controls, (4) public disclosure of government involvement in commercial banks, (5) constraints on connected lending, (6) higher bank capital ratios, (7) presumptive rules for corrective action by the supervisors, and (8) consolidated supervision plus co-operation between home- and host-country supervisors. Subject to the qualifications set out below, these standards and their voluntary adoption are a very good idea.

But extraterritorial bodies, such as the currently emerging regional groupings of national supervisors (usually encouraged by and modelled after the Basle Committee on Banking Supervision) or the IMF and the World Bank,[17] have no power to enforce the domestic adoption of such standards. If any sanctions, such as expulsion from the regional grouping, exclusion from international financial markets, or even from (World Bank or IMF) financial assistance programmes, were prescribed for countries that did not meet the standards, then most emerging countries would claim to be doing so. Whether the extraterritorial body would be in a reasonable position to assess such claims, at least without undesirable intrusion and wrangling, is uncertain.

D. Problems with the application of developed economy supervisory tools and methods to emerging financial markets

In a *perfect* world, the framework for regulation and supervision would be uniform across all countries, emerging and developed; there would be an agreed-upon set of core principles. In practice, however, there may need to be a transitional period in emerging markets during which the effectiveness of international standards may be constrained. In the same way that limited access to international capital markets and lack of markets for banks' assets complicate the management of crises in emerging markets (see Chapter 7), factors like lack of liquid markets for bank shares and concentration of ownership – both real and financial – constrain the effectiveness of developed country standards in the short run.

Because the environment in most emerging markets is inimical to creating a sound banking system, many commentators have argued that supervisory tools developed for developed economy banking systems must be considerably strengthened before they can be applied to emerging markets. The reasoning is that bank balance sheets in emerging markets must be more solid than those in developed economies to withstand the vicissitudes of the economic environment. Thus, for example, it is often argued that the Basle capital standards, in which banks must meet an 8 per cent capital-to-risk-weighted asset requirement, should be strengthened to 10 per cent or more in emerging markets. Similarly, what is considered a prudent level of loan loss reserves relative to loans in developed economies must be increased to meet a different standard of prudence in emerging markets.

The recommendation for strengthened ratios is always accompanied by the recognition that tougher standards are meaningless if accounting systems and auditing procedures permit banks to misrepresent the quality of their loan portfolios, the quality of their earnings, or the quality of their capital (Dziobek et al., 1995). It is widely argued that banks in emerging markets should be held to international standards for the definition of non-performing loans: once interest is ninety days past due, it can no longer be accrued and the loan must be recognised as non-performing. This requires not only that banks report non-performing loans according to international standards but also that they have legitimate loan classification and documentation procedures in place.

If loans are misclassified or subject to loose classification standards,[18] loan loss reserves will be inadequate and capital ratios will be overstated. Loan loss reserves are accumulated through provisions, which are deducted from income. If provisions are understated, banks can report higher profits than they have actually earned. Hence, retained earnings, an item in the capital account, will be overstated.

Another factor that can lead to the overstatement of capital accounts is overdependence on the use of asset re-evaluations as part of the capital account. This occurs when regulators permit banks to realise increases in the market value of assets, such as fixed assets or equity investments, in the reporting of the value of assets relative to liabilities, which increases the ratio of capital to assets. Assets that are typically reported at market value tend to be subject to wide variations in price, especially in volatile markets. Hence, banks that appear sound one day can be woefully undercapitalised the next.

The problems raised above may appear manageable. Why not take the tools that have been developed – capital requirements, CAMEL ratings, loan classification, etc. – and apply them more rigorously than in developed economy markets? Why not enforce provisioning as in these markets and require banks to comply with international accounting standards?

Of course, the rules are being rewritten in many emerging markets to conform more closely to international standards. But, given the particular features of emerging markets described above, rewriting the rules is not enough. The difficulty is a shortage of the necessary skilled personnel. The shortage extends beyond the lack of trained supervisory personnel; unfortunately, it extends into many of the organisations being supervised as well. Because the banks themselves cannot report properly, the supervisor's job is even more burdensome than it would otherwise be.

These difficulties are, in principle, solvable with time and resources: for example, training programmes are frequently held for bank supervisors in developing countries.[19] The effectiveness of these programmes can be criticised; perhaps more hands-on assistance is needed, where knowledgeable personnel actually work closely with supervisors in developing countries as they go about their tasks. Nevertheless, training needs are recognised and attempts are being made to remedy deficiencies.

There are, however, more fundamental issues that are more difficult to deal with: does the emerging country's economic environment itself reduce the efficiency of supervisory tools created for developed economy banking systems? To answer this question, we must consider how the environment in developed economies assists the regulators in maintaining a stable banking system. Indeed, in many developed economies, the presence of thick and active capital markets complements the job of regulators and supervisors. For example, in those developed economies with solid banking systems, markets for bank equity are large and efficient, which permits regulators to ensure that capital is of sufficient quality to absorb bank risk. In many of these economies, institutional investors, such as pension funds, mutual funds and insurance companies, are large participants in the market for bank equity. These investors are subject to prudent person rules that encourage them to hold well-diversified portfolios. Hence, bank stocks are widely held. This is true even in small developed economies, since their capital markets are well integrated into larger world markets.

The importance of this condition for risk absorption is best illustrated by considering the consequences of its absence. In such a case, bank ownership is concentrated, and, very likely, the stock is held by individuals who finance their holdings with loans. If bank dividends are inadequate to cover their loan payments, the investors can easily pressure management to increase risk, in an attempt to raise dividends. After all, if an investor faces the loss of his or her equity stake for non-payment of a loan, the investor might as well risk the bankruptcy of the bank in an attempt to meet his or her payments. This strategy is increasingly attractive to the extent that the public perceives that bank liabilities are protected by a public safety net, since bank liability costs will not fully reflect the increased risk. In addition, a small group of individuals may actually finance their holdings of bank stock with loans from the bank itself or from related parties. As a result, a position in bank stock is partially offset by a liability to the same institution, which reduces the net loss suffered by the investor in the case of bankruptcy of the bank.

The lack of true equity markets in emerging economies often leads to a situation where bank owners can satisfy the capital demands of regulators with little difficulty and at little risk to themselves, e.g. by borrowing from their own, or associated, banks. Thus, bank capital in these markets is usually highly elastic, and it can be increased to support phenomenal loan growth, while meeting capital standards. Of course, the capital is, in reality, not much good for absorbing the risk of bank portfolios; that is, the 'quality' of capital in this environment is low.

Conditions in the equity market, therefore, affect the ability to rely on capital standards. But market problems go deeper than this. Markets for collateral on defaulted loans are virtually non-existent in most emerging countries. This is more than a legal problem. Concentration of wealth implies that when a crisis occurs, there are no unaffected wealth holders who can step in and buy up assets. With no market for collateral, recovery rates on defaulted loans are extraordinarily poor. Hence, many banks put little effort into loan collection, since the only economic pay-off, assuming that properties can legally be repossessed from their owners, is a demonstration effect to other borrowers, and this benefit is only important if a bank can survive the crisis.

Poor equity markets and a lack of markets for collateral imply that strong banks in emerging markets have developed alternative ways to ensure the quality of their operations. Because banks are the only financial institutions existing in many of these markets, well-run banks with the capacity to survive crises are extremely valuable to their customers. Strong banks are capable of protecting some of their preferred clients from the worst ravages of sharp interest rate increases by rationing credit at below-market rates when the macroeconomic environment leads to tight money conditions. They are able to provide such services by paying deposit interest rates significantly below interbank market interest rates. In contrast, in many developed economies, deposit rates and interbank rates are well arbitraged, at least for wholesale customers.

These rates are not arbitraged in emerging markets because deposit customers, who are also potential loan customers, value the staying power of a strong bank. Hence, customers are reluctant to break a banking relationship just to gain higher deposit rates for fear of losing access to credit when money market conditions are extremely tight. This same incentive permits banks to maintain high spreads and high potential profits. In this situation, borrowers also have increased incentives to repay loans, even when the legal system is dysfunctional. Otherwise, they would lose a valued long-term relationship with the bank.

E. Effective regulatory systems in emerging financial markets: dealing with the transition

In the long run, it is extremely important to move emerging markets towards conditions that permit regulatory systems similar to those now found in developed economies. The most important reason for this is implied in the discussion immediately above. If bank credit, which effectively means almost all credit, is limited primarily to those borrowers with incentives to maintain long-term relations with banks, new and risky customers will face a very difficult time getting access to credit.

But emerging markets face an immediate problem: dealing with the transition. That is, they need to create a framework in which a stable banking system can operate while the conditions necessary for a broader financial system are being developed. To do this, regulators must use their most effective tools, and an important tool is the market for short-term bank liabilities, which, somewhat surprisingly, usually works much better than bank equity markets. Bank supervisors can exploit the short-term market, both as a source of information and as a policing device.

As a policing device, the short-term market can be used to restrain the incentives that equity holders have to increase risk at the expense of the (implicit or explicit) public safety net. As indicated above, equity holders who finance their investment with loans have incentives to force their bank to increase risk if dividends are inadequate to cover loan payments. If short-term liability markets are functioning properly – that is, risk is priced in these markets, the ability to raise dividends through risk taking is considerably reduced. This argues for removal of deposit insurance from wholesale bank liabilities as well as avoidance of 'too big to fail' policies. Well-functioning liability markets can also be used as sources of information about bank risk, as private investors will have incentives to assess bank risks. Regulators and supervisors can, of course, observe this information in the market.

In economies with underdeveloped equity markets, retained earnings, if based on reasonably good accounting standards, are probably more reliable forms of equity than capital injections, for the reasons described in Section D above. Thus, it is imperative that banks be given sufficient opportunities to earn profits and retain earnings to increase equity. As indicated above, opportunities for strong banks to earn healthy profits are great in illiquid markets because customers value the long-term relationship. However, these incentives can be undermined if the central bank follows policies that keep money markets more liquid than underlying economic conditions would warrant. If central bank policy is too liberal, potential loan customers will have the expectation that they can always cover cash-flow shortages with a bank loan. This will cause them to engage in imprudent business decisions, and it will also give them incentives to arbitrage deposit rates against interbank and other money market rates.

Meanwhile, it is never too early to begin constructing the accounting and legal infrastructure necessary for a maturing financial system to operate effectively. Thus, we believe it is important to begin creating a legal environment in which property rights to collateral on defaulted loans are clear. These rights should extend to movable property, such as inventory, as well as to real estate. However, we cannot expect changes in the law to affect the environment in which banks operate until several years have passed. Market participants must see how the judicial system interprets the new rules before they will have much confidence in them. It is also important to build a legal framework in which a more open and arm's-length equity market can function (e.g. by legally protecting minority shareholder rights). Again, this legal structure will be fully useful only when conditions for more open markets exist, but it is important to begin planning for this event.

We also believe it is important to begin moving towards international accounting standards. The starting place is the introduction of international standards for classifying loans as non-performing. Many commentators argue that these standards should be introduced gradually, so as not to reveal weaknesses of particular banks that could result in bank runs. Evidence is strong, however, that investors already know quite a bit about the relative qualities of banks, so this fear is probably overblown. Forcing banks to increase reserves for loan loss by adopting more rigorous definitions of non-performing loans would give regulators a way to force owners to inject more capital into their banks. While it is clear that this capital is not likely to be of the highest quality, the very process by which regulators place pressure on bank owners will enhance their authority.

In moving towards internationally accepted standards, however, it is best to keep the accounting system simple while everyone is learning the process. Accuracy in reporting must take precedence over thoroughness.

What about capital standards? It is difficult to make a judgement about an appropriate ratio when both the numerator and the denominator that form the ratio are in doubt. The concept of risk weighting must be simple. Marking-to-market for assets cannot reasonably be expected in the short run. Hence, asset classification must be broad. Also, it is useful for banks to learn the importance of reconciling the income statement and changes in the capital account. Therefore, we conclude that, during the transition, a capital standard is a useful tool, but it is more of a device to assess how bankers are accounting for risk and to identify the sources of bank capital than a risk-controlling mechanism.

F. The sequencing of liberalisation[20]

In the former Socialist/Communist countries, prior to their shift towards a more market-based economy, all the main banks were state owned; and in many other emerging countries, many, or most, of their major commercial banks were also state owned. As noted above, their asset portfolios were substantially distorted by planning and political diktat, often with large required holding of government debt and directed lending to the main SOEs in the country. But at least the state-owned banks were, almost entirely, protected from credit risk, since the government stood behind the SOEs, and thereby from insolvency and failure.

The process of liberalisation commonly removes that protection from the TSBs.[21] The recent historical record of banking sector problems, e.g. as reported by the IMF's authors in Lindgren *et al.* (1996) and in European Commission (1997), reveals that a large proportion of systemic problems in emerging countries occurred in the aftermath of a major programme of liberalisation[22] (see Table 6.1 in the Appendix to this chapter).[23] A common feature of economic liberalisation, both in formerly Communist and in developing countries, is that it opens up the SOEs both to a new set of prices for inputs and outputs that reflect world price levels, rather than the previously administered prices, and to much tougher (international) competition.[24]

The consequence has been that many have become loss making. This has raised the loan losses of the TSBs, and the TSBs are usually not in a position to cope. The loans to the SOEs are generally not collateralised, and in any case the TSBs usually do not want to, are not legally able to, and would not be allowed by the government to close down the SOEs in bankruptcy. Instead, the TSBs, by inclination and tradition, and often with government prompting, see their role as keeping the SOEs afloat by pumping in yet more (soft) loans; thus

> if the central bank restricts credit, the effect may be that what little credit there is does not go to the most profitable venture, but to the banks' weaker clients – because otherwise these clients would fail, and drag the banks with them.
>
> (European Commission 1997: 2)

Moreover, the TSBs are not trained to search out good loan prospects among the SMEs.

Meanwhile, inhabitants of formerly Socialist countries commonly believe that the success of capitalism is found in financial wizardry (especially via stock markets) rather than in the spur of competition on efficiency and innovation. So liberalisation has often been accompanied by bouts of financial speculation. Since the ensuing rise in asset prices is then often regarded as justified by the liberalisation programme itself – indeed some may think that asset price increases are the *raison d'être* of liberalisation – the commercial banks may be overly prone to lend on the basis of collateral that possibly has overblown value and that certainly is likely to be highly volatile. Indeed, in some cases the commercial banks may even directly participate in speculative purchases. This behaviour has been observed in banks in developed countries, so it is not surprising that those in emerging countries can be also subject to 'irrational exuberance'.[25] When liberalisation is followed by an asset price bubble, the financial system is particularly at risk.[26]

Finally, lack of familiarity with free competitive commercial banking among both the public and the putative bankers may allow new bank-type institutions to be set up whose purpose is to channel funds either to the connected enterprise of the new bankers themselves, or (knowingly) into highly risky and speculative investments (even just Ponzi games). For a time, and generally during any asset price bubble, such high-risk banking enterprises do well, but with downturns, they usually collapse.[27]

Clearly no one would wish to stop, or to defer, liberalisation just because it is commonly associated with financial fragility. But it should lead to steps to mitigate such risks. A major concern is how to wean the TSBs from continuing support of loss-making SOEs. It is not much help to recapitalise the TSBs, e.g. by replacing their existing bad debts to SOEs by government bonds, if the TSBs then just continue to extend more loans to SOEs. Perhaps the loss-making SOEs that the government wishes to support could be directly financed by a special 'bad bank' under the direct control of the Ministry of Finance, i.e. an appendage of government and not a commercial bank at all.

Beyond that, the central bank should appreciate how volatile financial markets will be in emerging countries. Authorisation of deposit-taking institutions and monitoring need to be particularly strict and careful in the early years of liberalisation programmes. Since asset prices can fall, as well as rise, asset price increases should make the central bank tighten loan to value ratios and collateral requirements.[28]

As McChesney Martin once said, 'It is the role of the Central Bank to take away the punch bowl just when the party is getting going'. Socialist countries have been short of such parties in the past, so the need to take away the 'spirits' at the correct time is both more difficult and more necessary.

Appendix

Table A6.1 Financial sector liberalisation[1]

Argentina (1980–82): In 1977, before the crisis, the financial sector grew faster than GDP. After the removal of controls on interest rates, real rates became positive, doubled and became volatile. Entry barriers and branching restrictions were removed in 1977. The economy was opened to trade and capital flows in 1976 and 1981. The exchange rate was devalued and then allowed to float in 1981.
(1989–90): Prices and the exchange rate were freed in 1989.
(1995): Capital flows were completely liberalized under the Convertibility Law of 1991 and the Argentine peso was pegged to the U.S. dollar. Industry is being privatized.

Bangladesh (1980s–present): Two state-owned banks were privatized, credit controls were terminated, and interest rates were largely deregulated in late 1984; foreign exchange markets were unified in 1991–92; restrictions on current transactions were lifted in 1994.

Bolivia (1994–present): Liberalization was not a factor, although permission for dollar deposits and transactions contributed to capital inflows.

Brazil (1994–present): During the second half of 1994, there was a consumption boom. The disinflation process was accompanied by rising real wages and a lower inflation tax. Credit to individuals increased by 91% in the third quarter of 1994 relative to the previous quarter, and by nearly 14% in the fourth quarter of 1994.

Chile (1981–86): Comprehensive liberalization of the economy included the removal of price controls, privatization of most state-owned enterprises, trade liberalization, and financial reform. Domestic interest rates remained high, however, in both nominal and real terms.

Czech Republic (1991–present): In transition from a controlled to a market economy. Enterprise privatization is ongoing and 80 per cent of assets are in private hands; banks have been privatized, but the state retains an important ownership interest in the largest banks.

Egypt (1991–95): The liberalization of trade, interest rates, and prices is under way; limited privatization is ongoing.

Estonia (1992–95): In transition from a controlled to a market economy.

Finland (1991–94): Capital controls and restrictions on lending were removed and credit rationing was ended in the mid-1980s. An asset-price boom followed. Foreign

Table A6.1 Cont.

banks were allowed to enter in 1982. The banking industry engaged in very heavy competition for market share after deregulation in the mid-1980s. In this process, banks' margins were reduced and interest rates did not compensate for banks' risk exposure.

France (1991–95): Regulatory reforms were undertaken from the mid-1980s.

Ghana (1983–89): The exchange system was liberalized in 1986–87. Most interest rates were decontrolled in 1987. Most controls on sectoral credit allocation were abolished in 1988. The agricultural lending requirement was lifted in 1990.

Hungary (1987–present): The economy is in transition from a controlled to a market economy. Interest rates were deregulated in 1990. Banks are being privatized and competition increased.

Indonesia (1992–present): The financial sector was deregulated in the late 1980s, and reserve requirements were reduced.

Japan (1992–present): Interest rates were deregulated and capital movements were freed. The authorities continued to exercise some moral suasion, however.

Kazakstan (1991–95): In transition from a controlled to a market economy. The liberalization of prices has been completed; for interest rates and trade, it is under way. Privatization is also under way.

Kuwait (1990–91): There has been a relaxation of financial and interest rate policies and limited divestiture of public ownership.

Latvia (1995–present): In transition from a controlled to a market economy. Beginning in mid-1992, directed and subsidized credits and interest rate controls were ended. The current account became convertible and all restrictions on capital movements were removed.

Lithuania (1995–present): In transition from a controlled to a market economy.

Malaysia (1985–88): Interest rates were deregulated in 1978–82, but moral suasion continued and controls were temporarily reimposed during the crisis. The exchange rate floated with intervention. Capital flows were fairly free, but approval was needed to borrow foreign exchange.

Mexico (1994–present): Most interest rates and quantitative credit controls were eliminated in 1989. In 1991–92, banks were reprivatized. Financial liberalization and the strengthening of public finances (which reduced the public sector's resort to bank credit) resulted in a shift of lending in favor of riskier borrowers. Total loans increased in real terms by about 25% a year between 1991 and 1994.

Norway (1987–93): The financial sector was initially heavily regulated. Interest and exchange rates were deregulated in the 1980s and credit restrictions were removed. Asset prices subsequently rose sharply.

Pakistan (1980–present): The economy was overregulated, but interest rates were decontrolled in 1995 and some state banks were privatized. Bank borrowers were successful in delaying necessary reforms and also in thwarting their implementation. Slow progress in fiscal consolidation contributed to delays in liberalizing the financial system.

Paraguay (1995–present): Liberalization began in the late 1980s and was mostly completed by the early 1990s.

Table A6.1 Cont.

Philippines (1981–87): Liberalization began in the 1980s. Interest rates were freed in 1980–81. Foreign entry was eased. Universal banking was permitted, giving banks and thrifts new activities to conduct. Capital markets were fairly free.

Poland (1991–present): In transition from a controlled to a market economy. Interest rates were deregulated in 1990. Nine state banks were commercialized in 1991 and 4 of these banks had been privatized by the end of 1995.

Russia (1992–present): In transition from a controlled to a market economy. Broad-based liberalization was begun in 1992. By 1995, most prices had been decontrolled and both interest rates and exchange rates were market determined. Many state-owned banks have been privatized, as have 90% of all small and medium-sized firms, but the Savings Bank, with 40% of ruble deposits, remains state owned.

Spain (1977–85): Interest rates were liberalized gradually between 1974 and 1981. Bank licensing and activity restrictions were eased in 1974. Capital flows were freed and exchange rate determination was based on a managed float.

Sweden (1990–93): Lending restrictions and interest rate controls were lifted in 1985. An asset-price bubble followed.

Tanzania (1988–present): Sharp exchange rate adjustments occurred from 1986–90. Interest and exchange rates were substantially deregulated in the early 1990s.

Thailand (1983–87): Most lending rates, but not deposit rates, were freed. Capital flows became fairly free and prime companies borrowed heavily abroad. Exchange rates were fixed in relation to a basket of currencies.

Turkey (1994): Liberalization and reforms in the banking sector were ongoing throughout the 1980s. Interest rates were deregulated and the lira was made convertible.

United States (1980–92): Interest rates were deregulated in the late 1970s and early 1980s. Legislation in 1980 and 1982 give thrifts power to engage in new activities, and bank licensing was temporarily eased in the mid-1980s.

Venezuela (1994–present): Interest rates were deregulated and credit controls eased in the late 1980s. There was a shift to indirect instruments of monetary policy.

Zambia (1994–present): The economy was excessively controlled until liberalization began in the late 1980s, when controls on external payments, interest rates, and exchange rates were removed.

[1] Years in parentheses denote the period of banking problems.

Source: C.-J. Lindgren, G. Garcia and M. I. Saat (1996), *Bank Soundness and Macroeconomic Policy* (Washington, DC: International Monetary Fund). (Reproduced by kind permission of the International Monetary Fund.)

7 Managing financial crises in industrial and developing countries

A. Introduction

At least since the Great Depression in the United States, there has been almost universal agreement that, because banks play a crucial role in the payments system, the public have a stake in maintaining the integrity of the banking system. So, almost all countries have established supervisory and regulatory mechanisms for prudential and systemic risk-control purposes. However, in spite of prudential regulation, the evidence indicates that when a crisis threatens a major segment of a country's banking industry, funds and facilities set aside to deal with the problem are inadequate to maintain the integrity of the system, and substantial additional public funds often must be used. In some quarters, the arguments for the protection of bank solvency have been extended to include a government role for preserving the values of broad classes of non-bank financial assets as well, thus potentially opening up additional avenues for the expenditure of public funds to promote financial stability.

Moral hazard problems may be exacerbated during the resolution of banking problems because the application of public funds can create adverse incentive effects that lead to an aggravation of the crisis, and subsequently to a much larger expenditure of public resources to accomplish the objective. Thus, care must be taken in structuring programmes to rescue banking systems in systemic crisis. This chapter sketches a set of principles for sound bank restructuring policies that should help to reduce the risks inherent in using public funds to rescue private banking systems. It also argues that, because of the risks inherent in bail-out programmes, such programmes should be strictly limited.

Principles must also confront reality: there are always constraints that prevent even the most dedicated and knowledgeable bank regulators from imposing solutions based only on sound principles. These constraints are more severe and more fundamental to the marketplace in developing countries than in developed ones, but this fact does not diminish the challenges faced by policy makers even in countries with strong fundamentals favouring success. Therefore, we discuss how underlying conditions affect the ability of policy makers to fashion the best solution.

The fact that policy makers face obstacles, however, does not imply that they are doomed to failure. The challenge is to manoeuvre within the constraints, and, where possible, to loosen the constraints, to fashion a restructuring policy close enough to the principles to provide a workable solution. This suggests that an understanding of how principles should be applied under constraints can be obtained only by analysing carefully how policy makers have manoeuvred under a variety of circumstances. The chapter describes solutions under various constraints and assesses their effectiveness, considering the severity of the initial conditions.

The chapter is organised as follows. Section B establishes a framework for carrying out a successful financial restructuring programme, which includes defining objectives and principles for execution of the objectives. The section identifies three basic principles for effective bank crisis management and one principle for managing non-bank financial crises. This section also illustrates how differing constraints faced by regulators in industrial and developing countries affect the application of principles to achieve a successful restructuring programme. Section C uses the framework to evaluate bank restructurings in several industrial countries. Political constraints in these markets have forced policy makers to modify principles in application, even though underlying economic conditions have been favourable to a principled solution. Section D uses the framework to evaluate two bank restructuring efforts in Latin America in the early and mid-1980s that had very different outcomes – Argentina, which emerged from its crisis with a much weakened banking system, and Chile, which used its restructuring programme to strengthen its banking system – and to evaluate Mexico in the 1990s.[1] This section demonstrates that the nature of the constraints faced by regulators and the willingness of policy makers to adhere to basic principles of effective crisis management explain sharply contrasting outcomes. Section E briefly considers the efficacy of using public funds to preserve the value of non-bank financial assets. Section F concludes.

B. Principles and constraints in managing financial crises

(i) Three basic principles for managing banking crises

When a large portion of a country's banking system is threatened with insolvency, funds set aside to resolve isolated bank failures, such as deposit insurance funds and emergency central bank credit, are usually inadequate for the task at hand. Thus, in systemic crises, if the integrity of the banking system is to be maintained, public funds often must be used to resolve bank failures.

Whether the regulatory system has an explicit deposit insurance programme or not, maintaining the integrity of the banking system inevitably requires that some bank liability holders be protected from the consequences of bank failure. Hence, the commitment of public funds for restructuring implies a transfer of resources from the public sector to the banking system. The objective of public policy is to ensure that the transfer is limited to those parties whose protection from bankruptcy is necessary to preserve the integrity of the banking system.

If policy makers are to execute a bank restructuring programme that fulfils the objectives above, they must follow three basic principles. The first is to *ensure that parties that have benefited from risk taking bear a large portion of the cost of restructuring the banking system.* For example, bank stockholders should be first to lose their investment along with holders of large, long-term liabilities such as subordinated debt.[2] Also, delinquent borrowers must not be given favourable treatment at public expense. Executing this principle not only limits current restructuring costs by forcing private parties to bear part of the loss but also creates incentives to restrain risk taking in the future, which strengthens the banking system in the long term.

The second principle is to *take prompt action to prevent problem institutions from extending credit to highly risky borrowers or capitalising unpaid interest on delinquent loans into new credit.* Execution of this principle reduces the moral hazard risk in bank restructurings that arises when institutions with low and declining net worth continue to operate under the protection of public policies designed to maintain the integrity of the banking system. This principle implies that, when possible, insolvent institutions should be removed from the hands of current owners, either through closure or through sale.

Because executing the first two principles requires adequate funding to pay off some liability holders of institutions with negative net worth, the third principle for a successful restructuring is that a society *muster the political will to make bank restructuring a priority by allocating public funds while avoiding sharp increases in inflation.*

To execute a successful rescue programme, policy makers must adhere faithfully to all three principles. However, the economic environment in which regulators must operate affects their ability to carry out the principles. Even if a society has mustered the will to fund a bank rescue, it may face a resource constraint severe enough to jeopardise the success of the restructuring programme. For example, an economy may not be able to access debt markets for funds. In this case, to finance bank restructuring it may be necessary to reduce fiscal expenditure in other areas in order to avoid inflation. Obviously, as the funding constraint becomes tighter, the task of assigning priorities becomes more difficult.

A second constraint affecting the implementation of the principles is the availability of markets for financial institutions or for financial assets held by these institutions. Such markets can be useful for minimising public expenditure because they permit private investors to recognise the franchise value of a failed bank's customer base and its distribution system. Revenues from the sale of these valuable assets can be used to offset public absorption of credit losses.

If markets are large and funding is abundant relative to the size of the problem, regulators have a variety of choices available to resolve banking problems. These choices can be classified into three broad categories: private sector merger or sale, take-over and management by the regulatory authorities, and, as a last resort, bail-out of an existing institution with ownership left largely in place.

Under the first option, private sector merger or sale, irrecoverable loans are charged off,[3] which, if loan reserves are inadequate, may require a write-down of bank capital, often to the point where the value of liabilities exceeds the value of assets. When the institution is sold or merged, the price a buyer is willing to pay may not result in an adequately capitalised institution. Often, therefore, public money must be used to pay off the excess liabilities or to extend credit to the private sector in order to finance acquisitions. Under this option, when private investors are unwilling to pay a positive price for the customer base and the distribution system of the failed bank, the regulator closes the institution and sells the financial assets of the institution to help pay off depositors.

The second option, take-over by the authorities, is used when regulators have sufficient know-how to operate financial institutions and the market for impaired institutions is not large enough to absorb the supply of such institutions, either because the market is underdeveloped or because the crisis has made banking properties unattractive even at very low prices. If delinquent loans are to be charged off and capital written down, this option usually requires a greater injection of public funds than the first option because regulators do not receive an up-front payment for the franchise value of customers and the distribution network. However, if regulators have experience in managing failed banks, they may eventually be able to recoup the franchise value through earnings on their investment. The government can postpone some of the cost by permitting seized institutions to operate temporarily at capital levels that would be inadequate for privately owned banks. This policy has risks, however, as governments, like private owners, may take excessive risks with inadequately capitalised institutions. Moreover, the success of this alternative lies in ensuring that banks are returned to private ownership as soon as market conditions permit.

The third option, a bail-out, must be used when funds that can be committed quickly are scarce, markets are undeveloped or are illiquid at the time of the crisis, and regulators do not have the know-how to manage banks. Of the three methods of resolution, a bail-out is the most complicated to execute in accord with the principles of sound restructuring because insolvent institutions must be left in the hands of their present owners, who are given public funds to maintain the viability of their institutions.

(ii) Differences in constraints between developed and developing countries

Regulators in developing countries face more extreme constraints in terms of resources, markets and know-how than their counterparts in developed ones.

Even if a developing country has followed a very conservative fiscal policy before the onset of a banking crisis, policy makers face a daunting task in obtaining adequate funds for a restructuring programme.

In contrast to industrial countries, developing countries rarely possess a domestic long-term bond market, although many have access to international bond markets. When international markets perceive that a crisis is imminent, however, access to long-term bond markets dries up. For example, during the financial crisis precipitated by the devaluation of the Mexican peso in December 1994, Brady bond spreads over comparable US Treasury securities increased from 1 percentage point to 4 percentage points for Mexico and from 2 percentage points to 4.5 percentage points for Argentina between December 1994 and the end of February 1995.

This would seem to leave the issuance of short-term debt as a more common funding option in developing countries. However, the risk in the short-term market is that the government must not only cover interest payments but also principal payments if the debt cannot be rolled over. Thus, the slightest hint of deterioration in the government's capacity to service its debt may shut the government out of the market, which, in turn, increases the pressure for inflationary finance.

In addition, the market for bank assets is much more limited in developing countries. This is due to more than a lack of skilled professionals, who could perhaps be imported. It is also due to a lack of the legal and market infrastructure necessary for secondary markets to develop, a point that is illustrated by recent attempts by US real estate investors to purchase properties in default in Mexico.[4] Finally, the financial system might be too small to support a market with sufficient 'critical mass' to survive.

Regulatory know-how is sometimes in short supply in developing markets as well (Chapter 6). Even in markets with skilled professionals in bank supervision, if bank regulators do not have political independence, they may not be able to sell banking properties through arm's-length transactions. This problem also arises in the developed world – as scandals surrounding Savings and Loan restructuring in the United States suggest – but they are less important than in the developing world because other constraints are less severe.

Thus, the constraints on bank supervisors in developing countries make the necessity of the bail-out option much more likely in these countries than in industrial countries. Nonetheless, restructurings, even under the most severe constraints, are more likely to be successful if policy makers attempt to enforce the three general principles outlined above. It is the capacity of the authorities to adapt principles to local conditions, more than the severity of the constraints, that often determines whether a bank restructuring effort will succeed.

(iii) A principle for managing non-bank financial crises

While fashioning an efficient solution to a banking crisis is difficult even in the best of circumstances, it creates less anxiety than doing nothing. After all, the potential disaster from not intervening has taken on a folklore of its own: loss of confidence in bank deposits and payments systems can lead to the breakdown of the formal economy, precipitating a major economic depression.

What about policy intervention to preserve the value of non-bank financial assets? Arguments to support intervention in these markets are not scarce. For example, stock, futures and commodities exchanges usually have formal settlement systems attached to them. If a major player in one of the settlement systems should fail to deliver, could this not lead to the same chain reactions that are so feared in banking, and does this not justify interference for the same reasons as banking crises require interference?

The fourth principle for effective management of financial crisis is to *avoid the temptation to view non-banking financial crises as requiring the same response as banking crises.* Minimising moral hazard risks in bank regulation is costly. Banks must be closely supervised, and supervisory ratios, such as capital requirements, must be carefully monitored to prevent evasion of the rules through accounting gimmickry. It is not feasible for most societies, especially developing countries, to expend similar resources on supervising the markets for non-bank financial assets.[5] Nevertheless, society has an interest in the proper functioning of the institutional arrangements surrounding non-bank financial markets. For example, it is desirable to have clearing mechanisms for stock and commodity exchanges that can allocate losses in an orderly manner. If these institutions are to function without strict government supervision, private parties must be made to understand that they will suffer severe losses if risk reduction measures do not work adequately. The best way to drive this message home is to demonstrate that the government will not support the values of broad classes of non-bank financial assets in a crisis.[6]

The next two sections discuss bank rescue efforts in several developed and developing economies. As will be evident from the examples, policy makers in developed countries have the luxury of ample funds to resolve banking problems. This does not, however, always lead to policies based solidly on the three principles.

C. Lessons from bank restructuring in the United States, Japan and the Nordic countries

Banking crises struck the United States in the late 1980s and Japan and the Nordic countries (Finland, Norway and Sweden) in the early 1990s. None of these countries faced severe constraints on the amount of potential funding available to rescue failed banking organisations. The United States was able to attract substantial capital from overseas because worldwide investors perceive US Treasury securities to be among the highest-quality investments available. Savings in Japan far exceed domestic demands, and the country has become the largest net exporter of capital. During their banking crises, the governments of the Nordic countries enjoyed access to long-term capital markets at favourable interest rates, although domestic short-term interest rates moved erratically. In fact, long-term bond prices in Norway and Sweden rose substantially in the early 1990s, compared with their prices in the late 1980s, as illustrated in Figure 7.1. However, neither Japan nor the Nordic countries had markets for failed bank assets as resilient and deep as those available to US regulators.

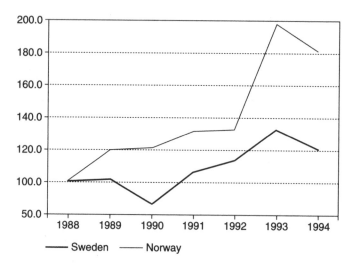

Figure 7.1 Government bond prices: Norway and Sweden (1988 = 100)
Source: IMF, *International Financial Statistics*

The similarities of the initial conditions of these countries, however, did not presage similar outcomes. Japan is still struggling to come to grips with its banking crisis, primarily because of political difficulties in allocating the costs of restructuring to various members of the banking community. In contrast, the United States and the Nordic countries fashioned a solution that imposed losses on bank shareholders and preserved the value of bank deposits, although, in the case of the United States, policy makers made some costly mistakes before designing a principled restructuring programme. This section outlines the steps that each country took to deal with its crisis and then draws general conclusions about why some restructuring efforts have been more successful than others.

(i) The Savings and Loan crisis in the United States

The case of the US Savings and Loan rescue and restructuring plan is an example of how access to funding and the availability of markets permit bank supervisors to apply these principles successfully. However, this example also demonstrates that, unless policy objectives are clearly defined and the political will can be mustered to commit funds, relatively lenient constraints can mitigate against good policy. Indeed, political constraints are the most common reasons why banking crises are not solved in principled ways in industrial countries.[7]

The US Savings and Loan crisis had its origins in two fundamental changes in US financial markets. The first was the broadening of the base of potential investors for mortgage-backed securities. The second was a rapid increase in nominal interest rates resulting from inflation. The first event reduced the economic value of institutions dedicated solely to directing funds to the residential housing market. The second increased the spread between open-market interest rates and the interest rate ceilings on Savings and Loan deposits, making it difficult for these institutions to raise funds through the deposit market.

As a result of these fundamental market changes, many institutions lost their net worth during the late 1970s and early 1980s. The magnitude of the losses involved exceeded the resources of the insurance fund available to insulate small depositors from the impact of bank failures. In violation of the third principle, the political will to provide additional public funds to cover the loss was not present. Hence, regulators attempted to solve the problem by manipulating accounting rules and pumping emergency funding into institutions in trouble.

Even with the lack of funding, regulators could have placed controls on the expansion of Savings and Loans with zero market net worth if they had established supervisory guidelines for asset growth relative to an institution's capital base. However, the political power of the real estate industry and regulatory lethargy combined to prevent any application of the principles of sound crisis management. Because the second and third principles were not followed, the owners of these institutions, having nothing to lose, took additional risks in hopes of recovering their investment.

By the late 1980s, when it became obvious that the programme in place only magnified the cost of restructuring, the authorities obtained sufficient public funds to deal with the situation in accordance with sound restructuring principles. For example, they were able to seize and sell failed institutions. Bidders assessed the value of a bank's assets as well as the franchise value of its distribution network. If bids were too low, regulators paid off depositors from sale of assets and government funds and closed the institution.

The policy accomplished two objectives consistent with the first principle: it forced stockholders of failed institutions to take losses, and it forced borrowers in default to lose their collateral. (It failed to force the holders of large claims on the S&Ls to take losses because they had liquidated their positions and left during the prolonged period of political indecision.) The policy worked because funds sufficient to close failed institutions could be raised without generating inflationary fears, and there was a market for the seized assets.

(ii) The banking crisis in Japan

The banking crisis in Japan was precipitated by the collapse of real estate and equity prices in early 1990. During the 1980s, financial institutions, led by the largest commercial and long-term credit banks, lent heavily to firms and individual investors engaged in real estate speculation. The methods by which these investments were made were somewhat complicated. Banks and other financial institutions made loans directly to participants in the real estate market. In addition, a significant portion of financial institutions' exposure to real estate occurred through related companies, known as jusen, or housing finance corporations. These companies were not subsidiaries in the strict sense of the word, as it is illegal for a Japanese financial institution to own controlling shares in another financial institution. They were affiliated with large banks, however, in that large banks supplied management expertise and directed customers to make investments in these institutions. Customers making investments in the jusen were primarily financial institutions. Many of these were smaller financial institutions, such as co-operatives. It is this tangled web of business relationships that has made it difficult to assess responsibility for much of the bad-loan problem in Japan.

When jusen and similar finance companies could not service their debts because of defaults on real estate loans, losses began to pile up on the balance sheets of the companies that had invested in the jusen. To their credit and consistent with the second principle, the authorities did not permit financial institutions to increase their lending to failed jusen, but their methods of preventing this from happening were, by non-Japanese standards, somewhat unorthodox. Under ordinary circumstances, jusen and similar firms would have been forced into bankruptcy, and their lenders would have recognised these losses on their own balance sheets. If the losses had exceeded the net worth of individual lenders, they too would have been forced into bankruptcy. Since most of these lenders were, in fact, depository institutions, the authorities would then have had to deal with the public policy question of how to rescue those that would have failed.

Table 7.1 The jusen resolution package (billion Japanese yen)

	Burden to be shared	*Loans outstanding to the jusen companies*
Founder banks	3,500 (abandonment of claims)	3,500
Lender banks	1,700 (abandonment of claims)	3,800
Agricultural financial institutions	530 (donation)	5,500

Source: Ministry of Finance Japan (1996)

Instead, the Japanese authorities decided not to force any of the depository institutions into bankruptcy as a result of the jusen problem. Total loans outstanding to jusen equalled approximately 13 trillion yen, about half of which were assumed uncollectible. The authorities contributed 685 billion yen to resolving the bad-loan problem. The banks founding the jusen, mostly large commercial and long-term credit banks, were asked to abandon their entire claims on jusen, which equalled some 3.5 trillion yen. Other banks, which had merely lent money to jusen, were to abandon claims equal to 1.7 trillion yen, representing less than half of their total exposure to these institutions. Agricultural co-operatives, which had made loans equal to about 5.5 trillion yen, were asked to contribute only 0.5 trillion yen to the bail-out (see Table 7.1). The latter institutions were treated lightly because they argued that they did not have the financial strength to absorb a more substantial share of the losses, and they were able to bring political backing to support their case.

There were two reasons why this solution was chosen rather than bankruptcy and resolution of individual financial institution problems. First, politically, the authorities could not afford to permit the demise of the agricultural co-operative system. These institutions, like S&Ls in the United States, have long ago lost their original purpose, which was to channel credit to the agricultural, fisheries and forestry industries. The credit needs of these industries have diminished to almost nothing. It was for this reason, of course, that these institutions aggressively lent funds to the jusen. The agricultural lobby in Japan proved to be a much more formidable opponent of financial reform than was the real estate industry in the United States, where assets held by S&Ls fell by 25 per cent between the inception and the end of the crisis. Hence, the solution to the jusen problem, while consistent with the second principle in the short run, failed to adhere to this principle in the long run, in that a set of institutions with incentives for risk taking were preserved.

Second, the authorities were acting on a traditional mechanism of dispute resolution. Explicit ownership rights have only a tenuous connection with responsibility. Founder banks did not own the jusen, but they had the responsibility of full ownership because their clients acted upon the knowledge that founders would behave as full owners. The authorities saw their role as merely enforcing a well-known implicit contract.

Thus, ultimately, the solution departed from the first and second principles. It failed to eliminate a failing set of financial institutions from the market, leaving open the strong possibility that they will take risks at public expense again. The policy also did not follow the first principle in so far as the allocation of losses across institutions was not a legal- or market-based process. If markets for failed institutions are to become operative in Japan, legal liability needs to be based on actual financial contracts rather than on notions of implicit responsibility. If the assets of failed institutions are to be sold, potential buyers must be able to predict their potential liability accurately.

This latter problem arose in the resolution of the failure of isolated regional banks and co-operatives, where the political issue of preserving a class of institutions did not exist. In each of these cases, public money funnelled through a newly established deposit insurance fund was used to cover the bad assets. However, the liability of the public fund was not assessed after the assets and distribution systems of the failed institutions were auctioned to the highest bidder. No such auction took place. Instead, a major 'main bank' institution was asked to provide funding for the establishment of a new bank serving the customers and holding the good assets of the failed bank. Thus, there was no market process to determine the value of the failed institution. This method of resolution does not ensure that the assets of a bad bank end up in the hands of the most competent or efficient managers available, nor does it minimise the cost to the public funds.

Why are the Japanese authorities so reluctant to remove failed financial institutions from the control of their former owners or former partners? A possible answer is that crisis resolution based on the principles described above would have disrupted fundamental business relationships in Japan. The political trade-offs necessary to obtain an efficient resolution of the crisis have been too costly. The Japanese government has announced a 'big bang' financial reform in the next few years (Ministry of Finance Japan, 1997). This may provide an opportunity to deal with the political opposition that is currently hindering crisis resolution.

(iii) The Nordic countries

Norway and Sweden handled their banking crises in similar ways.[8] They both used government funding, funnelled through deposit insurance agencies, to pump equity into banks whose capital had fallen dangerously low as a result of making provisions for non-performing loans. By 1993, the government of Norway had become the owner or majority shareholder in the three largest commercial banks in the country. In Sweden, the government made capital injections into two large commercial banks, while letting non-commercial bank-affiliated companies go bankrupt.

In Finland, the government provided all commercial banks with an injection of preferred stock to meet capital requirements. If any bank failed to meet interest payments on these shares for three consecutive years, the shares would be converted to voting shares, and the government would, in effect, take over the bank.

The common element in all these schemes was that the government ensured that banks could maintain their commitments to all liability holders and meet demands for new credits. As is consistent with basic principles, private shareholders lost control, at least temporarily, of institutions that had failed. At the same time, each government demanded that banks receiving aid submit restructuring plans to return to profitability. In Sweden, bad assets were separated from good assets through good-bank/bad-bank schemes. The government took responsibility for funding the bad bank. However, in no case was an effort made to auction off failed banks to private investors, primarily because domestic markets were too small to find investors for large banks. However, the question still remains why a bidding process open to foreigners was not initiated.

The absence of bidding for the franchise value of failed institutions constrained the ability of authorities to minimise the immediate payout costs of the banking crisis. Nevertheless, these governments seem to have managed take-overs of domestic banks in a professional manner, ensuring that efficiency and profitability requirements were established. It remains to be seen how long-run incentives of bank stockholders are affected by these programmes. In those cases where the government took only partial equity stakes, which occurred in several cases in Norway and Finland, it is not clear whether all private shareholders actually lost the value of their investments in banks. In Sweden, the government bought the shares of private shareholders of a majority-owned government bank that was in trouble. In all cases, private ownership rights were diluted, but this was a small price to pay given that, under ordinary circumstances, private shareholders would have lost their entire investment.

We conclude that the Nordic countries reacted promptly to restrain the behaviour of failed institutions. While to a large extent they followed the principles of effective crisis management, they could have done more to ensure that private investors, who were not depositors, lost wealth.

D. Lessons from bank restructuring in developing countries

While banking crises are a recurrent problem in both industrial and developing countries, the variety of experiences with bank rescue efforts in Latin America provide excellent case studies in crisis management. During the 1980s, regulators in Latin America often resorted to inflation and interest rate controls to resolve bad-debt problems. These methods were employed because countries entered banking crises with large fiscal deficits and with no political will to reduce them, in violation of the third principle. Argentina in the early 1980s and Mexico and Peru in the mid-1980s are prominent examples. Depositors took severe losses because of inflation, and in each country it took more than five years for investors to recover confidence in the financial system.

There are, however, other examples in Latin America demonstrating that, even under tight constraints, regulators have sometimes been able to fashion a policy that has remained sufficiently close to the principles to be successful. The most noted example of this is Chile in the early and mid-1980s. While funds to close failing banks were limited and markets were not available to sell large impaired institutions, regulators fashioned a recapitalisation and loan rescheduling programme that minimised incentives to capitalise unpaid interest or to expand balance sheets by taking increased risk. This case will be dealt with in detail below.[9]

In contrast to the 1980s, commitment to fight against inflation has been a prominent feature of the 1990s in Latin America. This is evident in the approach that a number of countries have taken to deal with the severe banking problems that erupted in the region in the mid-1990s.

The next two sections deal with three cases of banking crisis resolution in Latin America: Argentina and Chile in the 1980s and Mexico in the 1990s. The brief sketches of these experiences indicate that abiding by the three principles of bank crisis management are the most important determinants of success. However, the constraints imposed on regulators are more severe in developing countries than in industrial countries.

(i)   Crisis resolution in the 1980s: the cases of Argentina and Chile[10]

In a number of Latin American countries, a banking crisis followed in the wake of the debt crisis of the 1980s. As case studies in crisis resolution, the experiences of Argentina and Chile during the 1980s stand out for their contrasting results: Argentina's crisis ended in hyperinflation and substantial disintermediation, as evidenced by a sharp decline in the ratio of bank deposits to GDP, whereas Chile's crisis ended with a strengthened banking and financial system. This leads to the question of how much of the differing result was due to initial constraints and how much was due to the tenacity of the regulators in applying the three principles under severe constraints.

a. Constraints and designs

Chile experienced a severe banking crisis beginning in 1982 and, after an inadequate attempt to deal with the crisis, by 1984 had put into place a bank restructuring programme that is heralded for its singular success.[11] Nevertheless, the basic outline of Chile's programme was not unique: the programme originally proposed in Argentina in 1981 contained many of the same elements, as a brief description of each programme indicates.[12] Indeed, the design of both programmes was fully consistent with the first and second principles. As will be discussed below, however, it was the implementation rather than the design of each programme that accounts for the different outcomes. In carrying out their programmes Chile followed the third principle closely, whereas Argentina did not.

By late 1981 in Argentina and by 1984 in Chile, regulators in both countries recognised that they had to prevent banks from capitalising interest on loans to borrowers who were in default. They also realised that they had to force stockholders of risky institutions to bear part of the cost of cleaning up the system.

The programmes the regulators designed included mandatory restructuring of approximately half of the loans of the banking system. Each programme tied the principal of restructured loans to an index that reflected the rate of inflation, and each programme required the payment of a predetermined real interest rate. Both programmes permitted the banks to place loans with the central bank in return for a long-term bond. Under the Argentine programme, banks were permitted to discount restructured loans with the central bank, and they were required to purchase a government bond with the proceeds. In the Chilean programme, the banks were required to purchase a central bank security with the funds received from the transfer of restructured loans to the balance sheet of the central bank. In both countries, banks were required to buy back loans sold to the central bank at the price at which they were sold, plus, in most cases, accumulated interest, all by a specified date.

With the exception of a few small banks in Chile, the programmes did not include the sale to new owners of banks with depleted capital, nor did they include a government take-over of failed institutions. The programmes in both countries, therefore, can be classified as bail-outs in so far as existing banks would be, in effect, recapitalised. As discussed in Section B, regulators choose bail-outs when they face severe funding constraints and inadequate markets for bank assets, and they lack know-how to manage seized financial institutions. In managing their crisis in the early 1980s, both Chilean and Argentine authorities were faced with all three of these problems, but the funding constraint was probably the most onerous obstacle to establishing a good restructuring programme.

In the case of Chile, the accumulation of foreign debt in the late 1970s and 1980s hampered the authorities' ability to tap non-inflationary sources of funds to deal with banking problems. Indeed, in spite of its strong fiscal position, Chile was limited in its capacity to tap domestic savings to fund bank restructuring, because much of its savings were needed to service the high ratio of foreign debt to GDP (Table 7.2). The funding constraint became more onerous with the onset of the debt crisis in 1982, which effectively shut Latin American countries out of private international debt markets. Thus, in the absence of markets for bank assets, Chile was forced to seek funds from multilateral agencies in order to restructure its banking system.

Table 7.2 Fiscal deficit and long-term debt (percentage of GDP)

	Fiscal deficit (−)			*Long-term debt*	
	Argentina	*Chile*		*Argentina*	*Chile*
1979	−2.6	4.8		20.5	37.7
1980	−2.6	5.4		22.0	35.4
1981	−6.0	2.6		29.6	40.7
1982	−4.8	−1.0		34.2	62.6
1983	−7.9	−2.6		36.5	82.0
1984	−3.4	−3.0		33.4	99.5
1985	−5.5	−2.3		50.2	122.6
1986	−2.0	−0.9		44.8	114.9
1987	−2.9	0.4		49.2	95.1
1988	−1.9	−0.2		40.7	72.4
1989	−0.4	1.8		76.4	52.8
1990		0.8		36.0	51.9
1991		1.5		26.9	46.0
1992		2.2		21.9	38.6
1993		1.9		24.5	38.0

Sources: IMF, *International Financial Statistics*; World Bank, *World Debt Tables*

In sharp contrast, the funding constraint faced by Argentine regulators arose from that country's large fiscal deficit relative to GDP rather than its international debt burden, which was substantially less than Chile's as a percentage of GDP (Table 7.2). Allocating tax money to resolve banking problems was given a low priority, since these funds were used to finance government spending on other projects.

As discussed below, differences in the nature of each country's constraint had a crucial impact on how each programme was implemented. Since the bank regulators of neither country solely determined domestic priorities, they faced a common problem: a shortage of non-inflationary funds to shut down insolvent institutions and pay off liability holders. Hence, it is no surprise that authorities in both countries followed a strategy of recapitalising existing institutions by extending loan maturities and easing payment schedules. However, the success of a restructuring programme ultimately depends on authorities' ability to convince bank liability holders that the banking system can be returned to solvency, and that the value of their investment will be maintained in real terms. The Chilean authorities eventually succeeded in making this case whereas the Argentine authorities did not.

b. Implementing strategies

Why did the outcome of the Argentine restructuring programme differ so sharply from the Chilean one in spite of the similarity in the original designs of the programmes? The record indicates that, in implementing its programme, Argentina departed from the third principle: its authorities did not place a high priority on funding the restructuring programme with real resources; instead, banking problems were solved through inflation. In contrast, Chile clearly discarded the policy option of inflation, which was the major reason for the success of its programme.

It is important to recognise, however, that the difference in constraints played a key role in the outcomes. Inflation could not have eliminated the bad-loan problem in Chile because a large portion of bank liabilities were to foreigners[13] and denominated in foreign currency. Argentina's bad-loan problem was largely denominated in domestic currency. The fact that Chile's funding constraint was more external imposed a greater element of market discipline on the implementation of the programme.

To meet foreign commitments, Chile had to manage its banking system back to solvency. This policy had the added benefit of restoring domestic investor confidence in the banking system by the late 1980s, almost five years before such confidence returned in Argentina. The remainder of this section briefly discusses how the actual implementation of each programme was carried out.

As indicated above, regulators in both countries attempted to recapitalise banks by extending loan maturities, which implies a slower pace of principal repayment than was originally contemplated and, consequently, an increase in the funding commitment of banks. Hence, even with strong funding constraints, regulators had to find a source of funding for their programmes. In both cases, resources for bank restructuring programmes were channelled through the central bank to the banks. Hence, the magnitude of the funds required to restructure loans can be estimated by considering the extent to which gross central bank loans to each banking system as a percentage of total loans made by banks increased as the restructuring effort progressed. As indicated in Figure 7.2, in 1982 in Argentina, the central bank supplied gross loans to the banking system equal to 39 per cent of banks' loan portfolios, compared with about 9 per cent in 1981, whereas in Chile, in 1985 gross central bank loans equalled 87 per cent of total loans, compared with about 6 per cent in 1981.[14]

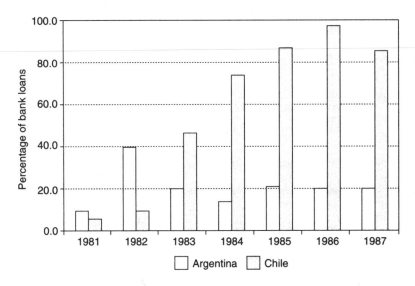

Figure 7.2 Banks' gross borrowings from the central bank
Sources: Superintendencia de Bancos (Chile), various issues; IMF, *International Financial Statistics*

The original constraints faced by regulators in each market made it difficult to fund the restructuring effort; hence, each central bank borrowed a large portion of the funds necessary to bail out insolvent banks from solvent banks in its own system. Of course, in order for solvent banks to lend funds to the central bank, they had to reduce credit to their own borrowers.

As indicated in Figure 7.3, in Argentina, the net credit position of banks with the central bank as a percentage of central bank credit to banks equalled –22 per cent in 1981 and increased to just over –12 per cent in 1982.[15] This implies that, in 1982, 88 per cent of central bank credit to banks was funded by the banks themselves. For Chile, the data begin in 1983 because prior to that date detailed asset breakdowns are not available. In

Chile, in 1984, at the inception of the second restructuring programme, banks' net position with the central bank was –21 per cent declining to –25 per cent by 1987, implying that 75 per cent of central bank credit to banks was funded by banks.

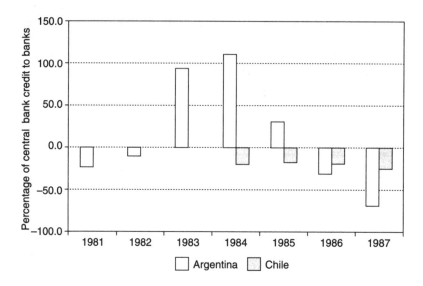

Figure 7.3 Banks' net position with the central bank (percentage of central bank credit to banks)
Sources: Superintendencia de Bancos (Chile), various issues; IMF, *International Financial Statistics*

In the case of Argentina, central bank loans to impaired banks were funded with reserve requirements on bank deposits, whereas in Chile they were funded by central bank bonds purchased by solvent banks.[16] Thus, in both cases, the central bank absorbed the credit risk of lending to impaired banks by acting as intermediary between banks lending funds and banks borrowing funds.

Events changed dramatically in Argentina in 1983. In contrast to developments in 1981 and 1982, by 1983 the banks became net lenders to the central bank, as indicated by the fact that banks' net position increased to positive 90 per cent. The central bank used the funds from the banks to fund the fiscal deficit, as central bank loans to the public sector increased from 11 per cent of GDP in 1982 to 27 per cent of GDP in 1983.[17]

Since the central bank was no longer lending to the banks, it had to find another method for dealing with problem loans. This method was to impose interest rate ceilings on bank loans during a period when inflation reached almost 500 per cent per year. As a result of these policies, the real value of loans was inflated away, falling from 51 per cent of GDP in 1982 to 39 per cent in 1984. Real interest rates on deposits were also negative, falling to about –50 per cent by 1984.

In short, in Argentina, in violation of the third principle, there was no political commitment to control the fiscal deficit, with the result that, in real terms, no funds could be committed to the bank bailout. The first two principles were also violated since the negative real interest rate on loans provided a subsidy to borrowers and heavily penalised depositors, a party bearing little responsibility for the crisis. Stockholders, on the other hand, emerged from the crisis with much of their wealth preserved in real terms. Depositors fled the banking system, and deposits to GDP declined from 22 per cent of GDP in 1981 to 14 per cent of GDP in 1985 (Figure 7.4).[18]

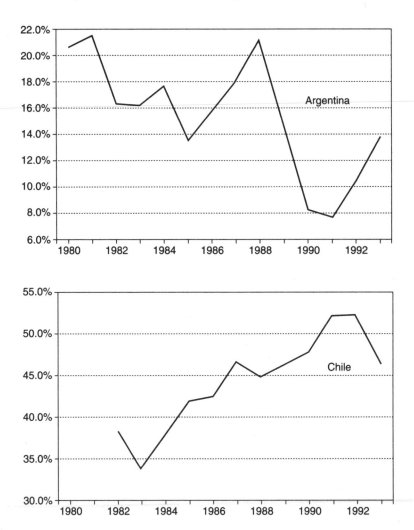

Figure 7.4 Deposits to GDP: Argentina and Chile
Sources: IMF, *International Financial Statistics*; *Superintendencia de Bancos* (Chile), various issues

In contrast to Argentina, Chile worked its way out of its bad-loan problem gradually. It was not until 1992 that the banks became net lenders to the central bank. During this period, Chile experienced only moderate inflation, and real interest rates on loans and deposits remained positive. As mentioned above, an element of market discipline inhibiting an inflationary solution in Chile was the large percentage of bank liabilities to foreigners, mostly to US banks, denominated in US dollars. Foreign borrowings as a percentage of bank financial liabilities plus capital accounts on the eve of the crisis in Chile were 53 per cent in 1982, compared with 24 per cent in 1981 in Argentina.

If the foreign liability holders were to be paid, the Chilean restructuring programme had to work. During the crisis, many borrowers who had borrowed foreign currency from banks were unable to earn foreign currency to repay their loans. Hence, banks could not service their own foreign liabilities. To help banks repay these liabilities, the central bank absorbed the foreign exchange risk for the banks.

In the first step in this process, many foreign currency loans held on the balance sheets of banks were converted into indexed peso loans to relieve borrowers of foreign exchange risk. However, this left the banks with an imbalance of foreign currency liabilities. For example, in 1985, foreign currency loans remaining on bank balance sheets totalled $2.0 billion while liabilities to foreigners denominated in foreign currency (mostly rescheduled loans from US banks) equalled $6.3 billion. In other words, foreign currency liabilities were funding indexed peso assets.

As the second step in the process, to remove most of the risk created by this imbalance from the banks, the central bank issued foreign currency bonds to the banks, and, at the same time, made loans to the banks denominated in indexed pesos. For example, in 1985, all banks held foreign-currency-denominated bonds and deposits issued by the central bank equal to $3.6 billion on the asset side of their balance sheet. At the same time, the banks borrowed $5 billion in indexed pesos from the central bank, excluding loans sold to the central bank.[19]

This device was available to all three categories of banks operating in the market – foreign-owned banks, the state bank and private domestic banks – but it was the private domestic banks, where the bad-loan problem was focused, that most extensively used the programme. In 1985, private domestic banks had indexed peso loans of $4.2 billion on their balance sheets and indexed peso deposits of only $1.1 billion. At the same time, these banks had foreign liabilities of $4.6 billion and foreign currency loans of $1.3 billion. Private domestic banks were net lenders of over $3.1 billion to the central bank in foreign currency and net borrowers of $3.8 in indexed pesos, excluding loans sold to the central bank.

By 1987, the net borrowing position of the domestic private banks with the central bank equalled $4.3 billion. Approximately one-third of this figure, or $1.4 billion, was covered by loans to the central bank from the state bank and foreign banks, which, by year-end 1987, were net creditors of the central bank. Approximately $1.2 billion of the $1.4 billion were funded by foreign currency bonds issued by the central bank to the state bank and foreign banks.

The central bank funded the remaining $3.2 billion through its liabilities to non-banks. In 1987, the central bank was able to issue $2.6 billion in domestic currency securities to the non-bank public. To avoid financing the remainder with inflation, it had to fund about $600 million from foreign sources, again mainly borrowings from multilateral agencies. As a result, foreign sources covered $1.8 billion, or 42 per cent of the cost, with the remaining $2.8 billion funded in the domestic market.

The proportion of the cost funded by foreign sources was much higher in 1985 (82 per cent of the total) even though at that point the total cost appeared smaller. In 1985, the central bank did not have sufficient access to the domestic non-bank funding market to cover much of its share of the cost. The rapid increase in the importance of non-bank domestic funding in the Chilean restructuring programme that occurred after 1985 demonstrates that, in contrast to Argentina, domestic investors gained confidence that the restructuring programme would return the banking system to solvency.

It is sometimes argued that this confidence was somewhat artificially created by Chile's mandatory pension system, which purchased much of the central bank's debt in 1987. It must be noted, however, that if domestic investors remained suspicious of the financial system, some would have fled the banking system to offset their mandatory investment in pension funds.[20] That this did not happen is demonstrated by the fact that, from 1984 onward, deposits increased rapidly as a percentage of GDP (Figure 7.4).

While the loan restructuring programme extended payment schedules of borrowers with problems meeting such schedules, it adhered closely enough to the first principle that, as of year-end 1994, the banks were able to repurchase about half of the restructured loans sold or placed with the central bank. However, two large banks still have large unpaid liabilities to the central bank and, even today, loans placed with the central bank still equal more than 8 per cent of GDP.

As a result of relatively close adherence to the principles, even while under severe constraints, Chile achieved a stable banking system by the late 1980s with deposits increasing relative to GDP, at a time when deposits to GDP in Argentina had dropped precipitously to less than 8 per cent from 19 per cent early in the decade (Figure 7.4).

The Chilean experience demonstrates that a successful programme to restructure banks must be backed up with adequate real funding to buy sufficient time to prove to domestic investors that bank liabilities will be paid off in real terms. To obtain this result, a programme must contain elements to encourage borrowers to meet their commitments and incentives for bank managers to return their banks to solvency. However, even carefully devised programmes can be successful only if policy makers pursue policies conducive to low inflation and macroeconomic stability. As the Chilean experience demonstrates, when investors become convinced that their domestic financial assets are safe, they will be willing to provide a good portion of the real funds needed for a successful restructuring programme.

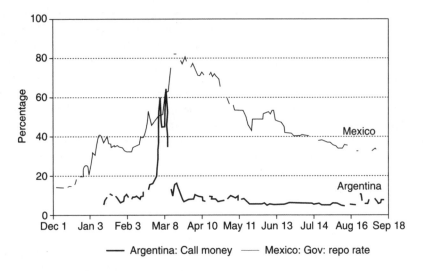

Figure 7.5 Interest rates: Argentina and Mexico (1 Dec. 1994–18 Sept. 1995)
Source: Bloomberg Business News

(ii) Restructuring the Mexican banking system in the mid-1990s

Having implemented strong stabilisation programmes as well as financial and other economic reforms in the early 1990s, many Latin American countries experienced large capital inflows. In December 1994, however, large outflows of capital from Mexico resulted in a balance of payments crisis and a sharp devaluation of the Mexican peso.[21] The crisis of international investor confidence in Mexico spilt over into several other Latin American countries, most notably Argentina (the so-called Tequila effect). To stem capital flight both countries increased domestic interest rates, which led to concerns that bank borrowers would not be able to meet their obligations.

By early March 1995, the peso interbank interest rate in Argentina reached a peak of almost 70 per cent, and in late March 1995 the repurchase agreement rate on government securities in Mexico reached over 80 per cent (Figure 7.5). The fears concerning the quality of the banking systems in these two countries were further fed by the impression that both systems contained pockets of institutions that had been weak before the financial crisis. In Argentina, the crisis proved to be a crisis of bank liquidity rather than a systemic banking crisis. In Mexico, on the other hand, the liquidity crisis evolved into a full-fledged banking crisis. The constraints Mexican bank regulators faced as they designed programmes to restructure their banking system and their progress in executing these programmes are the subjects of this section.

a. Constraints

Despite the reduction in investors' confidence in their financial system that followed the eruption of the crisis, Mexican regulators started the resolution of their banking problems under much more favourable conditions than was the case in the early 1980s for a number of Latin American countries. Policy makers' know-how in designing effective restructuring programmes was much improved as a result of absorbing the lessons of success and failure from the 1980s. Also, although still below industrial country standards, bank reporting and supervisory conditions were much improved.

On the funding side, the fiscal situation in Mexico was much healthier than in the early 1980s. Moreover, since the fight against inflation had become a priority, Mexico committed itself to solving the crisis with non-inflationary policies. Nevertheless, just as in the early 1980s, private funding for restructuring efforts practically vanished with the onset of the crisis, indicating that perceptions about country risk remained fragile in the early 1990s. Moreover, despite the reforms of the early 1990s, markets for long-term funds have not yet developed in many countries, and the market for insolvent banks remains thin. Although constraints on resolving bank problems have eased since the early 1980s, funding constraints are still relatively severe compared with conditions in industrial countries.

b. Programme design

As is discussed in the preceding section, in determining whether a restructuring programme follows the three principles of banking crisis resolution, the analyst must consider the following aspects of the programme: how it is funded, who bears the cost of resolution, and whether it controls the growth of impaired institutions. Conceptually, the restructuring programme in Mexico addresses each of these aspects in a manner that is consistent with adherence to the basic principles. However, in practical execution, it has been much more difficult to abide by the three principles.

Consistent with the first principle, the authorities in the early stages of the crisis intervened in the most seriously impaired banks in the system in a timely manner. Thus, they removed control of bankrupt banks from owners that might have attempted to expand their balance sheets in a gamble that growth would restore their banks to solvency. One of these impaired banks has recently been sold to a foreign bank, and parts of other banks have been sold as well. For the first nine months of 1996, credit growth in the non-intervened banks has been quite modest – below the inflation rate as well as below the average interest rate on short-term government bonds (CETES) over that period (Table 7.3).[22]

Table 7.3 Mexico: credit growth in non-intervened banks (January 1966 to September 1996; per cent, annualised)

Credit growth	16.21%
Inflation	25.40%
CETES (twenty-eight days)	32.67%

Sources: Banco de México, *Indicadores Económicos*; Comisión Nacional Bancaria y de Valores, *Boletín Estadístico de Banca Múltiple*

By late 1995, it became clear to the authorities that non-intervened banks needed some relief from non-performing loans, or, under any reasonable definition, these banks too would become insolvent. Their response was to establish two programmes to relieve banks of the burden of non-performing loans. The first programme permitted banks to sell loans net of loan loss provisions to the bank insurance fund (FOBAPROA, Fondo Bancario de Proteccion al Ahorro). To be eligible for this programme, bank owners had to inject 1 peso of capital or subordinated debt into their bank for every 2 pesos of loans sold to FOBAPROA. In addition, they had to promise to contribute an additional 20 to 30 per cent of the loan portfolio sold if losses on the portfolio exceeded those provided for by the provisions applied to loans sold. As of September 1996, this programme represented almost 30 per cent of performing loans at non-intervened banks (Table 7.4).

Table 7.4 Mexico: bank restructuring programmes (percentage of total performing loans)

FOBAPROA loan purchase programme	27.9%
UDIS restructured loan programme	23.0%

Source: Comisión Nacional Bancaria y de Valores, *Boletín Estadístico de Banca Múltiple*

To fund the net loans on its balance sheet, FOBAPROA has issued zero coupon bonds with twelve-year maturities that accumulate interest at the ninety-one-day CETES rate. These bonds are held on the balance sheets of banks participating in the programme and are non-marketable. Because this programme does not require any cash payments to the banks until the bonds mature, it does not generate an inflationary increase in the money supply.

The second programme parallels the basic Chilean restructuring programme in that it permits the indexation of principal for restructured loans through the use of a unit of account known as unidades de inversion (UDIs). As in the case of Chile, Mexican banks have not had access to UDI funding to match-fund the indexed loans. The solution to the problem has been to pass these restructured loans to a trust account that is funded by UDI deposits that are an asset of the government. In turn, the government issues a zero coupon bond, with interest rate tied to the CETES rate, that is bought by the bank transferring loans to the UDI trust.[23] The zero coupon bond is repaid from the income and principal payments on the loans in the trust. The banks are responsible for provisioning the trust, and, to the extent that loans are not repaid, the bonds are not redeemed. Hence, technically, banks continue to absorb the credit risk. This programme represented about 23 per cent of performing loans at non-intervened banks in September 1996 (see Table 7.4).

As in the FOBAPROA programme, the banks do not receive any immediate cash flow from the programme, so, technically, the programme does not require an expansion in the money supply. However, because over half of bank loans have been either sold to FOBAPROA or placed in UDI trusts (Table 7.4), the lack of cash flow on these bonds has potentially placed banks in an illiquid position. The Mexican authorities believe that most banks do not face an illiquidity problem because depositors have been willing to leave accumulated interest in their accounts. While this is true for the banking system as a whole, it is not the case of all individual banks. Some banks have been depending heavily on the interbank market for funding, which has, to some extent, been supported by an expansionary monetary policy. One indication of this is that since January 1996, the interbank and CETES rates have fallen by over 20 percentage points.

In attempting to assess the magnitude of the Mexican banking crisis, it is interesting to compare the size of the Mexican loan restructuring programmes to date with those in Chile. As indicated in Table 7.5, the Mexican loan restructuring programmes represent about the same portion of total loans as in the Chilean system, but they represent a much smaller portion of GDP. It is also important to note that, in Chile, the restructured loan problem was centred on a particular group of banks (domestically owned private banks), which make up about half the loans in the total system. Thus, the central bank was able to use funds from strong banks to cover some of the costs of the restructuring programme. In Mexico, the problem was spread more evenly across banks.

Table 7.5 The extent of bank restructuring programmes in Mexico and Chile

	Mexico (Sepember 1996)	*Chile (December 1987)*
Relative to performing loan	51.0%	54.8%
Relative to GDP	14.5%	44.2%

Note: The amount includes the loans sold and restructured. For Mexico, the data for non-intervened banks are used. For Chile, the data for total financial system are used

Sources: Comisión Nacional Bancaria y de Valores (Mexico), *Boletín Estadístico de Banca Múltiple*; Superintendencia de Bancos e Instituciones Financieros (Chile), *Información Financiera*

E. Preserving the value of financial assets outside the banking system

As is stated in Section B, the fourth principle of effective management of financial crisis is for the authorities to avoid the temptation of supporting the value of non-bank financial assets in a crisis. However, this temptation will be particularly large in cases when a significant proportion of bank assets is formed (or is backed up in the form of collateral) by securities whose prices are experiencing a sharp decline.[24] This raises the issue of whether it is good policy to rescue banks indirectly by supporting the value of securities owned by the banks or whether it is preferable to let asset prices seek their market level and deal with the consequences for bank balance sheets as they occur.

In this regard, it is useful to consider the circumstances surrounding the bankruptcy of Barings, the UK's oldest merchant bank, in February 1995.[25] Largely unbeknownst to management, an employee of Barings had taken open positions on exchange-traded futures contracts on the Nikkei 225 stock index traded in Singapore, Osaka and Tokyo. In late February, Barings was forced to announce that, as a result of movements in the index against its position, it was insolvent. The Bank of England did not rescue the merchant bank; instead it sent it into receivership.

While Barings was not a commercial bank, its failure had potential consequences for the solvency of settlement systems of several futures exchanges, a matter of great concern when a commercial bank fails. Regulators fear that bankruptcy of a single member of a settlement system can cause other members to default on their settlement positions, generating a systemic financial crisis.

Barings' bankruptcy did cause it to default on several transactions for borrowed securities in Japan, but the exchanges on which Barings traded its futures contracts were able to cover the defaulted positions. This demonstrates that market participants can and should be expected to protect themselves against the possibility that another participant may fail to deliver on its promises. While regulators can cajole exchanges and other parties to establish and follow rules to protect market integrity, the best incentive to make sure these rules are put into place and followed is to let markets know that bankruptcies have private costs.

If regulators support banks by ensuring that the prices of assets they hold remain stable, incentives to protect bank balance sheets from the consequences of both inadequate internal risk-control management and market movements will diminish significantly. In such situations, even though regulators might insist on stringent capital requirements and conservative provisioning policies, some banks will seek to evade these rules through such devices as accounting gimmickry. Effective control of risk, in the end, requires that it be in the economic interest of financial institution owners, managers and major liability holders. Experience shows that there is no substitute for an occasional bankruptcy to drive this point home.

F. Concluding remarks

Five major lessons for successful banking crisis management emerge from the analysis presented in this chapter. First, the do's of good banking crisis management must begin with three basic principles: ensure that parties responsible for the crisis bear most of the costs of restructuring, prevent problem banks from expanding credit to delinquent borrowers, and avoid financing the programme with inflation by making the restructuring programme a high priority. An examination of experiences in restructuring banks in a variety of developed and developing countries indicates that the most important element for a successful programme is a strong commitment to adherence to the three principles. The Chilean and US experiences stand out as evidence for this.

Second, while the three basic principles for bank crisis resolution are the same for industrial and developing countries, constraints differ significantly: they are much more severe in developing than in industrialised countries. These constraints include the availability of funding, the availability of markets to dispose of non-performing assets and institutions, and the know-how to manage a restructuring programme. In developed countries constraints on executing sound programmes are more often political rather than economic. Since the severity of constraints determines the shape of a restructuring programme, the attributes of successful programmes differ between industrial and developing countries.

Third, the experiences of Chile in the 1980s and Mexico in the 1990s indicate that, in developing countries, it is highly probable that regulators must devise programmes to extend maturities of loans in resolving crises. When constraints are severe, the crisis is likely to be associated with high nominal and real interest rates, and many borrowers are not able to meet their payments commitments without an extension of time. However, the Chilean experience shows that, unless the banks themselves are ultimately held responsible for extended maturity loans, many of them will not be repaid.

Fourth, regulators need to avoid the temptation of supporting the prices of non-bank financial assets in a crisis. The market discipline imposed on borrowers by the free fluctuation of the prices of securities would be lost if there were expectations that the government would intervene should the price of securities experience a sharp fall. The case of Barings is a good example of how, under the correct set of incentives, market participants can protect themselves against turbulent financial periods.

Fifth, regulators must operate under the assumption that their power to overcome constraints imposed by economics or politics is often quite modest. They must keep their regulatory tools relatively simple and should probably expend more effort in enforcing the tools they have than in seeking more complex and sophisticated means of controlling risk. Market powers to subvert regulatory intentions are strong; the wise regulator will use the market as an agent of risk control wherever possible. Hence, it is wise to permit financial systems to suffer bankruptcies from time to time so that the market sees the value in making simple regulatory tools effective.

8 The institutional structure of financial regulation

A. Introduction

Research in regulation has tended to concentrate on defining appropriate objectives and on issues related to efficiency in the conduct of regulation and supervision. With notable exceptions (e.g. Goodhart, 1996b; Taylor, 1995, 1996), questions of institutional structure have received comparatively little attention. In several countries, however, institutional structure has now become a major issue of policy and public debate. Increasing emphasis is being given to the general question of whether the efficiency of regulators and supervisors in achieving their objectives may be influenced by the particular institutional structure in which they operate.

Debate about institutional structure has opened up in several countries. In the UK, one of the first major policy initiatives of the new Labour government elected in May 1997 was to announce plans to reorganise totally the institutional structure of financial regulation by sweeping away specialist agencies and vesting all regulation (including banking supervision) into a single agency (see Hartmann, 1997b; Securities and Investments Board, 1997). In Australia, questions related to the institutional structure of financial regulation were on the agenda of the Wallis Committee (1996), which also recommended major changes. Institutional structure is also being considered actively in South Africa, where changes are envisaged following a series of official reports and discussion papers. Other countries are discussing the issue as well.

While the debate in each country inevitably reflects country-specific factors and the currently prevailing institutional structure, there are more general reasons why the debate has recently emerged:

- In many countries, the structure of regulatory agencies was devised for a different structure of the financial system than now exists, and structural change and financial innovation have challenged many of the assumptions made at the time current structures were created. This raises the issue of whether institutional structure should mirror the evolution of the structure of the financial system and the business of regulated firms.
- Over time, changes in institutional structure have in many instances been

made as a response to particular financial failures, and thus a pragmatic, piecemeal structure has emerged. It is appropriate from time to time to review what has emerged and to consider whether a more coherent structure can be put in place.

- The emergence of financial conglomerates has challenged traditional demarcations between regulatory agencies and has made the business of regulation more complex. A particular issue is whether a structure based on specialist agencies supervising different parts of the business of financial conglomerates might lose sight of the institution as a whole. The issue is discussed in the annex to this section.
- In many countries the objectives of regulation have become more complex as, for instance, issues of conduct of business have become more significant. This is most notably the case in the UK, where several agencies are currently responsible for the conduct of different types of financial business and institutions. This raises the issue of whether an excessive number of institutions unnecessarily adds to complexity, uncertainty, and the costs of regulation. Such was clearly the view taken by the incoming Labour government in the UK in 1997.
- Financial innovation and the emergence of new financial markets have added to the complexity of the financial system in general as well as the risk characteristics of financial firms. In particular, the systemic dimension to regulation and supervision may no longer be exclusively focused on banking.
- The increasing internationalisation of financial operations has accentuated the international dimension to regulation, which in turn has implications for the institutional structure of agencies at both national and international levels.

In general, the emergence of financial conglomerates and the increasing international dimension to financial operations of regulated institutions have combined to challenge some of the traditional assumptions about the institutional structure of financial regulation and supervision.

There are several issues to consider when focusing on institutional structure:

- What is the appropriate number of regulatory agencies?
- In the absence of a single 'mega' regulator, what structure of agencies is most appropriate, which functions and firms are to be allocated to which agencies, and how are the objectives for each agency to be defined? In particular, how should *functional* and *institutional* dimensions to regulation be allocated between different agencies?
- What degree of co-ordination should there be between different agencies, and what mechanisms are needed to ensure efficient and effective coordination, co-operation and information sharing?
- Does institutional structure have a significant bearing on the costs of regulation?

- In so far as regulation has consequences for competition, what is the role, if any, of competition authorities in the regulatory process?
- What role, if any, is to be given to self-regulation and mechanisms for practitioner input?
- Given the international dimension to regulation, what institutional mechanisms are most efficient at facilitating international co-ordination and co-operation between national regulatory agencies?
- How independent or accountable should regulatory agencies be?

(i) Alternative approaches

There are three broad approaches to the structure of regulation: *institutional, functional* and *objective*. In the institutional approach, regulation is directed at financial institutions irrespective of the mix of business undertaken. Different regulation applies to different types of institutions (e.g. banks, insurance companies), and specialist regulatory agencies are responsible for different types of financial institutions. This approach is particularly appropriate when considering prudential issues, which must necessarily focus on institutions because, after all, it is institutions and not functions that become insolvent. Functional regulation focuses on the business undertaken by institutions irrespective of which institutions are involved. Thus, life assurance is regulated as an activity in the same way regardless of whether banks or specialist life assurance companies are conducting the business. This approach requires specialist functional regulators.

The distinction between institutional and functional regulation and supervision is of little significance when financial institutions are specialised in narrow business areas, for then functions and institutions are co-extensive. Thus regulating banks is the same as regulating the business of banking, and regulation designed to focus upon particular functions immediately identifies the relevant institutions. When, on the other hand, financial institutions are diversified, the distinction between function and institution is more complex.

If an exclusively institutional approach is adopted, two problems are likely to arise. The first is a competitive neutrality issue, namely that different institutional regulators might adopt different functional regulation for the same activity. The second is socially wasteful duplication, as described by the Governor of the Bank of England: 'Each institutional regulator would need to apply the business rules appropriate for every function – which would be hugely inefficient in terms of regulatory resources' (George, 1996).

The obvious problem with a purely functional approach is that the position of the institution as a whole may be obscured, especially with respect to overall risk and solvency, because no agency is clearly responsible for the prudential management of the institution as an entity. In this case, prudential regulation of the total might be compromised unless each function has dedicated capital applied to it, which would be inefficient in terms of overall capital allocation.

In practice, a matrix approach is needed when financial institutions conduct a wide range of business. Institutions need to be regulated both on a functional basis for conduct of business purposes and on an institutional basis for prudential reasons. Even if a single agency is responsible for both functional and institutional regulation and supervision, the matrix approach still applies. The specialist divisions within the single agency need co-ordination, just as co-ordination is needed between different agencies in the absence of a mega regulator. The basic problems of information sharing, consistency and co-ordination apply equally between specialist divisions of a single agency as between different agencies.

The third approach is to focus regulation on the objectives being sought, with institutional structure following as a consequence. This approach is considered in Section C.

The remainder of this section considers whether the institutional structure of regulation is a significant issue. This forms the background to a discussion in Section B of alternative criteria for constructing a set of regulatory agencies. Section C considers a structure based specifically upon the objectives of regulation. Section D considers the international dimension to regulation. Section E offers an overall assessment.

(ii) No single model

A review of international experience indicates a variety of institutional structures for financial regulation (see the Appendix to this chapter). Some countries, such as Sweden, Canada and Denmark, have reduced the number of regulatory agencies and in some cases created a single mega-agency. This is now planned for the UK. Others have opted for multiple agencies and in some cases have increased the number. Differences in institutional structure are the result of several factors: historical evolution, the structure of the financial system, political structures and traditions, and the size of the country and financial sector. With respect to this last factor, for instance, if there are economies of scale in regulation, then a single agency might be appropriate for a small country. McDonald (1996) also notes the complications introduced in some countries where there are both national and regional dimensions to the structure of regulatory agencies. The Appendix offers a brief overview of the structure of regulatory institutions in several countries.

All this suggests that there currently is no obvious and universally applicable 'ideal model'. It also appears that there are problems with each of the different structures currently in place in different countries. Therefore, a set of imperfect institutional arrangements might be inevitable.

While structures must necessarily reflect the country-specific environment, it is nevertheless instructive to consider whether there are general principles that can inform discussion about the appropriate institutional structure.

(iii) Is institutional structure a significant issue?

There are several reasons why issues relating to the institutional structure of regulatory agencies are important and are not just minor administrative matters:

- Above all other considerations, institutional structure may have an impact on the overall effectiveness of regulation and supervision because of the expertise, experience and culture that develop within particular regulatory agencies. It might be the case that focused, rather than diversified or conglomerate, regulators are more effective simply because their mandates are clearly defined. It is partly for these reasons that, notwithstanding issues of ideal structures, there are transitional costs associated with any change in the structure of institutions and the allocation of responsibilities. There is a danger, though it is not inevitable, that expertise, collective memory and experience can be lost when changes are made to the structure of regulatory agencies. For example, there have been reports of difficulties in maintaining staff in the separate supervisory entities during the uncertain transition period leading up to the unification of supervision within the proposed UK mega regulator.
- Closely related to effectiveness is the question of clarity of responsibility for particular aspects or objectives of regulation. This in turn raises the question of interagency rivalry and disputes.
- Seldom is there a single objective of regulation. When multiple objectives are set, they can lead to conflict. Although this is true irrespective of institutional structure, different structures may be more or less effective at handling conflicts. A particular issue is whether conflicts are better handled within a single agency or between different agencies, where responsibilities for particular objectives are more clearly defined. Are transaction costs lower when conflicts are resolved within a single agency?
- Different structures may imply different costs of regulation. On the one hand, if there are economies of scale and scope in regulation, there might be advantage in having a small number of agencies, or even a single authority. On the other hand, if a single regulator encompassing a variety of financial institutions adopts an inappropriate regulatory regime (perhaps because its remit is too wide and unfocused), the *compliance* and *structural* costs of regulation could rise even though the purely *institutional* costs of regulatory agencies might be lower. This is discussed further in Section B.
- Overlap and underlap are major issues. Does a particular structure cause unnecessary duplication of regulatory activity and hence increase costs to firms? Do some aspects of business or some institutions fall through the net altogether?
- A multiple agency regime, especially if it allows an element of choice to regulated institutions, creates a potential for regulatory arbitrage and

inconsistent regulation between different institutions conducting the
same type of business.

- Public perceptions and credibility may also be significant issues, especially with respect to conduct of business. Consumers may be unclear
about which agency is responsible for which issues, or they may not
know where to register complaints.

For these reasons, the institutional structure of regulatory agencies has a significance beyond simple bureaucratic tidiness. However, the importance
should not be exaggerated, for in some ways institutional structure is a comparatively easy part of the regulatory process. It is not difficult to devise a
whole range of viable institutional structures. As put by the Governor of the
Bank of England: 'There are many ways of skinning this particular cat . . .
and in any event no structure can be set in stone – the markets continue to
evolve and so too must the regulatory structure' (George, 1996).

*Institutional structure does not in itself guarantee what really matters: the
effectiveness of regulation in achieving its objectives in an efficient and cost-
effective manner.* Our starting point, therefore, is that, without a clear
analytical foundation based on the rationale and objectives of regulation, any
institutional structure is likely to be *ad hoc* and arbitrary and may even compromise the objectives of regulation. It is for this reason that questions related
to institutional structure come at the end of this series of chapters.

(iv) Appendix to Section A: financial conglomerates

We have identified the problems of allocating functional and institutional regulation when financial institutions conduct a wide range of business.
Historically, financial systems in many countries have been based upon functionally defined institutions: banks, insurance companies and securities
traders, with each being regulated and supervised separately by dedicated
prudential regulatory agencies. In many countries this has given way to financial conglomerates because, across the board, institutions have diversified
away from their traditional specialist activities. A useful working definition of
a financial conglomerate is given in the De Swaan Report of the Tripartite
Group of Bank, Securities and Insurance Regulators (*The Supervision of
Financial Conglomerates*): '[a financial conglomerate is] any group of companies under common control whose exclusive or predominant activities
consist of providing services in at least two different financial sectors (banking, securities, insurance)'.

One of the issues with financial conglomerates is whether mixing different
types of business (e.g. banking, insurance, fund management, securities trading) raises or lowers the overall risk characteristics of the institution. If the
risks attached to different parts of the business are weakly or, even better,
negatively correlated, then, depending on the magnitude of the separate risks
and the size of each component business, the overall risk profile of an

institution is reduced when different business areas are mixed within the same institution. This, however, creates something of a dilemma for the regulator: the *probability* of a failure is reduced, but the potential *cost* in the event of a failure may be increased because a wider range of business is affected.

A second issue is how financial innovation has eroded some of the traditional distinctions between different types of financial products and contracts.

In combination, these two issues challenge some of the traditional approaches to regulation and supervision that become more complex when financial institutions encompass a wide range of business activities with different and complex risk characteristics. Several official reports[1] have focused on the particular supervisory problems posed by financial conglomerates. In particular, the traditional distinction between functional and institutional approaches is less clearly delineated. A financial conglomerate must necessarily be subject to several conduct of business regulatory regimes because of the diverse nature of its business. Most countries have specialist prudential regulators for banks, insurance companies and securities traders. It follows that, in the absence of a merging of hitherto independent supervisory agencies, financial conglomerates may be subject to several prudential and conduct of business agencies.

Financial conglomerates raise several regulatory and supervisory issues: the nature of the group structure may be complex; there may be a lack of transparency due to complex intragroup exposures; in the absence of effective firewalls, there is a risk of contamination and contagion due to intragroup exposures; specialist supervisors may not always have access to necessary information; and so forth. Above all, there is a danger that prudential regulation based on *solo* principles might fail to capture the risk characteristics of the institution as a whole. In effect, the totality of risks may be *greater* than the sum of the parts, while the totality of effective risk capital available to cover risks may be *less* than the sum of the parts contained within each business of the conglomerate. A key supervisory issue, therefore, is whether there are risks arising within the group as a whole that are not adequately addressed by any of the specialist prudential supervisory agencies that undertake their work on a solo basis.

One approach to these problems is to replace the separate banking, insurance and securities prudential regulators by a single, conglomerate regulator to mirror the emerging structure of a significant number of – though by no means all – financial institutions. There may be a case for an institutional structure of regulation that mirrors the structure of regulated institutions. A later section, however, argues that the structure of regulatory agencies should more appropriately mirror not *institutions* but the *objectives* of regulation.

The issues raised by the emergence of financial conglomerates have been comprehensively reviewed and analysed in the De Swaan Report of the Tripartite Group (De Swaan, 1995). This informal group of regulators was formed to address issues related to the supervision of financial conglomerates and, specifically, 'whether the traditional organisation, procedures and instruments of prudential supervision enable the objectives of the various supervisory authorities to be met' (De Swaan, 1995). The report was emphatic that a group-wide perspective is needed in the supervision of financial conglomerates. However, it endorsed the dominance in current arrangements for solo supervision to be the main focus for the supervision of the component parts of conglomerates and did not judge that there was any pressing need to create conglomerate prudential supervisory agencies. In the words of the report:

> The group takes the view that the potential problems of intragroup exposures are best tackled as an element of solo supervision, not least because the parent regulator's perspective is likely to be quite different from that of a subsidiary's regulator.

However, the report also recognised the need for close co-operation, collaboration and exchange of information between the different prudential supervisory agencies of a financial conglomerate. Solo supervision alone would not be sufficient. As put in the report:

> The Tripartite Group very quickly came to the unanimous view that, while the *solo* supervision of individually regulated entities should continue to be the foundation for effective supervision, there is a need for the various supervisors to establish a co-ordinated approach to supervision so that a prudential assessment can also be made from a group-wide perspective.

It is widely accepted that the key issues of regulation and supervision of financial conglomerates are exchange of information between different specialist agencies, co-ordination of regulatory requirements and liaison of their activities, and effective mechanisms for co-ordinated action when problems with a regulated firm arise. In Australia, the Council of Financial Supervisors, a co-ordinating body that brings together the heads of the country's main supervisory agencies, has identified the co-ordination of prudential supervision of financial conglomerates as one of its major roles. It has specifically agreed a set of 'guidelines for co-operation among agencies involved in the supervision of entities in financial conglomerates' (Council of Financial Supervisors, 1996).

The Tripartite Group surveyed six alternative approaches to monitoring the risk characteristics and solvency of financial conglomerates as a whole. The group judged that monitoring could be achieved either through balance sheet consolidation or by a *solo–plus* approach. In the balance sheet consolidation approach, the assets and liabilities of the component companies are aggregated, and capital adequacy requirements are defined in terms of the group's aggregate position. However, qualitative judgements are also made about any additional capital requirement for the group as a whole over and above a simple summation of the components. Under the solo–plus alternative, capital requirements are related to the balance sheet positions of each component of the group (the solo component) after which adjustments are made with a view to the conglomerate as a whole (plus component). This allows for any double-counting of capital within the group.

The group recommended that lead regulators be used to facilitate solo–plus regulation without creating a single prudential agency. (This arrangement is already the norm in many countries.) The lead regulator is responsible for taking a group-wide perspective on the risk profile of the financial conglomerate and for co-ordinating the process of supervision, both on a regular basis and in crisis situations. The lead regulator is also responsible for assessing the capital adequacy of the group as a whole, transmitting and demanding relevant information to and from other supervisors, and generally co-ordinating any necessary action that involves more than one supervisory agency. Large (1996) and H. Davies (1997) have also argued strongly for lead regulators, partly with a view to facilitating international co-ordination and consistency of regulation. Davies, for instance, envisages the lead regulator as having several tasks, including the following: performing quantitative and qualitative assessment of international financial groups as a whole, taking the primary role in the management of emergencies, acting to ease the exchange of information between different regulators, and suggesting ways to improve co-ordination and supervision.

B. Institutional structure of regulation

(i) The criteria for institutional structure

In order to prevent institutional structure from being a purely arbitrary and *ad hoc* process, several key issues need to be considered:

1 The objectives of regulation: institutional structure should not obscure the ultimate objectives or impede their attainment.
2 The clarity of regulatory agencies' remit.
3 The costs of particular institutional structures.
4 The accountability of regulatory agencies.
5 Questions related to the efficiency of the regulatory process and the extent to which different institutional structures are more or less efficient at achieving their objectives.
6 The merits of a degree of competition in regulation.
7 Issues related to the concentration of power in regulatory agencies.

While these considerations do not point unambiguously to any unique institutional structure, each is significant to the questions of agency structure.

Questions about the costs of regulation are frequently raised when institutional structure is considered. This is a more complex issue than sometimes assumed. Table 8.1 identifies three types of cost: *institutional* (costs of running regulatory agencies), *compliance* (costs imposed on firms through regulation), and *structural* (costs such as excess burdens and stifling of innovation). Institutional structure and the costs of regulatory institutions themselves are a comparatively small proportion of the total, and focusing on the institutional costs takes attention away from other dimensions of the costs of regulation.

Table 8.1 Costs of regulation

1	Institutional	Cost of agencies Monitoring costs
2	Compliance	Costs imposed on regulated firms
3	Structural	Possible impairment of competition Stifling of innovation Forced choice on consumers: consumers might choose (if given the option) not to pay regulation costs Moral hazard of implicit contracts (the consumer believes more protection is offered than is in fact the case) Regulatory capture Regulatory escalation: regulation becomes excessively burdensome over time Public choice theory problems

An inappropriate institutional structure, although it may reduce the institutional costs of regulation, may raise overall costs if it leads to inappropriate regulation. Put another way, the wrong institutional structure may cause an increase in compliance and structural costs that exceeds the savings in institutional costs associated, perhaps, with economies of scale. For example, a mega regulator may appear to reduce institutional costs, but if that regulator fails to make appropriate distinctions between wholesale and retail business, then the overall costs of regulation may increase to the detriment of the industry and consumer.

The key issue is whether institutional structure itself determines the type of regulation practised. *The overall objective must be to create an institutional structure that reflects the objectives of regulation and that promotes those objectives most effectively and efficiently.* We argue below that this is achieved when different regulatory agencies focus on particular objectives. The goal is not simply to create a tidy regulatory structure.

(ii) Single v. multiple agencies: the case for a mega regulator

One school of thought argues in favour of a single regulatory agency for the full range of financial services and markets. Such a mega-agency would be responsible for systemic, prudential and conduct of business regulation (for both wholesale and retail business) even though different considerations are involved in each case. This has been the approach of the incoming government in the UK in May 1997 (Hartmann, 1997b; SIB, 1997). Several arguments favour such a structure:

- There might be economies of scale within regulatory agencies, especially with respect to skill requirements. If so, the smaller the number of agencies, the lower should be the institutional costs. A single regulator might be more efficient because of shared resources. However, institutional costs are a comparatively small proportion of the total costs of regulation, and other costs of regulation (compliance and structural) rise if inappropriate regulation is adopted.
- Similarly, there might also be economies of scope (or synergies) to be reaped between different functional areas of regulation.
- There might be merit in having a simple structure of regulatory institutions, a structure that is readily understood and recognised by regulated firms and consumers.
- There might be advantage in having a structure that mirrors the business of regulated institutions. To the extent that financial institutions have steadily diversified, traditional functional divisions have been eroded. Although there are other ways of addressing overall prudential requirements for diversified institutions, a single, conglomerate regulator might be able to monitor the full range of institutions' business more effectively and might be able to detect potential solvency risks emanating from different parts of the business.
- A single agency should, in principle, avoid problems of competitive inequality, inconsistencies, duplication, overlap and gaps, all of which can arise in a regime based upon several regulatory agencies. However, there is no guarantee of this. In practice, different aspects of functional regulation will be conducted by different divisions within a single agency, and problems of co-ordination will still arise.
- If expertise in regulation is in short supply, such expertise might be more effectively utilised if it is concentrated within a single agency.
- Accountability of regulation might be more certain with a simple structure, if for no other reason than that it would be more difficult for different agencies to 'pass the buck'.
- The monitoring costs imposed on regulated firms might be reduced in so far as they would need to deal with only one agency.

Taylor (1995), referring specifically to the UK, argues that the multiplicity of regulatory agencies causes problems associated with regulatory overlap and underlap, duplication, duplicate rule books, potential for regulatory arbitrage, lack of co-ordination between regulatory agencies, bureaucratic infighting, and lack of transparency in the regulatory system. In his words, 'These examples show why structure does, and should, matter if we wish to create an efficient, effective system of financial services regulation'.

(iii) The case against a mega regulator

There is clear merit and a certain prima-facie appeal to the mega regulator proposal. However, several reservations may be made about a mega regulator:

- One of the arguments alleged to be in favour of a single regulator is that, as firms have increasingly diversified, the traditional functional distinctions between institutions have been eroded. While this is generally the case, it does not mean that all institutions have converged on a common financial conglomerate model. There remain, and will remain for the foreseeable future, major differences between banks, securities firms and insurance companies in the nature of their business, the type of contracts they issue, and hence the nature and form of asset transformation. Firms in all subsectors have diversified, but almost invariably their core business remains dominant. The natures of the risks are sufficiently different to warrant a differentiated approach to prudential regulation. As the Reserve Bank of Australia stated:

> For instance, insurance companies have long-term liabilities with ill-defined value, while their assets are generally marketable with readily ascertainable values. Banks, in contrast, tend to have relatively short-term liabilities, with assets which are difficult to liquidate and to value. Consequently, the applicable prudential supervisory regimes are different and there would be few (if any) efficiencies in bringing their supervision together.
>
> (Thompson, 1996)

- A single regulator might not have a clear focus on the objectives and rationale of regulation, and might not make the necessary differentiations between different types of institutions. Even if the different regulatory requirements of different types of firms were managed within specialist divisions of a mega regulator, it is not self-evident that supervisors within the same organisation but responsible for different types of business would necessarily communicate and co-ordinate more efficiently and closely than they would within different, specialist regulatory agencies.
- It is possible that significant cultural conflicts within the organisation could emerge if a single agency were responsible for all aspects of regulation (systemic, prudential and conduct of business), and for all types of financial institutions. Would, for instance, a single conduct of business regulator adequately reflect the fundamentally different requirements, rationale and approach needed for the regulation of wholesale as opposed to retail business? The Reserve Bank of Australia, on the subject of a mega regulator combining both prudential and conduct of business regulation, has argued as follows: 'The differences in objectives and cultures would produce an institution which was difficult to manage and unlikely to be clearly focused on the various tasks for which it had responsibility' (Thompson, 1996).
- A mega regulator would be extremely powerful, and its power might become excessive. As argued by Taylor in his Twin Peaks approach:

> [a single regulator] with a remit covering both prudential and conduct of business regulation in banking, securities and insurance and with

the power to undertake civil proceedings against those it suspected of insider dealing or market abuse, could potentially become an over-mighty bully, a bureaucratic leviathan divorced from the industry it regulates.

- A potential moral hazard could result from a public perception that the risk spectrum among financial institutions had disappeared or become blurred. In particular, the distinction between, on the one hand, deposits that are redeemable on demand at face value and, on the other hand, investments (e.g. life assurance), where the value of the institution's liability is a function of the performance of the institution in managing its assets, could become obscured.
- There is a danger that a large mega regulator might become excessively bureaucratic in its procedures.
- The creation of a single regulator would involve a loss of potentially valuable information simply because a single approach was adopted. In effect, there is merit in having a degree of competition and diversity in regulation so that lessons can be learned from the experience of different approaches. In some respects, the case for not having a monopoly regulator is the same as with any monopolist.
- Further, there is the question of whether there are, in fact, economies of scale to be derived in a mega regulator. The economics literature demonstrates quite clearly that diseconomies of scale can also arise in some circumstances. Put another way, X-inefficiencies may arise in a monopolist regulator. It is not self-evident that a single mega regulator would in practice be more efficient than a series of specialist regulators with clearly defined objectives.

As always, the arguments are finely balanced. However, we argue in Section C for a different approach based on the objectives of regulation.

In May 1997, only two weeks after giving operational independence for monetary policy to the Bank of England, the new Labour government in the UK announced a fundamental set of changes to the institutional structure of regulation. The incoming government inherited a complex and fragmented structure of regulation and supervision. There were separate prudential regulators for banks (Bank of England), insurance companies (Department of Trade and Industry) and building societies (Building Societies Commission). With respect to conduct of business regulation, following the 1986 Financial Services Act a two-tier structure was established with the Securities and Investments Board overseeing a set of three specialist self-regulatory organisations (SROs).

The main changes announced by the new government were:

1 Prudential regulation and supervision of banks would be transferred from the Bank of England to an enlarged Securities and Investments Board (SIB), since renamed the Financial Services Authority.

2 At a later stage, and after legislation has been passed, the SROs will be merged into an expanded agency, thereby ending the two-tier system that the government believed to be inefficient, confusing for investors, and lacking in accountability and a clear allocation of responsibilities.
3 The Bank of England is to retain its role as lender of last resort (though this is still subject to review) and its responsibility for systemic stability.
4 The prudential regulation of other financial institutions will also be transferred to the new agency (Financial Services Authority).

Since the new, single regulator will be responsible for both prudential and conduct of business regulation and supervision, as well as for all financial institutions of markets, the UK is clearly adopting the mega regulator concept. This plan will greatly simplify the regulatory structure by abandoning the questionable two-tier structure and reducing the number of separate regulatory agencies.

The first issue the planned new agency needed to address was how it would organise its own internal structure. It considered a range of options: by regulatory function, by regulated group, by type of business, or by dividing along prudential and conduct of business lines. In a report commissioned by the Chancellor of the Exchequer from Sir Andrew Large, the agency argued that:

> the guiding principle has been to balance the need, on the one hand, for consistency and co-ordination in policies and objectives and in the regulation of comparable financial activities against, on the other, the need for appropriately differentiated delivery of regulation, taking into account the specific nature of the regulated business and its customers, and the risks involved.

(iv) Alternative divisions

If a single agency is rejected, what other structure of agencies is most efficient and what criteria should be applied? There is no single way of dividing the cake. Problems of co-ordination will emerge in any structure of multiple agencies. This will be true of any structure that does not involve an all-embracing agency and, as already noted, will in practice also be true within a single mega regulator. There is no perfect way of demarcating responsibilities between regulatory agencies; there will always be problems at the boundaries. To some extent, a pragmatic approach is needed, because a perfect institutional structure is unattainable.

There are many possible distinctions that can be made between different types of financial institution, and these distinctions may dictate the type of institutional structure created. They are:

1 between systemic, prudential, and conduct of business regulation;
2 between different types of institution;

3 between banks on the one hand, and all other institutions on the other if, for reasons outlined earlier, banks are thought to be special in some sense or another;
4 between those institutions that might be judged to have a systemic dimension as opposed to those that do not;
5 between the regulation of institutions that do involve elements of depositor or investor protection schemes and those that do not; and
6 between wholesale and retail business.

Perhaps, in addition, questions related to competition policy need to be reflected in the institutional structure of regulation.

There is, therefore, no simple way of categorising institutions and regulatory agencies. Each of the distinctions may warrant a different approach to regulation and possibly different regulatory agencies. Some would argue that this itself justifies a single, all-embracing regulatory agency.

In Section A, three alternative ways of categorising regulatory arrangements were suggested: by institution, by function, or by objectives. In reality, a strict dichotomy between functional and institutional regulation is misleading, for the two serve different purposes. In practice, it is institutions and not functions that fail or become insolvent, and therefore institutions *per se* need to be regulated for safety and soundness. It is the overall institution that must be the focus of such regulation. Functional regulation, on the other hand, is concerned with how an institution conducts the various aspects of its business and how it behaves towards customers. If competitive neutrality of regulation is to be maintained, such functional regulation must apply to particular aspects of the business irrespective of which type of institution is conducting it. Thus, while regulation for the solvency of banks and insurance companies may be different (and conducted by different agencies), the conduct of insurance business needs to be the same whether conducted by banks or by insurance companies.

C. Institutional structure based on the objectives of regulation

The ultimate criterion for devising a structure of regulatory agencies should be the effectiveness and efficiency of regulation in meeting its basic objectives. Accordingly, the most appropriate basis for organising institutional structure is to focus directly on the *objectives* of regulation, because:

- Regulatory agencies are probably most effective and efficient when they have clearly defined, and precisely delineated, objectives and when their mandate is clear and precise.
- Accountability is likely to be more effective and transparent when it is clear precisely what regulatory agencies are responsible for.
- A clear internal management focus is more likely to be created when the objectives of the agency are clear and precise.

- There will be times when the objectives of regulation are in conflict; one of the issues to consider is what structure is most efficient at resolving conflicts. In a single agency, conflicts are internalised. However, Taylor (1995) argues that this is undesirable because the resolution of conflicting objectives involves judgements about important issues of public policy, and these judgements and decisions should be made at the political level, in a publicly accountable way. One merit of focusing institutional structure upon regulatory functions is that it requires significant conflicts between different objectives to be resolved at the political level.
- Prudential, systemic, and conduct of business dimensions to regulation require fundamentally different approaches and cultures and there may be doubt about whether a single regulator would, in practice, be able to encompass them effectively. Again as noted by Taylor:

  There are already profound differences between the style and techniques appropriate to prudential and conduct of business regulation, and these are likely to become more pronounced as prudential regulation moves further in the direction of assessment of firms' own internal risk control systems. It would be difficult to combine two such different cultures within a single organisation.

- There is doubt whether the fundamental distinction between wholesale and retail business, and the different approach to regulation that is appropriate to each, would be adequately reflected within a single regulatory agency. Making different agencies responsible for wholesale and retail business (even though the distinction is fuzzy at the margin) could reduce the potential for specific regulations to be extended beyond their appropriate sphere.

A counterargument is that, in practice, a single agency would be structured internally for different functional responsibilities. However, this in itself would add to internal transactions costs and some of the arguments in favour of a single agency would be weakened in the process.

(i) Twin Peaks

Taylor (1995, 1996) and Goodhart (1996b) have proposed an approach to regulation and supervision based upon systemic stability and consumer protection. Both authors distinguish the two objectives of regulation, and they argue that systemic considerations include a wider range of financial institutions beyond banks.

In his Twin Peaks concept, Taylor argues for a single prudential supervisory agency (Financial Stability Commission) and a single conduct of business agency (Consumer Protection Commission). The former would apply prudential measures to ensure the soundness of the system, the capital adequacy of banks, and control of risk. It would encompass all types of financial institution (including securities firms, fund management institutions, insurance companies) from which a systemic crisis 'might conceivably develop'. As Taylor argues: (1) a wide range of financial institutions are systematically significant; (2) existing regulatory arrangements (in the UK) raise issues of competitive neutrality between different types of financial institutions; (3) the emergence of financial conglomerates requires a group-wide perspective; and (4) there is a need to pool rare regulatory expertise. In particular, Taylor argues: 'A regulatory system which presupposes a clear separation between banking, securities and insurance is no longer the best way to regulate a financial system in which these distinctions are increasingly irrelevant' (Taylor, 1996). The case for Twin Peaks is summarised by Taylor as follows:

> The proposed structure would eliminate regulatory duplication and overlap; it would create regulatory bodies with a clear and precise remit; it would establish mechanisms for resolving conflicts between the objectives of financial services regulation; and it would encourage a regulatory process which is open, transparent and politically accountable.

Taylor recognises that there would be grey areas within the overall structure proposed, but he believes that 'any system is bound to have its anomalies and illogicalities; it is sufficient that the *Twin Peaks* model has fewer than the alternatives'.

A counterargument has been given by the Deputy Governor of the Bank of England:

> I must say that we are not persuaded. Certainly there has been a degree of convergence between banks and securities firms. But in our view, there is still a reasonably clear distinction to be made between banks and other financial institutions, and their prudential soundness, or lack of it, can have rather different implications for the rest of the market. . . . [W]e are not convinced that the substantial upheaval and cost involved would be warranted. The model assumes that both a wide range of firms are systemic and that all systematically significant firms should be regulated by the same institution. By contrast, we believe that banks remain unique in this respect (at least for the time being) and, were a single institution to conduct prudential supervision for everything from banks to insurance companies, it would still need to tailor the rules to meet the characteristics of particular types of business. In effect, the new regulator could quickly become a collection of separate 'Divisions', . . . the costs of change would be substantial.

> (Davies, 1996)

Something like a Twin Peaks approach was recommended by the Wallis Committee of Inquiry in Australia in April 1997. The Committee recommended that a single conduct of business regulator cover issues like disclosure requirements, consumer protection, financial advice, and integrity of market conduct. A Corporations and Financial Services Commission would be formed through a merger of existing conduct of business regulators. Under the Wallis proposals there would also be a single prudential regulator for all financial institutions. The proposals were designed to address the problems perceived to result from an *institutional* approach to regulation.

Currently the Reserve Bank of Australia is the prudential regulator of banks, but not of other financial institutions. The Wallis Committee argued against the central bank's being the single prudential regulator. However, it also argued that systemic stability (with respect to the payments system) would remain a responsibility of the Reserve Bank of Australia. The central bank would retain powers of lender of last resort to the institutions involved with the payments system. Whether retaining this responsibility is viable without the bank's also being responsible for prudential supervision remains to be seen.

Two separate issues are involved here. One is whether there should be a single prudential regulator for all financial institutions. The other is whether the central bank should be a prudential regulator. Our judgement is that it would not be appropriate, and could be hazardous, to make the central bank responsible for the prudential regulation of all financial institutions. We note in the Appendix to this chapter that no country, with the exception of the Singapore Monetary Authority, has this arrangement. However, there is a much stronger case for having the central bank be responsible for the regulation of banks: this would keep the prudential regulation of banks separate from that of other institutions (and we argue for this below).

While institutional structure should focus upon the objectives of regulation, the Twin Peaks model is too all embracing and does not recognise the significant differences between institutions and types of business with respect to both prudential and conduct of business regulation.

(ii) An alternative system

Earlier we noted that regulation has three dimensions: systemic, prudential and conduct of business. One way to construct a system of regulatory agencies is to base it on the objectives of regulation. One structure could be:

1 A systemic regulator.
2 A separate prudential regulator for securities firms, insurance companies, and other non-bank institutions where continued solvency is a regulatory issue.
3 A single conduct of business regulator for retail financial business.
4 A single conduct of business regulator for wholesale business.
5 Self-regulation for exchanges, except that they would be subject to 6 below.
6 A competition agency with a clear role in regulation, although it would not be a specialist agency dealing only with financial services.

In this construction, the mandate of each agency is clearly defined. This structure is summarised in Table 8.2, which includes the range of institutions and the nature of regulation to be covered in each agency. While the focus on objectives is similar to Goodhart's and Taylor's focus, a more differentiated structure of institutions is suggested.

Table 8.2 Model for the regulation of the financial system

Focus	Regulator	Coverage	Nature of regulation
Systemic risk: Prudential supervision of deposit-taking financial institutions	Central bank or banking commission	Banks Building societies Credit unions	Institutional
Prudential supervision of other institutions	Financial commission	General insurance companies Life assurance companies Superannuation entities Collective Investments[1]	Institutional

Retail conduct of business	Retail investments commission	Conduct of product providers and advisers in respect of:
		    financial advice
		    competence
		    disclosure
		    complaints handling
		
		Oversight of complaints handling schemes
			Functional

Wholesale conduct of business	Financial markets commission	All financial intermediaries and brokers including fund managers, pension funds and collective investments Rules, agreements, codes about: interprofessional and interinstitution dealings; market transactions; and market integrity Rules for fund management	Functional

Table 8.2 Cont.

Focus	Regulator	Coverage	Nature of regulation
Financial exchanges	Exchanges	Members of exchanges	Functional and largely self-regulation
Competition	Competition authority	Competition implications of regulation	Functional

¹ If prudentially supervised.

As we noted earlier, prudential regulation is required even when no systemic considerations arise, and it needs to be addressed by a regulatory agency. Conduct of business regulation (how business is conducted, and how financial firms behave with respect to their customers, as opposed to how they maintain their solvency) raises fundamentally different issues and requires a different approach. Because there is a fundamental distinction between wholesale and retail business – the nature of market imperfections and failures is different in the two areas – the rationale, approach and conduct of regulation need to be different for each. We briefly consider the role of each of the agencies identified above.

a. Systemic regulator

A key issue is which institutions are to be subject to the systemic regulator. As we argued earlier, this is relevant when the failure of an institution has a systemic dimension (because the social costs of failure exceed the private costs), which happens because of the potential for bank runs. The case for subjecting banks, and only banks, to systemic regulation and a specialist systemic regulator derives from the nature of the contracts that banks issue on each side of the balance sheet. Two essential characteristics of banks entail a need for systemic regulation:

1 Banks issue money-certain liabilities on one side of the balance sheet that are used to fund money-uncertain assets on the other side. In other words, a key characteristic of a bank is asset transformation. If there is a run on the bank, a solvent bank can be made insolvent (because the value of its assets may fall below the book value).
2 A bank's liabilities can be withdrawn on demand or at short notice.

These two essential characteristics warrant banks' being subject to a systemic regulator. In practice, this means that the systemic regulator should cover all deposit-taking institutions (including, where relevant, building societies), whereas in some countries (e.g. the UK and Australia) this is currently not the case (because, for example, banks and building societies are prudentially regulated by different agencies). It is sometimes argued that only large banks need be subject to the systemic regulator, because the damage done by the failure of a small bank is very limited and is unlikely to lead to systemic problems. Yet systemic problems can arise through the failure of even small banks. It is not possible to determine in advance when the failure of an institution will lead to a potential run and therefore systemic costs.

Insurance companies, however, would not fall under the jurisdiction of the systemic regulator because neither of the two essential bank characteristics apply to them. In fact, an insurance company's asset transformation is opposite to that of a bank: it effectively transforms illiquid liabilities into liquid assets (whereas the bank transforms liquid liabilities into illiquid assets). For these reasons, systemic regulation should not be applied to all institutions. However, this is not to argue that there is no case for prudential regulation of other institutions: for reasons outlined earlier, the failure of any institution imposes costs on consumers even if there is no systemic dimension.

It might be thought that, because systemic and prudential considerations require similar types of regulation (e.g. capital adequacy), a single prudential regulatory agency would suffice for all financial institutions, although insurance companies and securities firms do not create the type of systemic problems that arise with banks. The advantages of a single agency are: economies of scale, possible synergies between the regulation of banks and other financial companies, a simplified structure of agencies, and ease of consolidated regulation when banking, securities and insurance are mixed within the same firm. However, there are also arguments in favour of keeping the systemic regulator of deposit-taking institutions different from the prudential regulator of other institutions:

- It is still true that the precise form of regulation for systemic reasons is different from that for prudential reasons. While functional distinctions between institutions have become blurred *at the margin*, banks retain special key characteristics.
- Including securities firms and insurance companies (and other institutions) within the jurisdiction of a systemic regulator (e.g. the central bank) could have the effect of spreading the coverage of the safety net and thus extending the associated moral hazard. If insurance companies were prudentially regulated by the same agency that is responsible for systemic regulation, the regulator could experience pressure to act also as a lender of last resort to insurance companies. This is especially likely because some insurance companies are wholly owned by banks. The regulator might find it difficult to separate the two types of firms with respect to access to the safety net. Lamfalussy (1992) makes this point in a passage considering whether central banks should

be the prudential supervisor of banks, and possibly other financial institutions:

> Why should central bank supervision stop with an ill-defined group of intermediaries, namely banks? If it were extended to other institutions *where* should it stop? The 'globalization' (encompassing a wide range of institutions) of supervisory duties in the hands of central banks would not only enlarge the areas covered by the moral hazard risk; it would also put an excessive operational burden on them. There is surely a point beyond which the drawbacks would begin to offset the advantages derived from effectively ensuring systemic stability.

- Similarly, consumers might form the *perception* that insurance companies would have equal access to the safety net with banks. And, if the safety net is extended to insurance companies, it can be asked whether there is any logical limit to the scope of the safety net.
- If consumers' judgement is influenced by their perception that there is a safety net associated with insurance companies, a moral hazard could be created with respect to their purchases of insurance products.
- With respect to the problem of the mix of banking and insurance within the same organisation, an alternative solution (practised in most countries, although not in the universal banks in Germany) is to firewall the two companies. In other words, the insurance activity of a bank is conducted by a properly constituted insurance company with dedicated capital, with the clear requirement that the insurance company be viable in its own right, and that the failure of the bank would not impair the insurance company, and vice versa. This is a standard way of proceeding, and therefore there is no obvious benefit for the insurance side to be prudentially regulated by the same agency that is involved with regulating the bank for systemic reasons. For instance, in the UK, only an insurance company can conduct insurance business, and, if it is owned by a bank, the insurance company must be managed and capitalised entirely independently of the bank.

Overall, mixing of prudential and systemic regulation would breach the basic principle that there be a clear delineation between regulatory agencies based on the underlying objectives of regulation.

Another issue is whether the containment of contagion risk within a financial conglomerate, and the monitoring of an institution's overall solvency, would be undertaken more efficiently within a single prudential regulator. The argument against this has been put by the Reserve Bank of Australia:

> As long as prudential supervision of different members – such as banks and insurance companies – remains specialised, it is questionable whether a single agency would be more effective than two or three working together. An international consensus is emerging that, for most financial

conglomerates, a convenor or lead regulator should be nominated to organise group-wide financial assessments, exercise authority over special purpose holding companies and co-ordinate crisis response.

(Thompson, 1996)

Thus, while the regulation imposed for systemic and prudential reasons may be similar (e.g. the setting of capital adequacy requirements), it does not need to be (nor should it be) conducted by the same regulatory agency. The danger is that a single agency would impose the same requirements for different purposes, even if the objectives require a different approach in the detail. It is partly about the culture that develops within a regulatory agency.

However, the systemic regulator's approach to the regulation of banks will be influenced by whether banks conduct insurance business. Clearly, the systemic regulator must consider the totality of the institution; therefore, the systemic regulator's approach to regulating banks that have securities and insurance business may differ from its approach to regulating banks that do not. The solo–plus approach is the most appropriate way of handling diverse conglomerates, with different facets of their business requiring different approaches to regulation. Similarly, the 'lead regulator' concept, which is often employed when individual institutions are subject to the jurisdiction of more than one regulatory agency, has merit. Thus, when a financial conglomerate is either based in a bank or includes a bank, the systemic regulator (often the central bank) would act as the lead regulator.

b. Prudential regulator

Although there are considerably fewer systemic risks with non-bank financial institutions, prudential regulation is still needed for consumer protection reasons. Because the regulatory objective is the same for all non-deposit-taking institutions, a single prudential regulator could cover the requirements for all such institutions, such as insurance companies, life assurance offices, superannuation entities, and collective investment funds (Table 8.2).

c. Retail conduct of business regulator

Chapter 1 outlined the reasons why a distinction is made between wholesale and retail business in the financial sector, and why this indicates a different rationale and type of conduct of business regulation and supervision for consumer protection. The ultimate case for such regulation is to offset market imperfections, such as asymmetric information, principal–agent problems associated with financial advisers, the difficulty of consumers ascertaining the quality of financial products and contracts at the point of purchase, the need for monitoring because the value of a contract is determined by the actions of the supplier after the purchase, and the non-feasibility of retail consumers undertaking the monitoring.

All of these have the potential to compromise consumer welfare (Llewellyn, 1995a). The coverage of conduct of business regulation would include information disclosure, honesty and integrity, the manner in which financial advice is given to retail consumers, competence requirements, terms of marketing and advertising material, status disclosure of financial firms (e.g. whether a firm is selling only its own products or those of many companies), and so forth. Information disclosure is a major part of the regulatory process in the retail sector: investors cannot make informed judgements about the purchase of financial products unless they know the nature and terms of the product or contract, their true cost, the risk characteristics, and the basis upon which a product or advice is offered. An example of such a retail conduct of business regulator is the Personal Investment Authority in the UK.

It is recognised, however, that the distinction between wholesale and retail business may be fuzzy, and an arbitrary allocation may be required at the margin. This and related issues of jurisdiction would be handled by an interface unit of officials from the retail and wholesale conduct of business agencies. In the final analysis no model of institutional structure avoids the need for co-operation, co-ordination and active exchange of information between agencies. As already argued, this problem would also exist between divisions of a single mega-agency.

d. Wholesale conduct of business regulator

A distinct conduct of business agency would cover some of the same issues for wholesale business. However, for reasons noted earlier (Chapter 1, Section B(ii)), conduct of business regulation between professionals would be considerably less intensive and prescriptive than for retail business. It is this major difference of approach, and the nature of the market imperfections, that suggests the case for separating retail and wholesale business for such regulation. It is also feasible for this agency to be more practitioner based than in the retail agency, though pure self-regulation is potentially hazardous. This agency would also encompass issues centred on the integrity of financial markets. It is likely that supervision of markets would be based on codes of conduct and the agency would be responsible for monitoring adherence to such codes. There would be an important role for the competition agency to ensure that codes were not anti-competitive and did not condone unwarranted restrictive practices.

e. Regulation of exchanges

The regulation and supervision of exchanges raise different issues. A major issue is market integrity. The UK SIB in a discussion paper on 'The

Regulation of the UK Equity Market' identified several elements in the concept of market integrity:

Fairness, as it relates to equitable access to information and trading opportunities.

Orderliness, as it relates to prices reflecting investor perceptions of value without being arbitrary or capricious.

Efficiency, as it relates to meeting the needs of users, for example, for liquidity and ease of execution.

Freedom from abuse and misconduct, which requires appropriate rules and effective arrangements for the detection, investigation, and punishment of their violation.

Disclosure of information is at the centre of issues related to all aspects of market integrity. The focus of market integrity has been put well by McDonald (1996):

> Plainly, the notion of market integrity is designed to protect investors; not in the narrow sense of the relation between a particular company and its customers, but in the broad sense in which all investors, whether professional or private, have an interest in a fair, appropriately transparent, orderly and efficient market which is free from abuse and misconduct. Companies themselves require such a market, since if their decisions are based on inadequate or false information, so they make decisions which they would not otherwise have made, then the consequences of those decisions may be disastrous for the solvency of the company concerned. More transparent operations and less asymmetrical information, some of the elements in market integrity, help to promote more efficient financial markets and institutions, especially in the case of derivatives markets.

Professionals have a clear interest in market integrity. For this reason, a large element of self-regulation is appropriate for the general regulation of exchanges, and each exchange could have its own, largely self-regulatory, committee, though with an important non-practitioner representation. However, it would also be important for the competition agency to monitor the self-regulation of exchanges for any anti-competitive mechanisms. In the UK, for example, the Office of Fair Trading has had a significant influence on the regulatory practices of exchanges and this is to be welcomed and reinforced in all cases of self-regulation. As with some aspects of the wholesale *conduct of business* agency, codes of practice would be a feature of the regulation of exchanges.

An interesting issue also arises with respect to governance of exchanges, specifically whether they should be externally owned and controlled or, as is often the case in practice, operated as member co-operatives. The central question is: in whose interests are the rules made? This question is addressed by Hart and Moore (1995). The issue arises because there may be conflicts of interest between different members of the exchange, such as between small v. large transactors. Hart and Moore note, for instance, that there are many cases in which reforms have been hindered by an exchange's difficulty in securing consensus among its members. The authors find that there is no unambiguous answer to the basic question of ownership. On the one hand they show that, since an external owner is typically interested only in maximising profits, the owner has a tendency to make inefficient decisions tailored to the marginal user. This is, in effect, based on the familiar idea that a monopolist inefficiently restricts supply. On the other hand, a co-operative which has a collective decision-making mechanism is also likely to be inefficient because in a vote the views of the decisive voter are not necessarily those of the members as a whole. They show that 'the relative merits of a co-operative structure and outside ownership depend on the level of competition and the diversity of ownership' (Hart and Moore, 1995). They conclude, however, that, while the judgement will differ between different exchanges, the balance of the argument is shifting towards outside ownership largely because competition is increasing.

We argue that exchanges can be left largely to a regime of self-regulation. This was challenged by some of the participants at the Central Bank Governors' Symposium. One argued, from a Latin American perspective, that he was concerned by some of the irregularities found in some stock exchanges, and that regulation of capital market transactions was weak, with a deleterious effect on the development of such markets and on the economy.

f. Competition agency

In all cases of regulation, there is an important competition dimension. Regulation, however well intentioned, has the potential to compromise competition and to condone, if not in some cases endorse, unwarranted entry barriers, restrictive practices and other anti-competitive mechanisms. Thus, while authorisation is invariably one of the instruments of the regulator, this can act as an unwarranted entry barrier. In the UK, the competition agency (the Office of Fair Trading) has the power to consider rules made by regulatory agencies and to judge whether they introduce unwarranted anti-competitive requirements. If it so judges, a government minister is required to adjudicate. The point of the procedure is that there is a mechanism for considering the competition aspects of regulators' rules.

One of the major challenges to self-regulation in the UK came in 1986, when the Office of Fair Trading threatened to put the Rule Book of the Stock Exchange (itself a self-regulatory agency) to the Restrictive Trades Practices Court (Goodhart, 1989b). This was because many of the self-created rules of the stock exchange (minimum commissions, single capacity, entry barriers, etc.) were deemed to be powerfully anti-competitive. It was this threat and the subsequent agreement between the stock exchange and the government that led to one of the biggest structural changes ever in the UK financial system: the entry of banks into securities business. Thus, an active competition authority can have a powerful impact on regulation if there is a mechanism for its operation.

Since a significant component of consumer protection is a competitive marketplace, this is entirely appropriate. There is, therefore, a powerful case for a country's general competition agency to be actively involved in the regulatory regime, even if such involvement falls short of the power of veto.

(iii) A regulatory matrix

In the absence of a mega regulator, a financial institution will necessarily be subject to the jurisdiction of more than one regulator and, depending on its range of business, possibly to several agencies. To the extent that prudential supervision is deemed appropriate, the institution will fall under the jurisdiction of either the systemic or the prudential agency. It will also come within the jurisdiction of the retail and/or wholesale conduct of business agency and, if it operates on exchanges, the relevant exchange regulators. An indicative schema of this is outlined in Table 8.3.

Table 8.3 Regulatory matrix

			Conduct of business regulation		
	Systemic regulator	Prudential regulator	Wholesale[1]	Retail[1]	Exchange regulators[2]
Banks	✓		✓	✓	✓
Building societies	✓		✓	✓	✓
Credit unions	✓			✓	
General insurance companies		✓	✓	✓	✓
Life assurance offices		✓		✓	
Fund managers		✓	✓	✓	✓
Unit trusts and OEICs		✓	✓	✓	✓
Pension funds		✓	✓	✓	
Financial advisers			✓	✓	
Money and FX brokers			✓		✓
Securities brokers			✓	✓	✓
Friendly societies		✓		✓	

Notes: [1] Dependent upon the type of business undertaken.
[2] If members of an exchange.

(iv) The role of the central bank

When each country has decided on its optimal regulatory structure, the next question is the role of the central bank within that structure. The first issue we shall address is power. Of the seven countries that currently have in place a single, all-embracing financial regulatory authority, all but one have made the regulatory authority separate from the central bank; the sole exception is the Monetary Authority in Singapore. Such separation is not accidental. Particularly if the central bank has independent powers to set the interest rate – 'instrument independence', to use Fischer's phrase (Fischer, 1994) – the combination of a widespread regulatory function with monetary control might be thought to place excessive powers within the hands of unelected officials. Indeed, there is some slight tendency for there to be a negative relationship between independence to set monetary instruments and the central bank's direct operation of, and responsibility for, regulation. Consider, for example, the relative roles of the Bundesbank and the Bank of England prior to 1997; indeed the acquisition of monetary autonomy at the same time as the Bank's loss of a role in the supervisory and debt management functions in 1997 was not just a coincidence. The issue is power, not formal independence as such. When the European System of Central Banks is formed, the member national central banks will be required to be independent, but they will, individually, have little power over monetary policy. Therefore, we would expect them to seek to assume, and to guard jealously, their regulatory function. What else, indeed, would occupy these august and venerable institutions? While the shift of the Bank of England's supervisory role to the new mega regulator makes sense in the context of a separate sovereign UK monetary system, it would become more questionable when, and if, the UK should join the single-currency, euro area. In the United States, the separate Federal Reserve banks play their largest role in watching over the health and conditions of their local banks.

The next issue is possible conflicts of interest. This is frequently advanced by academic economists as the main argument against central bank participation in regulation, in the belief that a central bank with responsibility for preventing systemic risk is more likely to loosen monetary policy on occasions of difficulty (see Cukierman, 1992: Chapter 7; Brimmer, 1989; Heller, 1991). Indeed, there is a slight statistical relationship between responsibility for regulation and higher inflation, but this is, we suggest, due to the interaction within the central bank between dependence and the regulatory role. We see no reason why assistance to individual banks in difficulty need affect the aggregate provision of reserves or level of interest rates. Any lender-of-last-resort assistance can be offset in the aggregate by open-market operations. Furthermore, cases in which the banking systems of countries as a whole get into serious difficulty (United States 1930–3; Japan 1992 to date; Scandinavia late 1980s and early 1990s; UK 1974–5), are much more likely to be periods of deflation than inflation, and the really serious sins of omission are of insufficient support in such cases (often on a quasi-Austrian view of the benefits of purging past excesses). In our previous empirical and historical studies of this issue (Goodhart and Schoenmaker,1995a, 1995b), we have come across few attested cases where the concern of a central bank for the solvency of its banks has been a major factor in an excessively expansionary monetary policy.

Indeed, the question of conflicts of interest might in some cases be an argument *for* giving the central bank such regulatory responsibilities. The question here is: if not the central bank, then which other body will have such powers, and what conflicts of interest might it have? If the central bank does not play this role, will it then be given to a body more subject to direct political influence? If public policy conflicts do arise, they will do so irrespective of whether supervision is a responsibility of the central bank. Such conflicts may arise despite whatever institutional structure is created, and they must be resolved somehow. The key issue is whether the transactions costs of resolving conflicts are greater or less when resolution occurs internally rather than externally. A particular view on this issue has been put by the Reserve Bank of Australia:

> By supervising banks (the central bank) gains first-hand knowledge and 'feel' for financial market conditions and for the behaviour of those institutions which are a key element in the transmission of monetary policy changes to the general economy. This can be an important input into monetary policy decisions. There are more likely to be complementarities between supervision and monetary policy than conflicts, and any conflicts that do arise will need to be resolved however the various responsibilities are allocated.
>
> (Thompson, 1996)

An interesting perspective on the question of whether bank supervision should or should not be located in the central bank is given by Dr C. Stals (Governor of the Reserve Bank of South Africa). In his 1992 Annual Address to shareholders of the Reserve Bank he argued as follows:

> The Bank's responsibilities with regard to the function of bank supervision have over the past year involved it in various controversial issues which may well question the wisdom of the five-year old 'marriage' of the Reserve Bank and the Office of the Registrar of Deposit-taking Institutions . . .
>
> Unwarranted claims by investors with deposit-taking institutions and unregulated entities alike for financial assistance by the Reserve Bank, which have received wide publicity and unjustified support in the financial press, have actually forced the Reserve Bank into the position of being a defendant in time-consuming and costly litigation. It cannot be denied that these events have had a negative impact on the general standing of the Reserve Bank and, if carried too far, the credibility of the central bank as a monetary authority could be undermined.
>
> In the light of these developments, two fundamental questions arise. The first is whether the Reserve Bank, as central bank and monetary authority, should continue to involve itself in bank supervision. The second question is whether the Bank could be expected to provide, without any

legal obligation to do so, deposit insurance by acting as financial supporter of last resort . . .

In reappraising its position, the Reserve Bank will have to be guided by several considerations, including the following:

- the extent to which its credibility as a monetary authority could be undermined by its involvement in bank supervision;
- the likelihood that it will attract a moral obligation to provide financial assistance to a deposit-taking institution under its supervision when such an institution ends up in financial difficulty; . . .

Firm decisions have not yet been reached, but some preliminary conclusions are the following:

- the functions of bank supervision and lender (or financial supporter) of last resort should be separated clearly;
- practical ways of establishing an arms-length relationship between the Office for Deposit-taking Institutions and the Reserve Bank itself should be devised in order to allow the Registrar of Deposit-taking Institutions to focus exclusively on prudential supervisory matters, and the Reserve Bank to focus on the stability of the financial system.

The Reserve Bank of South Africa has devised something of a working compromise between the opposing arguments about the location of bank supervision. An 'arm's-length' relationship has been established between the Office of the Registrar (of banks), which is located within the Reserve Bank, and the Reserve Bank itself – particularly its role as lender of last resort. This has been accomplished partly by separating clearly The Bank Act (for the Registrar's functions) and the Act for the South African Reserve Bank, thereby distinguishing the respective responsibilities of the Supervisory Office and of the Reserve Bank as the main monetary policy authority. Despite being a Senior Reserve Bank Official, the Registrar has been given some autonomy in the administration and implementation of his or her functions, but also clearly defined restrictions when it comes to decisions on monetary policy. This seems to accept a degree of inevitability that, at least in the current circumstances of South Africa, the central bank must have some role in bank supervision, though an attempt has been made to guard against some of the potential hazards involved in such arrangements.

In many countries and at many times there have been close links between commercial bankers and politicians. Placing regulatory responsibility within the central bank is, for a variety of reasons, probably the most effective way of reducing the influence of politicians (or of commercial bankers) on the supervisory treatment of the commercial banks.

But this comes at a reputational cost. One of the maintained themes of this monograph is that regulation and supervision is a thankless task. The best that can be hoped for is not to be noticed. Failures become immediate public knowledge and engender heaps of blame, whereas successes are unknown, unrealised and unappreciated. A typical response, in the UK to the BCCI and Barings failures, was to assert that a central bank that can allow that to happen is unfit to have independent control of monetary policy. This is yet another reason why there may be some slight association between central bank independence and the delegation of the regulatory and supervisory function over banks to some 'independent' body.

We put the term 'independent' in quotes consciously, since no bank regulator could, or should, ever in practice be actually independent of the central bank (as distinct from regulators of non-bank financial intermediaries, or those with responsibility for (retail) conduct of business).[2] The central bank is the monopoly provider of the reserve base and lender of last resort. Any serious banking problems are bound to lead to calls for the central bank to use its reserve-creating powers. Moreover, the central bank, in its macro-policy operational role, must have a direct concern for the payments and settlement system, the money markets and the development of the monetary aggregates. Any serious problem with the health of the banking system will touch on one or more of these concerns. So there are bound to be – must be – very close relationships between the bank regulator and the monetary policy authority.[3] Establishing such relationships must be one of the priorities in the forthcoming reform of the regulatory structure in the UK.

If so, the need for co-ordination might suggest unifying the functions within the central bank. But, for a variety of reasons, including the need for confidentiality, the supervisory department (wing in the Bank of England) was usually held largely separate from the monetary policy department (wing).[4] Co-ordination is then regarded as necessary and actually achieved only between the top officials. But such regular meetings of top officials can be organised just as easily regardless of whether their subordinates are in separate or the same buildings, or whether their organisation is formally separate or not. Perhaps the only real difference is that disagreements between top officials would be settled (quietly) within the central bank in the case of unification, and outside the bank, presumably by the Minister of Finance, with more likelihood of publicity, in the case of separation. But it is hard to recall cases of publicly observed disagreements between central bank and separate bank regulators in countries with such separation.

A final issue relates to the finance of bail-outs, should such occur. Owing to fraud, mismanagement or simply incidents of extreme volatility in asset markets, some banks, including perhaps very large banks, may become insolvent. It used to be possible, at least on some occasions, to resolve such situations by a rescue, a 'lifeboat', organised by the central bank and paid for by a voluntary levy on the remaining commercial banks. The increasing diversity within, and competition among, the banking sector will make that almost impossible to arrange in future years. Such a rescue depended on the existence of a well-defined 'club' of banks that were prepared and able to spend shareholders' funds to protect the reputation and the privileges of the club. With a mixed bunch of niche, specialist, universal, domestic and multinational banks, agreement to pay out good money to revive an ailing competitor could not be achieved.

The implication is that any large rescues within the banking field will, in future, have to be financed by taxpayers' funds (see Goodhart and Schoenmaker, 1995a, 1995b).[5] If so, the central government, politicians and ministries of finance will have to be involved in any large failures and rescues. This, in turn, will have a bearing on the question of the relationship between the body charged with the maintenance of systemic stability and the central bank.

The bottom line in our view is that banking realities will force considerable co-ordination and interaction between the top officials dealing with monetary macro policy and with bank regulation. The question of whether the banking supervisory body is formally inside or outside the central bank is then essentially a subsidiary issue depending on perceptions of the appropriate locus of power and responsibility. These perceptions will vary depending on the accidents of history and culture. There is no single best approach under all circumstances, as is clearly evidenced by the variety of regulatory structures in being in different countries, and the lack of any tendency towards a single model.

D. The international dimension

The increasing globalisation of banking and finance means that autarky is no longer a viable approach in financial regulation: regulation determined at the national level can be undermined by developments in other regulatory jurisdictions, and regulatory requirements in one country have impacts on others. A general problem in banking and securities regulation is that the jurisdiction of national regulators is smaller than the geographical business area of regulated financial institutions. There is no overriding international regulatory authority, since supervision and prudential regulation is conducted at the national level, whereas the issues have an international dimension. Different legal systems are involved; the powers and authority of individual central banks and bank supervisors vary considerably, as do institutional structures in different countries. Steil (1992) puts it as follows: 'The global integration process in capital markets means that the system with which policy makers are concerned, extends over a multitude of regulatory jurisdictions'.

Herring (1997) notes four factors determining the appropriate size of the regulatory domain: (1) the extent of externalities; (2) the scope for a prisoner's dilemma amongst regulators (all jurisdictions may be better off by co-operating, but each believes it can gain by operating alone); (3) economies of scale in the administration of regulation such as may arise with information use; and (4) the extent to which benefits may derive from uniformity (e.g. lowering compliance costs).

Because of the potential externalities involved, co-operative strategies have the capacity to increase the effectiveness of regulation and limit the scope for regulatory arbitrage. This becomes an especially relevant consideration where financial conglomerates (particularly banks that undertake significant business in securities and derivatives trading) operate on an international basis. Increasing volumes of cross-border trading on international futures and options exchanges create particular hazards. The problems of Barings and Daiwa Securities illustrate such problems. Increasing attention has been given to the international dimension of the regulation and supervision of financial conglomerates. It has also brought forward increased co-operation between bank and securities regulators. A recent G-30 survey suggested that the monitoring of banks on a global basis by the home-country supervisor was the most important role for regulators in controlling systemic risk. The second most important role was judged to be communication and co-ordination between home and host regulators. (For a comprehensive review of the historical evolution of international regulatory collaboration, see White (1996) and Padoa-Schioppa (1996b).)

The central issues are, therefore, the extent to which international factors undermine the power of exclusively national regulation, and whether, in an increasingly integrated global financial system, some or all of the objectives of regulation can be achieved only by abandoning autarky, implying that the design of effective regulatory structures can be met more effectively – or only – through various forms of international co-operation.

The international dimension of regulation has both *competitive neutrality* and *systemic* implications. First, given that financial institutions and markets compete globally, regulation in national systems has the capacity to confer competitive subsidies or disadvantages. Second, this can have the effect of inducing regulatory arbitrage. This, in turn, creates a third potential hazard, namely international competition in laxity. In a highly interdependent global financial system the security of the whole may be only as secure as that of its weakest part, and hence all countries have an interest in the regulatory arrangements in all others.

In addition, international operations have the potential to increase the impact of systemic failures resulting from the increasing interdependence of national financial systems. On the other hand, the greater opportunity for diversification between countries may lessen somewhat the probability of failure in the first place. As we noted earlier, the wider the ambit of financial intermediaries (both geographically and functionally) the less likely they should be to fail (because of the benefits of diversification), but the more serious would probably be the ramifications if such a failure nevertheless occurred. The potential danger is that systemic stability can be threatened because of a failure in a poorly regulated jurisdiction. Thus, risks can be spread, partly through the international interbank market, and the failure of an institution can have repercussions in other countries. This perspective has been emphasised by the then President of the Federal Reserve Bank of New York:

The speed, volume, value, and complexity of international banking transactions have introduced new linkages and interdependencies between
markets and institutions that have the potential to transmit problems and
disruptions from place to place and institution to institution at almost
breakneck speed.

(Corrigan, 1992)

On the other hand, others have challenged the case for international harmonisation of regulation, though this is often part of a general challenge to
the regulation of banks. Thus, for instance, Benston (1994) argues:

The need to harmonise the regulatory structure is not supported by the
analysis. Analyses of the rationales for domestic banking regulation lead to
the conclusion that international banking and the cross-border operation
of banks do not pose special problems that would be mitigated by harmonisation of national banking regulations.

Be that as it may, the *systemic stability* objective relates to internationally co-
operative mechanisms to reduce the probability of default and the potential
for default of an institution in one country to have systemic effects in others.
An aim is to prevent any country gaining a competitive advantage by virtue
of having weak regulation for the safety and soundness of key institutions.
Thus competition in regulation, while it has merits in some areas, should not
apply to those regulatory requirements that specifically impinge on systemic
stability. However, if this is the main purpose of international collaboration,
then the field to be harmonised need not cover areas wider than those necessary to ensure the solvency of institutions. In particular, harmonisation of
conduct of business rules is *not* required.[6]

The focus of the *competitive neutrality* objective is somewhat different. It
implies international collaboration in those aspects of regulation that have
the potential to affect the competitive position of suppliers of financial services in different countries. The premise is that all forms of regulation have a
potential impact on the cost of providing services.

(i) Hazards in competitive neutrality

There are problems in adopting a competitive neutrality approach to international co-ordination of regulation:

- It can create significant distortions by trying to force into the same
  mould institutions that in practice are inherently different because of differences in the legal framework, accounting procedures, and other
  infrastructural and cultural factors.
- Thus, harmonisation may, in some circumstances, be inappropriate
  because of different institutional structures and business practices.
  For instance, the Investment Services Directive has certain provisions

requiring securities firms to publish data on prices and trading volumes on a rolling basis during a trading session. However, this may pose problems for dealer-markets (e.g. London) where immediate disclosure of certain transactions might itself affect prices and put market makers into a hazardous position (but see Board and Sutcliffe, 1995, 1997). This, on the other hand, would not apply in markets, such as Paris, that are order driven.

- With respect to competition between banks and securities firms, there are other issues that affect competitiveness, not the least being the access that banks have to safety nets associated with the lender-of-last-resort role and deposit protection schemes. Applying the principle of the second best, harmonising one aspect of regulation when other aspects are not equalised does not produce competitive neutrality. Because of the perceptions with respect to the safety net, banks may secure a competitive advantage even in those areas where, in principle, the safety net does not apply.

- Excessive harmonisation for competitive neutrality denies the benefits of elements of competition between regulators and removes potentially valuable information about the operation of different regulatory regimes.

- If competitive neutrality considerations should become dominant, the process of harmonisation is likely to become increasingly extensive as more aspects of regulation that potentially affect competitiveness are brought within the net. This potential for 'escalating harmonisation' can be seen in the EU's Investment Services Directive. Article 11 establishes the principle of host-country responsibility for various conduct of business rules. However, it also states: 'This is without prejudice to any decisions to be taken in the context of the harmonisation of the rules of conduct'. This seems to imply that present 'essential' harmonisation is only a prelude to a broader objective of possibly total uniformity in European securities market regulation.

- The steps towards harmonisation create an environment of bargaining and negotiation. Such negotiation produced the concept of the 'trading book' in the Investment Services Directive, which seems to have no rationale other than to meet the objective of competitive neutrality between banks and specialist securities firms.

- Competitive neutrality and systemic stability objectives may at times be in conflict. As noted by the Basle Committee (1993) when referring to its proposals related to the position risks of banks: '(They) contain features which bank supervisors acting on their own would not necessarily favour'. This seems to imply that competitive neutrality has been bought at the cost of inappropriately low standards for banks.

Competitive neutrality considerations are, however, relevant where systemic stability considerations might be undermined if, through regulatory arbitrage, banks are able to choose their regulatory regime through decisions about where to locate. Our point is that there are potential costs if competitive neutrality considerations are pursued slavishly and beyond the requirements of systems stability.

(ii) Alternative forms of international collaboration

As international financial integration erodes the viability of autarky, there is a prima-facie case for at least a limited form of international collaboration. In highly interdependent systems, co-operative strategies can yield welfare benefits in terms of enhancing the effectiveness of regulation. However, financial integration does not in itself create sufficient conditions for total regulatory harmonisation. A trend has emerged in banking, securities trading, and other areas of finance towards increasing degrees of harmonisation and encompassing a wider range of regulatory issues.

Substantial reservations can be entered about this seemingly inexorable tendency. In Chapter 4 it was argued that, partly because the costs of regulation are seldom made explicit and the consumer may believe them to be zero, there can be a tendency towards overregulation in the sense of an excessively cumbersome set of externally imposed rules. This in itself might caution against attempting to establish a global regulatory framework even if it were practically feasible. In particular, harmonisation need not cover all aspects of regulation in order for the objectives of regulation to be achieved, and harmonisation is only one form of international collaboration. Even in cases where autarky is either not viable or less efficient than international collaboration, harmonisation is not the only strategic response and may itself be less than optimum. It is also the case that harmonisation may make regulation uniformly bad. Herring and Litan (1995) make the point that consumer protection measures should be governed by national preferences.

Ultimately, the focus needs to be on the *objectives* of regulation (systemic stability and consumer protection) and the extent to which they can be secured more efficiently through international collaborative strategies. There is a danger that, once the principle of collaboration is accepted, harmonisation is pursued for its own sake and questions related to competitive neutrality come to dominate prudential requirements and systemic stability. Such 'international escalation' may take harmonisation beyond the point where benefits, in terms of increased effectiveness in regulation, exceed costs.

There are many reasons why, in some areas of finance, differences in regulation between countries are both viable and desirable. They allow for different social choices to be made with respect to objectives, for different institutional structures and potential for systemic hazard, and for differences in externalities and the social cost of institutional failure. Competition in regulation can be beneficial provided that systemic stability is not impaired and the externalities of one regime do not impose costs on others. It is not inevitable that competition in regulation would emerge as competition in

laxity if there are benefits of regulation that consumers recognise and are prepared to pay for. Herring (1997) also argues that competition among
regulators reduces the dangers of regulatory cartels being formed. On the
other hand, Dale (1996) argues that the major weaknesses of the regulatory
competition approach are that it does not deal with the danger of cross-
border financial contagion and that it may confuse depositors, counterparties
and investors. Similar issues are raised in Benink and Llewellyn (1995).

The principle of subsidiarity, which surfaced in the Delors Report on
European Monetary Union, can equally be applied to the international
dimension of regulation. For the reasons just outlined, the benefits that can
be derived from competition, and questions of accountability of regulatory
authorities, there is a strong case for regulation being framed at a local level
except when its effectiveness is significantly impaired, and where clear economic gains can be made by international collaboration which exceed the
benefits to be derived from local regulation. The position has been highlighted by Grundfest (1990): 'The major challenge for regulators will,
however, be to distinguish situations in which co-ordination is desirable from
those in which diversity yields greater benefits'. We add that decisions also
relate to the particular form of collaboration of which the fashion for harmonisation is at one end of a spectrum.

Competition and harmonisation are two polar cases along a spectrum.
The full spectrum of international regulatory collaboration encompasses
what might be termed: *systemic harmonisation, economic harmonisation, international co-ordination, co-operation, extraterritorial enforcement,* and
international competition.

Systemic harmonisation implies a high degree of harmonisation of regulation for systemic stability reasons, intended to make common regulatory
objectives effective. It reflects the weakness of autarky in achieving objectives
because of externalities at the international level. As each country has a
mutual interest in all other countries' regulatory arrangements, each has to be
confident about the integrity of regulation everywhere. There is, therefore, a
strong case for a degree of minimum harmonisation of standards for systemic
stability.

The case for *economic harmonisation* arises when there are differences in
regulation that serve no regulatory or other objective and may simply be a
product of history, but nevertheless impose unnecessary costs and inconve-
nience. The regulation of securities markets, for instance, is based on
arrangements which vary considerably between countries (see OECD, 1993).
Harmonisation in these cases, while not impairing any country's regulatory
objectives or detracting from consumer welfare, could reduce costs and incon-
venience involved when suppliers and consumers operate under different
regulatory regimes. Examples include arrangements with respect to information disclosure, registration procedures, and accounting conventions. While
the case for reducing unnecessary or unchosen differences in regulation is
strong, if the benefits of standardisation are significant the markets should be

able to devise their own mechanisms for securing regulatory convergence without the intervention of official regulatory authorities. Self-regulatory agencies are in a position to respond to market pressures if there are mutual advantages in standardisation and if no regulatory objectives are involved. This is one of the roles of IOSCO in the securities market.

Co-ordination aims not at harmonisation but at establishing a common set of *minimum* regulatory standards above which individual countries can make choices, and at the removal of evident inconsistencies and conflicts in regulation between jurisdictions.

Co-operative strategies relate to enforcement procedures and information sharing. With institutions conducting business in several regulatory jurisdictions, there are clear advantages in sharing information between host and home countries. However, problems can be encountered, such as confidentiality and legal power to divulge information to foreign agencies. Such co-operative arrangements are well established in the banking sector through the Basle Committee but fairly rudimentary in the securities industry, though IOSCO has made significant contributions. Co-operative strategies are also beneficial in enforcement, where the co-operation of foreign regulatory authorities may be essential for the enforcement of home regulation and the prosecution of infringements. Regulatory authorities have a mutual interest in co-operation to secure enforcement and, where necessary, prosecution. This has been well developed by the Securities and Exchange Commission, which has successfully negotiated a network of treaties, communiqués, accords, etc., with regulatory authorities outside the United States. In general, mutual recognition agreements and memoranda of understanding can be valuable contributions to effective recognition that nevertheless fall short of harmonisation.

A further option to address problems encountered with the international dimension to regulation is the application of *extraterritorial jurisdiction*. In some cases, though this may require the consent of host-country authorities, a home regulator may require certain regulatory standards to be met by institutions under its jurisdiction, even when the operations are being conducted by a foreign subsidiary of that institution which is formally under the jurisdiction of a host regulator. A host country would not normally allow a more lenient regulatory arrangement to apply, but it might acquiesce to more demanding standards being set.

There is no presumption that harmonisation is invariably the most appropriate approach. In practice, the debate should be about the mix of collaborative arrangements between regulators along the spectrum, with harmonisation at one end and *international competition* at the other end. The mix will vary for the different dimensions to regulation that are the subject of this monograph.

Even so, there may be a case for extending international collaboration to wider aspects of regulation than purely systemic stability considerations. Two areas deserve particular consideration: (1) where the objective is to create a single market in financial services across several countries, and (2) where cross-border transactions are undertaken and it is judged that consumers, perhaps unaware of differences in regulation, may assume that the same regulation applies as in their home country. The latter consideration is easier to handle when financial firms supply services to consumers by locating in the latter's home country. The generally accepted principle is that host-country regulation applies with respect to conduct of business rules even though it is home countries that are responsible for prudential regulation.

(iii)   Suggested guidelines

The increasing globalisation of finance and the interdependencies of national banking systems imply that autarky is not, in practice, a viable option for the regulation of banks and financial conglomerates. However, this does not mean that rigid harmonisation is the correct response, even though it has the merit of simplicity and precision. We also suggest that the appropriate collaborative response with respect to the spectrum between harmonisation and competition will depend in part on the specific regulatory issue under consideration.

Nevertheless, without imposing a strait-jacket, a set of general guidelines can be suggested to deal with the international dimension of regulated firms:

1 There should be agreed minimum standards for the safety and soundness of relevant institutions. This amounts to an international concerted approach in two areas: minimum capital adequacy standards and requirements for risk analysis and management systems.
2 Clear, certain and agreed mechanisms for the sharing of relevant information between regulators about the financial standing and business operations of firms under their jurisdiction are essential.
3 There must be international co-operation in the investigation of problem financial institutions.
4 When it is necessary to close an institution, the procedure should not be impeded by international barriers.
5 Every relevant institution needs an agency clearly responsible for its regulation, monitoring, and supervision. There should be no ambiguity in this.
6 There should be no scope for regulated institutions to escape minimum safety standards by locating in lax areas.
7 In order to avoid bureaucratic uncertainty, a lead regulator should be identified for all financial conglomerates with international business so that all other regulators know, without any uncertainty, who is the relevant regulatory agency. This requirement is not universally agreed upon. It has been noted recently that 'Reflecting some concerns on national sovereignty, members have agreed that international lead regulatory arrangements – whereby a "global lead regulator" would exist for a financial conglomerate

operating across borders – will not be provided for in domestic law' (Council of Financial Supervisors, 1996).

All of this falls far short of widespread and generalised harmonisation.

Whatever levels of collaboration are attempted, the problems are substantial. In the absence of any international legal basis, it is not clear what sanctions can be applied to errant jurisdictions or how internationally agreed standards are to be enforced. There are wide differences in national approaches to regulation, and this makes international agreement difficult to secure and even more difficult to enforce. At the national level, the authority and jurisdiction of regulatory agencies is clear. Power has been conferred by the political authorities, and the agencies have powers of enforcement (including through the courts). They also have the sanction of withdrawing authorisation from regulated institutions. The threat of these sanctions gives power to the regulator. This is not the case at the international level, as there are no legal mechanisms for enforcing internationally agreed standards and rules. The absence of clearly defined enforcement mechanisms means that co-operation is all the more important if agreements are to have effect. But the issue of effective sanctions remains. In the final analysis, the ultimate sanction against an unco-operative regulator is exclusion: for all other jurisdictions to bar its financial institutions from conducting business in their countries.

E. Assessment

The institutional structure of regulation has recently become an issue of public policy debate in several countries, which suggests a certain unease about prevailing structures. International experience indicates a wide variety of institutional regulatory formats, which signals that these are influenced by national characteristics, such as the structure of the financial system. It also suggests that there is no universal ideal model.

A key issue is whether the regulatory structure has an impact on the overall effectiveness and efficiency of regulation and supervision, since this should be the ultimate criterion when making judgement between alternative formats. It is for this reason that the objectives of regulation should be at the centre of the debate.

While institutional structure is important, in itself it does not guarantee anything about effective and efficient regulation and supervision, and it would be hazardous to assume that changing the structure of regulatory institutions is a panacea.

With the emergence of mixed financial institutions, the case for a conglomerate or mega regulator might have a certain prima-facie appeal, since it mirrors the emerging structure of financial systems. However, there are reservations to this, and we prefer a structure more closely focused on the objectives of regulation. Nevertheless, it is recognised that a perfect institutional structure is a chimera, and we have to accept the inevitability of working within an imperfect structure: it is not possible to capture fully an untidy marketplace in a perfectly neat set of regulatory boxes.

There is an increasing international dimension to regulation. The problem arises because the jurisdiction of national regulators is smaller than the geographical area of regulated financial firms: there is no overriding international regulatory authority. The increasing globalisation of banking and securities trading means that autarky is no longer a viable approach to regulation. Given the potential externalities involved, collaborative strategies of one sort or another have the capacity to increase the effectiveness of regulation, and limit the scope for regulatory arbitrage. The international dimension has both competitive neutrality and systemic dimensions. However, we have argued that financial integration does not in itself create sufficient conditions for total harmonisation of regulatory requirements between countries. The key is to decide which areas of regulation are to be undertaken primarily or solely at the national level as opposed to those which need overt international collaboration. Such collaboration need not imply a high degree of harmonisation, which is only one of a series of options. In particular, harmonisation need not cover all aspects of regulation in order for the objectives to be achieved. While it might be hazardous to leave systemic stability issues strictly within the jurisdiction of national authorities, there is merit in allowing national differences in areas where systemic stability considerations do not arise. Indeed, we have argued that there are many reasons why, in some areas, differences in regulation between countries are both viable and desirable. We have argued that the debate should be about the mix of different collaborative arrangements between national regulators.

Appendix

The structure of regulatory agencies in key countries

There is a substantial variety of institutional structures for regulatory and supervisory institutions throughout the world. This is so, for instance, in relation to the role of the central bank in bank supervision; the role of the central bank in the regulation and supervision of other financial business (notably securities and insurance); whether regulation is conducted by specialist or conglomerate agencies; whether regulation and supervision is based predominantly on *institutional* or *functional* criteria; and whether different arrangements are made for business conducted within financial conglomerates or by specialist institutions. The full spectrum of possibilities is represented.

Two sources of information are particularly helpful when considering the institutional structure of financial regulation in different countries. The most comprehensive annual listing, together with a brief history and description of the roles of each regulatory/supervisory agency, is to be found in *The Directory of Regulatory Agencies* published by Central Bank Publications in London; the first issue was published in 1996. A second major reference is the report of the Tripartite Group of Bank, Securities and Insurance Regulators (De Swaan Report): *The Supervision of Financial Conglomerates* published in July 1995.

A simplified categorisation of national institutional structures is given in Table A8.1 and summarised in Tables A8.2 and A8.3. However, caution is needed when interpreting such descriptions of structures, in addition to the general problem of encapsulating sometimes complex structures in a simple form. The nuances cannot be captured in a simple tabulation. First, the practice is often not always as precise as might be suggested by formal structure; demarcations of responsibilities are frequently not as precise as the structure of agencies might suggest. Second, there are varying degrees of co-ordination and co-operation between regulatory agencies where responsibilities overlap, and in some cases different agencies have joint responsibility in some areas. For instance, in Australia the co-ordination of supervision (including of financial conglomerates) is undertaken by a dedicated agency, the Council of Financial Supervisors. Third, the supervisory arrangements for components

Table A8.1 Regulators of banking, securities and insurance

	Securities	Insurance	Banking
Algeria			A
Argentina	C	D	(A)
Australia	C	D	A
Austria	H	H	H
Bangladesh	C		
Barbados			A
Belgium	E	D	E
Bermuda	A	D	A
Bolivia	C	D	
Botswana	C	D	A
Brazil	C	D	A
Bulgaria			A
Canada	C	F	F
Chile	G	G	B
China	C		A
Colombia	C	F	F
Costa Rica	B		A
Cyprus	A		A
Czech Republic	G	G	A
Denmark	H	H	H
Dominican Republic	A		A
Ecuador	C	F	F
Egypt	C	D	A
Finland	E	J	E
France	C	D	B
Germany	C	D	B
Greece	C		A
Guatemala	A		B
Hong Kong	C	D	A
Hungary	C	D	B
India	C		A
Indonesia	C		A
Ireland	A	J	A
Israel	C	J	A
Italy	C	D	A
Ivory Coast	C		
Jamaica	C		A
Japan	J	J	A/J
Jordan	C		A
Kenya	C		A
Korea	C	D	A
Lithuania			A
Luxembourg	A	D	A
Macau		F	F
Malaysia	C	A	A
Malta	H	H	H
Mauritius	C	D	A
Mexico	E	D	E
Netherlands	C	D	A
New Zealand	C		A

Table A8.1 Cont.

	Securities	Insurance	Banking
Nigeria	C		A
Norway	H	H	H
Oman	C		
Pakistan	C		A
Panama	C	D	
Paraguay	C	F	F
Philippines	C	D	A
Poland	C	D	A
Portugal	C	D	A
Russia	C	D	A
Singapore	A	A	A
Slovenia	C	J	A
South Africa	G	G	A
Spain	C	D	A
Sri Lanka	C	J	A
Sweden	H	H	H
Switzerland	E	D	E
Taiwan	C		A
Thailand	C	J	A
Trinidad & Tobago	C		A
Tunisia	C	J	A
Turkey	C		A
United Kingdom	C	J	A/B
United States	C	D	A/B
Uruguay	A		A
Venezuela	C		B
Zambia	C		A

Notes: A: Central bank/monetary agency; B: specialist bank regulator; C: specialist securities regulator; D: specialist insurance regulator; E: banking and securities regulator; F: banking and insurance regulator; G: securities and insurance regulator; H: combined banking, securities and insurance regulator; J: government department.
Source: Directory of Financial Regulatory Agencies (1996) London: Central Bank Publications

of financial conglomerates are often shared between agencies and are often different from the case when the same business is conducted by specialist institutions. For instance, in Italy when an insurance company forms part of a financial conglomerate it is subject to *solo* supervision by the insurance regulator, but when a financial conglomerate includes insurance and a securities investment firm, prudential supervision on a solo basis is conducted both by the insurance agency and the Banca d'Italia. Experience varies as to whether regulation is conducted on a consolidated basis.

Institutional structure is also complex in many countries because of the existence of both federal and regional/state agencies. This is notably the case in the United States, Australia and Canada. In Canada, for instance, while prudential supervision is conducted by the Office of the Superintendent of

Financial Institutions (formed in the late 1980s by the merger of the former specialist regulators of banks and insurance companies), securities regulation and insurance-related consumer protection are provided separately by provincial agencies. Moreover, securities companies and credit unions are supervised by both federal and provincial agencies in Canada.

A further complication is that many countries have adopted the lead regulator approach to supervision of diversified financial institutions.

There are substantial differences between countries in the composition of regulatory agencies (most especially with respect to the role of practitioners) and in their accountability. Practitioners play a significant role in several agencies in the UK and in the United States. In South Africa, the Financial Services Board is responsible for non-bank supervision and is advised by the Policy Board for Financial Services and Regulation which has a majority of practitioners.

Finally, the tables do not reflect the varying role of auditors in the supervisory process. In Switzerland, for instance, external auditors are the essential supervisory tool for assessing the risks of financial conglomerates. Nevertheless, and notwithstanding these qualifications, some general observations can be made from the data in the tables.

With respect to the supervision of banks (Table A8.2), it is evident that central banks dominate: in the sample of seventy-five countries, central banks are the bank supervisory agency in fifty-four (Table A8.1). In addition, in the great majority of cases (forty-six of the fifty-four) the central bank is responsible only for the supervision of banks and not directly for other business. In six countries (Bermuda, Cyprus, Dominican Republic, Ireland, Luxembourg and Uruguay) the central bank is also responsible for securities business (but not insurance), while in one country (Malaysia) it is also responsible for insurance but not securities. In only one country (Singapore) is the central bank (monetary agency) responsible for all three of banking, insurance and securities.

In those countries where the central bank is not responsible for bank

Table A8.2 Regulators of banks

	Central banks	Non-central bank agencies	Total
Only banks	46	6	52
Banks and securities	6	4	10
Banks and insurance	1	5	62
Banks, insurance and securities	1	6	7
TOTAL	54	21	75

Source: *Directory of Financial Regulatory Agencies* (1996) London: Central Bank Publications

supervision, in six cases (Chile, France, Germany, Guatemala, Hungary and Venezuela) bank supervision is undertaken by an agency which is exclusively dedicated to banks. In four other cases (Belgium, Finland, Mexico and Switzerland) the bank regulator is also responsible for securities (but not insurance), while in five cases (Canada, Colombia, Ecuador, Macau and Paraguay) it is also responsible for insurance but not securities. There are six countries (Austria, Denmark, Japan, Malta, Norway and Sweden) where a single agency (but not the central bank) is responsible for all three sectors: the mega regulator model.

When we consider the structure of regulatory agencies more generally, we find in Table A8.3 that specialist agencies dominate. In forty four of the countries in the sample there are specialist agencies for the separate supervision of banking (whether or not it is the central bank), securities and insurance. In ten countries the supervision of banking and securities (but not insurance) is combined, and in three countries securities and insurance (but not banking) are undertaken by the same agency. In six countries (Canada, Colombia, Ecuador, Macau, Malaysia and Paraguay) the supervision of banks and insurance (but not securities) is conducted by the same agency (in one case – Malaysia – the central bank).

Table A8.3 Structure of regulatory institutions[1]

Specialist institutions[2]	44
Banking, securities and insurance combined	7
Banking and insurance combined	6
Banking and securities combined	10
Securities and insurance combined	3

Notes:
[1] Sample of seventy countries.
[2] For either two or three of banking, insurance and securities separately.
Source: Directory of Financial Regulatory Agencies (1996) London: Central Bank Publications

In only seven countries is a single agency (in one case, the central bank) responsible for the supervision of banking, insurance and securities. This will rise to eight when the UK implements the proposal to place all financial regulation under the umbrella of a single agency. The concept of the mega regulator is found in only a very small number of countries. In these countries the practice is somewhat different from appearance. Thus, in Norway solo supervision is conducted by separate divisions of the mega-agency and co-ordination problems are internalised. Similarly, in Japan there is a single supervisor for all three sectors: the Ministry of Finance. However, there are different bureaux within it responsible for different sectors and institutions and Quinn (1996b) notes that: 'it is no secret that sometimes problems can arise in communicating with each other'. In fact, it is planned that the supervisory arrangements will be changed in Japan. A new supervisory agency is set to replace the Ministry of Finance to supervise the whole of the financial sector. The new Financial Inspection and Supervisory Agency will supervise all types of financial institutions and is scheduled to begin operations during 1998. Draft plans for this new mega supervisor are to be submitted to the Cabinet in March.

In Sweden the supervision of all financial entities is undertaken by a single agency: the Swedish Financial Supervisory Authority (SFSA) which was formed in 1991 by a merger of the Bank Inspectorate and the Insurance Inspectorate. It is responsible for the supervision of more than 2,500 institutions. However, again the internal organisation reflects the recognition that there are major differences between banking, securities and insurance. Diversified institutions are therefore subject to the supervision of several departments within the SFSA. Thus, while the authority was created through the merger of previously specialised agencies, it has in practice retained something of the specialist approach.

9 Summary of policy conclusions

A. Main analytical themes

There are several analytical themes in this monograph, and our specific policy conclusions flow from them. The themes are:

1 Distinction is made between *regulation* (the establishment of specific rules of behaviour), *monitoring* (observing whether the rules are obeyed), and *supervision* (the more general observation of the behaviour of financial firms). Each involves different issues. The balance among the three activities varies between countries, and over time. For instance, there is currently a shift in emphasis away from detailed and prescriptive regulation towards monitoring and supervision.

2 The primary concern of banking regulators is to protect the financial system against systemic instability. The nature of banks' balance sheets, with nominal-certain short-term liabilities and longer-term assets of uncertain value, and the manifold and often enormous interconnectedness between banks, makes them especially susceptible to contagious runs. The latter remains a controversial subject, but even if the probability of such systemic instability is actually now low, the disruption that would be caused by multiple bank closures is too severe to contemplate with equanimity.

3 Because of the nature of contracts between financial firms and their customers (e.g. many are long term and involve a fiduciary obligation), there is a need for continuous monitoring of the behaviour of financial firms. Because most (especially retail) customers are not able to undertake continuous monitoring, and because there are substantial economies of scale in such activity, an important role of regulatory agencies is to monitor the behaviour of financial firms effectively and efficiently on behalf of customers. In effect, consumers delegate the task of monitoring to a regulatory agency; therefore, to some extent, that agency can be viewed as supplying monitoring services to customers of financial firms. In terms of resources used, consumer protection usually takes up the greater part of the time and effort of regulators and supervisors. This in turn raises the

issue of the nature of any perceived implicit contract between the regulator and consumers of financial services.

4 Financial transactions involve a complex structure of explicit and perceived implicit contracts between firms and their customers, firms and the regulator, and the regulator and society. Accordingly, we emphasise the contractual nature of the relationship between the regulated firm and the regulator. Given different (asymmetric) information between regulators and firms, two dangers arise. First, the effective (implicit or explicit) contract may not be the optimal one ('adverse selection') when the regulator is misinformed about the characteristics (such as the effectiveness of internal controls) of a firm. Second, even with the most well-designed regulatory contract, a firm may sometimes have incentives covertly to break the contract ('moral hazard'). These dangers can cause market failures, which have to be addressed in the design of regulations, monitoring and supervision techniques.

5 Regulatory agencies (central banks or other bodies) are viewed as supplying regulatory, monitoring and supervisory services to various stakeholders, including financial firms, consumers and government. However, complications arise because, unlike most other services, they are not supplied through a market process but are largely imposed by the regulator, although there may be a consultation process. This leads to several problems: valuable information is lost about the type and the extent of regulation that consumers demand, and about how much consumers are prepared to pay for regulation. Above all (and this is probably the most serious aspect), regulation is largely perceived as being a free good.

6 If the perception that regulation is costless is combined with risk-averse regulators, there is an evident danger that regulation will be overdemanded by consumers and oversupplied by the regulator. A major issue, therefore, is how to guard against overregulation.

7 Regulation is not costless, but imposes a range of costs (*institutional, compliance* and *structural*, as outlined in Chapter 8), which are ultimately reflected in the price of financial services. If regulation is 'excessive' (if it exceeds what is needed to achieve its limited objectives) or if it focuses on inappropriate objectives, avoidable costs are imposed upon society, and these costs could exceed the costs that regulation is designed to avoid.

8 Chapter 8 is devoted to the institutional structure of regulatory agencies, a topic that many countries are currently addressing. Particular institutional structures do not in themselves guarantee what really matters: regulation achieving its objectives in an efficient and cost-effective manner. There are many ways to create an institutional structure of regulatory agencies, and a review of international experience reveals a variety of structures. It also indicates powerfully that there is no 'ideal model' that

can be universally applied. We therefore do not offer firm policy conclusions in this area, except to stress that the focus must always be on the ultimate objectives of regulation, and, given the particular circumstances of a country, institutional structure should be designed to maximise the likelihood that the objectives will be met in the most effective and efficient manner.

9 In the final analysis, regulation is about changing the behaviour of regulated institutions. One of the key questions that arises is the extent to which behaviour is to be altered by externally imposed *rules*, or through creating *incentives* for firms to behave in a particular way. Regulation can be endogenous to the financial firm (i.e. self-control) as well as exogenous. A major issue, therefore, is whether regulation should proceed through externally imposed, prescriptive and detailed rules, or by the regulator creating incentives for appropriate behaviour.

10 Financial systems are changing substantially, to an extent that may undermine traditional approaches to regulation, most especially the balance between regulation and supervision. In particular, globalisation, the pace of financial innovation and the creation of new financial instruments, the blurring of traditional distinctions between different types of financial firm, the speed with which portfolios can change through banks' trading in derivatives, and the increased complexity of banking business, create a fundamentally new – particularly more competitive – environment in which (still predominantly national) regulation and supervision are undertaken. They also challenge the different approaches to regulation, which, if they are to be effective, must constantly respond to changes in the market environment in which regulated firms operate.

Although financial regulation applies (albeit differently) to all financial institutions, and such regulation has both a prudential and a conduct of business dimension, our main (but not exclusive) focus is on banks, and the prudential (systemic) dimension in particular. However, many of the policy conclusions to which we now turn apply more generally, i.e. to other financial firms, and to conduct of business regulation.

B. Policy conclusions

The main policy conclusions of this monograph are organised under six headings:

(i) The basis of regulation
(ii) The general approach: incentive structures
(iii) Policy differentiation
(iv) Issues in developing countries
(v) The management of financial crises
(vi) The international dimension to regulation

(i)   The basis of regulation

1   *The objectives of regulation need to be clearly defined and circumscribed.*
Financial regulation should have only a limited range of objectives (more
limited than consumers sometimes assume). In the final analysis, the
objectives are to sustain systemic stability and to protect the consumer.
The case for regulation depends on market imperfections and failures
(especially externalities and asymmetric information) that, in the absence
of regulation, produce suboptimal results and reduce consumer welfare.
Regulation should not be overloaded with other and wider objectives,
such as social outcomes. Effective and efficient regulation is difficult
enough with limited objectives, and the more it is burdened by wider considerations, the more likely it is to fail in many of them.

2   *Expectations about what regulation, monitoring, and supervision can
achieve need to be kept to realistic levels.* There needs to be recognition
of, and an encouragement of consumer awareness of, the limitations of
regulation – that it has only a limited role, that even in this restricted
dimension it can fail, that not all risks are covered, and that the optimal
level of regulation and supervision falls short of eliminating all possibility of consumers making wrong choices in financial contracts. The
consumer cannot be, and should not be, protected against all possibility of loss. This is emphasised for three main reasons. First, in the
absence of such recognition, the demands placed upon regulation will
become so excessive that they can only be met by an overly expensive,
intrusive and rigid system, with costs that greatly exceed the benefits.
Second, there is the moral hazard that excessive and unrealistic expectations about what regulation can achieve will reduce incentives for the
owners and managers of regulated firms to monitor and control themselves, and for their customers to exercise due diligence. Third,
occasional regulatory lapses and failures are a powerful signal and disciplinary mechanism that should be regarded as the necessary cost of an
optimal regulatory regime. An optimal regulatory regime takes account
of the costs that regulation can impose on consumers and regulated
firms, including the danger of impairing competition, stifling financial
innovation, and impeding efficiency, and the higher price of financial
services imposed on consumers.

3   *Regulation should not impede competition, but should support it; by addressing information asymmetries, it can enhance competition in the marketplace.*
However well intentioned, regulation has the potential to compromise
competition and to condone, if not endorse, unwarranted entry barriers,
restrictive practices, and other anti-competitive mechanisms. Indeed, historically regulation in finance has often been anti-competitive, but this is
not an inherent property of regulation. Regulation and competition can
be complementary. For example, regulation can make competition more

effective in the marketplace by requiring the disclosure of relevant information that can be used by consumers in making informed choices.

4 *Regulation should reinforce, not replace, market discipline.* Where possible, market discipline (e.g. disclosure) should be strengthened. This means creating incentives for private markets to reward good performance and to penalise hazardous behaviour.

5 *There must be practitioner input into the regulatory process.* If regulation is to be realistic, the regulator needs to work closely with the profession, and there should be due consultation about regulatory issues. The relationship between the regulator and the regulated should not be antagonistic, and there is much to be gained by both sides appreciating the objectives, constraints and perspectives of the other. Regulation is likely to be more effective if it is not viewed as being unrealistically imposed upon the industry. The skill lies in involving practitioners without the regulator's being actually, or being perceived to be, captured; the boundary between appropriate accommodation of practitioner perspectives and regulatory capture is inevitably blurry.

6 *Regulatory agencies should be staffed with well-qualified people.* In some respects, the contest between regulatory agencies and regulated firms is unequal, in that frequently careers in the regulated firms are more attractive than careers in regulatory agencies. Regulatory agencies often serve as fruitful recruitment grounds for regulated institutions. For these reasons, regulators should be remunerated at a competitive market rate in order to attract and retain well-qualified personnel. Given the importance of regulation, paying regulators low salaries is likely to prove to be a false economy.

7 *The extent of deposit insurance should be limited.* In order to limit moral hazard, deposit insurance should not cover 100 per cent of deposits at banks, and it should be financed by the industry.

(ii) The general approach: incentive structures

Several of our policy conclusions relate to the balance between externally imposed regulation and the development of internal control mechanisms, and the desirability of creating proper incentives for both regulated firms and regulatory agencies.

8 *Regulation should be seen as a set of contracts.* Laws, regulations and supervisory actions provide incentives for regulated firms to adjust their actions and behaviour, and to control their own risks internally. They can usefully be viewed as *incentive contracts* within a standard principal–agent relationship, where the principal (whose authority may be created by law) is the regulator and the agent is the regulated firm. Within this general

framework, regulation involves a process of creating incentive-compatible contracts, so that regulated firms have an incentive to behave in a way consistent with the social objectives of systemic stability and investor protection. Similarly, there need to be incentives for the regulator to set appropriate objectives, to adopt well-designed rules, not to overregulate, and to act in a timely fashion (for instance, in the face of pressure for forbearance). If incentive contracts are well designed they will induce appropriate behaviour by regulated firms. Conversely, if they are badly constructed and improperly designed, they may fail to reduce systemic risk (and other hazards regulation is designed to avoid) or they may have undesirable side-effects on the process of financial intermediation (e.g. impose high costs). The central issue is whether all parties have the right incentives to act in a way that satisfies the objectives of regulation.

9 *Less emphasis should be placed on detailed and prescriptive rules and more on internal risk analysis, management and control systems.* For reasons outlined in the previous section (globalisation, financial innovation, etc.), externally imposed regulation in the form of prescriptive and detailed rules is becoming increasingly inappropriate and ineffective. More reliance needs to be placed on institutions' own internal risk analysis, management and control systems. This relates not only to quantitative techniques, such as value-at-risk (VaR) models, but also to the management 'culture' of those who handle models and supervise traders. Risks are too complex to be covered by simple rules, and there are several hazards in relying upon a prescriptive approach to regulation. There is no alternative to placing the primary responsibility for risk control on the shoulders of internal management, owners and auditors of regulated firms. There needs to be a clear shift of emphasis towards the reinforcement of internal managerial risk-control mechanisms, and a recasting of the nature and functions of external regulation away from generalised rule setting towards establishing incentives and sanctions to reinforce internal control systems. These incentives and sanctions need to include disclosure requirements and fiduciary rules for internal management (e.g. rules establishing the responsibilities of directors, managers, auditors, etc.). However, this does not imply that there is no role for rules. It is not a question of internal v. external regulation: both must be involved. The debate is about the balance between the two. It is our judgement that there needs to be a shift in emphasis towards internal risk-management systems and, therefore, that regulation should be designed to reinforce internal management incentives.

10 *There should be appropriate internal management incentives.* Ultimately, all aspects of the behaviour of a firm are corporate governance issues. Several procedures, processes and structures can reinforce internal risk-control mechanisms. They include internal auditors, internal audit committees, procedures for reporting to senior management (and perhaps to the supervisors), and making a named board member responsible for compliance

and risk analysis and management systems. Supervisors can strengthen the incentives for these by, for instance, relating the frequency and intensity of their supervision and inspection visits (and possibly rules) to the perceived adequacy of the internal control procedures. In addition, regulators can create appropriate incentives by calibrating the external burden of regulation (e.g. number of inspection visits, allowable business, etc.) to the quality of management and the efficiency of internal incentives. Other measures include:

(a) ensuring that appropriate sanctions are applied to internal management; and

(b) requiring large financial institutions to establish internal audit systems.

The key is that there need to be internal incentives for management to behave in appropriate ways, and the regulator has a role in ensuring that internal incentives are compatible with the objectives of regulation.

11 *Regulators should be publicly accountable through credible mechanisms.* Regulatory agencies have considerable power over both regulated firms and the consumer through their influence on the terms by which business is conducted. For this reason, agencies need to be accountable and their activities transparent. Difficulties arise when it is prudent for an agency's success in averting a bank failure or systemic crisis to remain secret. One possible solution is to create an audit agency, with the regulator's being required to report regularly to an independent person or body. The report would cover the objectives of the regulator and the measures of success and failure. The audit authority would have the power to force the regulatory agency to respond to any concerns raised. In due course, the regulator's reports to the agency should be published.

12 *Time-inconsistency and credibility problems should be addressed through pre-commitments and graduated responses, with the possibility of overrides.* A major issue for the credibility, and hence authority, of a regulator is whether rules and decisions are time consistent. Some circumstances may require a rule or a normal policy action to be suspended. Our prejudices are that there is a strong case for pre-commitment and rules of behaviour for the regulator. We favour a graduated-response approach because, for example, there is no magical capital ratio below which an institution is in danger and above which it is safe. Other things being equal, the potential danger gradually increases as the capital ratio declines. This in itself suggests that there should be a graduated series of responses from the regulator as capital diminishes. No single dividing line should trigger action, but there should be a series of trigger points, with the effect of going through any one of them being relatively minor, but the cumulative effect being large. The graduated responses should make no distinction between losses caused by idiosyncratic developments and losses caused by general market developments. There should also be a decision about what

market movements are so extreme as to merit government support to withstand them. Capital would be required to be held by banks to meet shocks up to the limit calculated in stress tests of proprietary models. However, even in a pre-commitment and graduated-response regime, there may be cases where predetermined rules should be overridden. The problem is that, if this is publicly known, the credibility of the regulator could be seriously compromised, especially since it is to create and to sustain such credibility that the pre-commitment rule is established in the first place. Can there be any guarantee that such an override would not turn regulation into a totally *ad hoc* procedure? Our preferred solution is to require that use of the override be reported to the regulator's audit commission.

13 *The incentive effect of pay structures should be a regulatory issue.* The potential for pay structures to influence the risk-taking propensities of key staff has been well established. It would, however, be an unacceptable intrusion, and also unfeasible, for the regulator to specify remuneration systems within regulated institutions. On the other hand, it is both desirable and feasible for firms' internal audit committees to be required to report to the regulator that they have considered the implications for the risk preferences of key personnel to be affected by their firm's remuneration systems and structures. Going a step further, it might even be advisable to include pay structures as one of the criteria in a risk-based examination scheme (see below).

(iii) Policy differentiation

Several of our policy conclusions are based on the appreciation that financial firms are not homogeneous in their risk characteristics, nor do they have risk analysis, management and control systems of equal quality and effectiveness. This suggests that it is inappropriate to have the same regulatory requirements for all regulated firms. Similarly, consumers of financial services are not homogeneous, and there may be a case for allowing consumers a degree of choice with respect to regulatory standards.

14 *The form and intensity of regulatory and supervisory requirements should differentiate between regulated institutions according to their relative portfolio risk and efficiency of internal control mechanisms.* While the objective of 'competitive neutrality' in regulation is something of a mantra, it is not satisfied if unequal institutions are treated equally. In this respect, 'equality' should relate to the risk characteristics of institutions. It might be argued that, in order to maintain competitive neutrality, two banks with different risk characteristics and differing quality of risk-management systems should be treated equally because they are both 'banks' and in competition with each other. However, in terms of satisfying the objectives of regulation, a suboptimal outcome is likely if they are subject to

identical regulatory requirements. One of the hazards of a detailed and prescriptive approach is that it will fail to make the necessary distinctions between non-homogeneous firms and apply the same rules to all; it reduces the scope for legitimate differentiations to be made. The adoption of an internal models approach, such as now introduced by G-10 countries after the Market Risk Amendment of the Basle Accord, recognises this point.

15 *In some areas the regulator could offer a menu of contracts to regulated firms, requiring them to self-select into the correct category.* Forcing a high degree of conformity in the behaviour of regulated firms can cause an information, and possiblly an efficiency, loss. If, alternatively, firms have a choice about how to satisfy the regulator's objectives and principles, they will be able to choose their own, least-cost way of satisfying these objectives. The regulator could offer a menu of contracts, rather than the same contract for all institutions. Equally, banks could offer their own contracts. An example of this approach is the variable add-on in the *multiplication factor* of the Basle internal models approach. Since this add-on varies with the performance of a VaR model during back-testing procedures, a bank has a choice between using a simple (less precise) model with a higher capital requirement for market risk or incurring costs in developing a better model and benefitting from a lower capital requirement. However, empirical tests of VaR models show that the fixed part of 3 in the Basle multiplication factor is already so high that there is little incentive to use the best models because of the relatively small variable add-on (between 0 and 1). Our suggestion, therefore, is to lower the fixed part of the multiplication factor and to increase the variable part. More qualitative measures of internal control and risk management quality could use *risk-related examination schedules.* Here, financial institutions can be given a risk rating (say, between 0 and 10) on the basis of a series of internal control indicators. The higher the rating, the greater the perceived overall risk, and the more frequent and detailed on-site examinations would be. A more far-reaching proposal is the pre-commitment approach, which enables a bank to pre-commit to a maximum trading loss and then to incur regulatory penalties or other sanctions in proportion to the amount the maximum loss is exceeded.

16 *There should be a reconsideration of the differences in the regulatory treatment of banking and trading books.* Now that market VaR models have reached an advanced stage, sophisticated players in international financial and banking markets are allocating substantial resources to the development of quantitative credit risk management techniques. Admittedly, credit risk evaluation and pricing still suffer from considerable gaps in data on default experiences and recovery rates. This probably means that adoption of an internal models approach for credit risk, analogous to that for market risk now cleared by the Basle Committee, is some way off.

However, imperfections in scientific methodology rarely prevent trading, as is demonstrated by the emergence of OTC credit derivatives markets. If these markets continue to expand at their current pace, a non-negligible part of banks' credit risk exposure could become tradable. Since regulators in the United States and UK have already expressed their willingness to make credit-default products eligible for the trading book, the danger of regulatory arbitrage between banking and trading books arises. This might force regulators to abandon the distinction even before credit VaR models are ready for an internal models approach. In the longer term, an internal models approach for both credit and market risk is probably desirable, particularly since the credit risk weightings in the 1988 Basle Capital Accord reflect only very imperfectly the differential riskiness of various counterparty exposures.

17 *With respect to conduct of business regulation, a major distinction should be made between wholesale and retail business.* Consumers of financial services are not homogeneous, and their requirements for conduct of business regulation and 'protection' are different. Market imperfections (most especially related to asymmetric information problems) are likely to be more pervasive in retail markets than in wholesale markets. Retail business should therefore be regulated more explicitly than wholesale business, although the distinction may be difficult to make in some areas. If the distinction is not drawn sufficiently powerfully, there is a danger that wholesale business will be excessively regulated. When professionals are dealing with each other, the need for conduct of business regulation is less evident, and greater reliance can be placed on industry codes of conduct.

18 *In some limited areas, consumers can be offered a choice between institutions subject to different levels of regulation.* Consumers are not homogeneous with respect to their demand for regulation or the price they are prepared to pay for its benefits. In some areas it is feasible to offer choice to the consumer. An example is the narrow bank proposal, which, despite its limitations, may be appropriate for some developing countries. Given the more extreme economic fluctuations evident in these countries, the maintenance of at least a safe core of narrow banks that can sustain the payments system and the real value of savings for the risk averse would seem to be a useful objective. More generally, there may be scope for offering limited choice in some areas of conduct of business regulation.

(iv) Issues in developing countries

The general analysis, rationale and principles of financial regulation are not fundamentally different between developing and developed countries. Most new technical developments (e.g. use of derivatives) are quickly applied in developing countries. Even so, developing countries have special problems and difficulties.

19 *The need for regulation is even greater in developing countries than else-where.* Externally imposed rules and ratios should be relatively more important in developing countries, since less reliance can be placed on internal mechanisms. So, there is a greater need for the relevant authority (preferably the central bank) to monitor and to supervise the banks, and to authorise all new deposit-taking institutions. At the same time, how-ever, the central bank itself is likely to face shortages of skilled personnel and of adequate data and (balance sheet) reports on banks.

Under these circumstances, there is an advantage in keeping regula-tions, and thus the need for monitoring, simple and straightforward.

20 *It is important to begin creating a legal environment in which:* (a) property rights to collateral on defaulted loans are clear – these rights should extend to movable property, such as inventory, as well as to real estate; (b) a more open and arm's-length equity market can function (e.g. by build-ing a legal structure to protect minority shareholder rights).

There is also a need to begin moving towards international accounting standards. The place to start is the introduction of international stan-dards for classifying loans as non-performing. The accounting system must be kept simple while everyone is learning the process. Accuracy in reporting must take precedence over thoroughness.

During the transition to a developed financial system, a capital stan-dard is useful, but it is more of a device for assessing how bankers are accounting for risk and for identifying the sources of bank capital than a risk-controlling mechanism.

21 *The process of liberalisation must be managed carefully.* Many systemic problems have occurred in the aftermath of major programmes of liber-alisation. Clearly, no one would wish to stop, or to defer, liberalisation just because it has been frequently associated with financial fragility, but steps could be taken to mitigate its risks. Authorisation of deposit-taking insti-tutions and monitoring need to be particularly careful and strict in the early years of liberalisation programmes. Since asset prices can fall as well as rise, asset price increases should make the central bank tighten loan-to-value ratios and collateral requirements.

(v) Management of financial crises

Regulation and supervision sometimes fail to maintain systemic stability, sometimes to a degree that requires official intervention. This has been true in both developed and developing countries. How such intervention is under-taken has signalling and incentive effects for the future behaviour of financial institutions. Maintaining the integrity of the banking system requires that some bank liability holders be protected from the consequences of bank failure, but this protection should be limited, since the application of public funds can create adverse incentives that aggravate the crisis. Caution is required in restructuring banks. Intervention guidelines are suggested in Chapter 7.

22 *There should be a clear bias (although not a bar) against forbearance when a bank is in difficulty.* As argued earlier, regulatory authorities need to build up a reputation for tough supervision and, when necessary, decisive action in cases of financial problems. Supervisory authorities may, from time to time, face substantial political pressure to delay action in closing a hazardous financial institution, but the need to maintain credibility creates a strong bias against forbearance, and there are many cases of unsuccessful forbearance that reinforce this conclusion. However, there are circumstances where this general presumption is appropriately overridden.

23 *Intervention authorities need to ensure that parties that have benefited from risk taking bear a large proportion of the cost of restructuring the banking system.* For example, shareholders should be the first to lose their investment, along with large holders of long-term liabilities, such as subordinated debt. Also, delinquent borrowers must not be given favourable treatment at public expense.

24 *Prompt action should be taken to prevent problem institutions from extending credit to high-risk borrowers, or capitalising unpaid interest on delinquent loans into new credit.* This principle is designed to reduce the moral hazard risk in bank restructuring that arises when institutions with low and declining net worth continue to operate under the protection of public policies intended to maintain the integrity of the banking system. This implies that, when practicable, ownership of insolvent institutions should be changed through sale, nationalisation or closure.

25 *Society must establish the political will to make restructuring a priority in allocating public funds, while avoiding sharp increases in inflation.* This follows from the previous two principles, in that their execution requires adequate funding to pay off some liability holders of institutions with negative net worth.

26 *Intervention agencies should not support the values of broad classes of non-bank financial assets in a crisis.* The optimal response to non-bank crises is different from the response to bank crises. This follows from the systemic centrality of the banking system.

(vi) The international dimension to regulation

The increasing globalisation of banking and finance means that autarky is no longer a viable option in financial regulation. Consequently, the extent to which the efficiency of regulation requires collaboration or harmonisation between national regulators is becoming a major issue.

27 *Harmonisation need not cover all aspects of regulation in order for the objectives of regulation to be achieved.* The bias towards harmonisation should be resisted, and harmonisation should not be extended beyond the point where it is necessary for the objectives of regulation to be achieved. In some areas of finance, there is merit in international diversity in regulation, not least because it yields valuable information about the operation of different regimes. The general principle of subsidiarity should be applied to financial regulation. Competition in regulation is also beneficial *provided* systemic stability is not compromised. There is, therefore, a strong case for regulation being framed at a local level unless its effectiveness is significantly impaired and clear gains can be made by international collaboration.

C. Concluding note

Perhaps the best way to end this monograph is to summarise our key perspectives:

1 Regulation is essentially about changing the behaviour of financial intermediaries. This needs to be seen and analysed in terms of a set of incentive contracts.
2 Financial systems have been changing substantially in a way that is undermining traditional approaches to regulation. More weight will now have to be placed on internal risk analysis, management and control systems, with an appropriate incentive structure introduced to this end.
3 Whereas regulatory services, if properly structured, are beneficial, the fact that they are not provided by a market process, but largely imposed, causes a variety of problems. In particular, if the perception that regulation is costless is combined with risk-averse regulators, there is an evident danger that regulation will be overdemanded by consumers and oversupplied by the regulator.

We were heartened to find that these views are in accord with the position taken by Alan Greenspan, who, in his keynote speech at the Conference on Bank Structure and Competition of the Federal Reserve Bank of Chicago on 1 May 1997, stated that:

I believe that in many cases, policymakers can reduce potential distortions by structuring policies to be more 'incentive-compatible' – that is, by working with, rather than around, the profit-maximizing goals of investors and firm managers. In light of the underlying uncertainties illustrated in my earlier examples, I readily acknowledge this is often easier said than done. Nevertheless, I believe some useful guiding principles can be formulated.

The first guiding principle is that, where possible, we should attempt to strengthen market discipline, without compromising financial stability . . .

A second guiding principle is that, to the extent possible, our regulatory policies should attempt to simulate what would be the private market's response in the absence of the safety net.

Appendix
Central Bank Governors' Symposium participants

Heads of delegation

Mr Eddie George
Governor
Bank of England

Mr Ian MacFarlane
Governor
Reserve Bank of Australia

HE Abdulla Hassan Saif
Governor
Bahrain Monetary Authority

Mr Lutfar Rahman Sarkar
Governor
Bangladesh Bank

Mr Calvin Springer
Governor
Central Bank of Barbados

Mr Keith Arnold
Governor
Central Bank of Belize

Mr Mansfield Brock Jr
Chairman
Bermuda Monetary Authority

Mr Quill Hermans
Governor
Bank of Botswana

Mr Gordon Thiessen
Governor
Bank of Canada

Mr Afxentis Afxentiou
Governor
Central Bank of Cyprus

Mr Dwight Venner
Governor
Eastern Caribbean Central Bank

Ratu Jone Kubuabola
Governor
Reserve Bank of Fiji

Mr Momodou Bajo
Governor
Central Bank of The Gambia

Dr Godfried Agama
Governor
Bank of Ghana

Mr Joseph Yam
Chief Executive
Hong Kong Monetary Authority

Dr Yaga Venugopal Reddy
Deputy Governor
Reserve Bank of India

Mr Colin Bullock
Deputy Governor
Bank of Jamaica

Sheikh Salem Abdul Aziz Al-Sabah
Governor
Central Bank of Kuwait

Dr Anthony Maruping
Governor
Central Bank of Lesotho

Dr Mathew Chikaonda
Governor
Reserve Bank of Malawi

Datuk Ahmad Mohamed Don
Governor
Bank Negara Malaysia

Mr Francis Vassallo
Governor
Central Bank of Malta

Mr Ernesto Gove
Deputy Governor
Banco de Moçambique

Mr Thomas Alweendo
Governor
Bank of Namibia

Mr Richard Lang
Deputy Governor
Reserve Bank of New Zealand

Dr Paul Ogwuma
Governor
Central Bank of Nigeria

Mr Leonard Kamit
Deputy Governor
Bank of Papua New Guinea

HE Sheikh Hamad Al-Sayari
Governor
Saudi Arabian Monetary Authority

Mr Birgir Gunnarsson
Governor
Sedlabanki Islands

Mrs Yvonne Gibril
Deputy Governor
Bank of Sierra Leone

Mr Lee Ek Tieng
Managing Director
Monetary Authority of Singapore

Mr Rick Houenipwela
Governor
Central Bank of Solomon Islands

Dr Chris Stals
Governor
South African Reserve Bank

Mr Palenage Amarasinghe
Deputy Governor
Central Bank of Sri Lanka

Mr Martin Dlamini
Deputy Governor
Central Bank of Swaziland

Mr Herman Kessy
Deputy Director
Bank of Tanzania

Dr Duangmanee Vongpradhip
Director, Office of the Governor
Bank of Thailand

Mr Thomas Harewood
Governor
Central Bank of Trinidad & Tobago

Mr Charles Kikonyogo
Governor
Bank of Uganda

HE Sultan Al-Suwaidi
Governor
Central Bank of the United Arab Emirates

Mr Sampson Ngwele
Governor
Reserve Bank of Vanuatu

Dr Antonio Casas-Gonzalez
Governor
Banco Central de Venezuela

Dr Jacob Mwanza
Governor
Bank of Zambia

Dr Leonard Tsumba
Governor
Reserve Bank of Zimbabwe

Bank of England

Mr Michael Foot
Executive Director

Mr Ian Plenderleith
Executive Director

Mr Alastair Clark
Executive Director

Sir Peter Petrie
Adviser

Mr Gordon Midgely
Deputy Director

Mr Oliver Page
Deputy Director

Mr Paul Wright

Mr David Swanney

Mr Lionel Price

Mr Tony Latter

Mr Clive Briault

Mr Simon Gray

Ms Edna Young

Ms Christine Walsh

Mr Mike Stephenson

Mr Peter Phelan

Mr Ronald MacDonald

Mr Derrick Ware

Mr Andrew Bulley

Mr Richard Chalmers

Mr Ian Michael

Mr Tim Smith

Mr Clifford Smout

Others

Professor Maxwell Fry
University of Birmingham

Professor Charles Goodhart
London School of Economics

Dr Philipp Hartmann
London School of Economics

Professor David Llewellyn
Loughborough University

Dr Liliana Rojas-Suárez
Inter-American Development Bank

Mr Herbert Carr
Senior Admin Officer
Central Bank of The Gambia

Mr Alexander Bernasko
Secretary to the Board
Bank of Ghana

Mr Francis Badasu
Deputy Chief
Bank of Ghana

Mr Andrew Boye-Doe
Special Assistant to the Governor
Bank of Ghana

Ms Miranda Yip
Senior Manager
Hong Kong Monetary Authority

Mr Nabil Al-Saqabi
Manager, Governor's Office
Central Bank of Kuwait

Mr Manoeli Ntholi
Banking Supervision
Central Bank of Lesotho

Mrs Francinah Mohasoa
Assistant Manager Accounts
Central Bank of Lesotho

Ms Lenia Banda
Director of Administration
Reserve Bank of Malawi

Mr George Kanyanda
Deputy Chief of Protocol
Reserve Bank of Malawi

Dr Zeti Akhtar Aziz
Assistant Governor
Bank Negara Malaysia

Mr Herbert Zammit
Deputy General Manager, Supervision
& Banking
Central Bank of Malta

Mr Urbans Karumendu
Senior Financial Analyst
Bank of Namibia

Mr Mahey Rasheed
Director, Foreign Operations
Central Bank of Nigeria

Dr Joseph Nnanna
Assistant Director, Governor's Office
Central Bank of Nigeria

Mr Mathew Onugha
Personal Assistant to the Governor
Central Bank of Nigeria

Mr Osuji
Central Bank of Nigeria

Mr Loi Bakani
Executive Manager, Economics Dept
Bank of Papua New Guinea

Mr Hendrik Van Gass
Assistant to the Governor
South African Reserve Bank

Mr P. M. Nagahawatte
Executive Director
Central Bank of Sri Lanka

Miss Bhimolban Bavovada
Chief Representative, London Office
Bank of Thailand

Mr David Opiokello
Executive Director Finance
Bank of Uganda

Mr German Utreras
Vice-President of International
Operations
Banco Central de Venezuela

Mr Matthew Chisunka
Assistant Bank Secretary
Bank of Zambia

Notes

1 THE RATIONALE FOR REGULATION

1 By Lindgren *et al.* 1996; also see the Bank for International Settlements (BIS) (1997: Chapter VIII), especially p. 142.
2 For precise definitions of our groupings, see the notes to Table A1.3.
3 See Dowd (1996a, 1996b: 679–87), plus the many references therein contained.
4 See Benston and Kaufman (1996: 688–97), noting the many references on p. 697.
5 See also Harris and Pigott (1997), especially Section II.
6 For those wishing to delve deeper into this field, Ruben Lee (1994) has recently discussed many of these issues in his book.
7 Harris and Pigott (1997: 38) note that:

> For the most part, the role and influence of the antitrust authorities have not been as influential as political and central agency decision-makers in influencing the structure and competitive circumstances of the financial services industry. As information networks and computer technology rapidly transform the financial services industry, and mergers lead to increased concentration in some cases, competition issues will grow in importance. It is particularly important that competition policy be applied throughout the sector, subject to overriding prudential or other public policy objectives. Authorities – both regulation and competition – should be aware of the potential anti-competitive effects of established firms denying access of potential competitors to the information network itself.

8 The impact of failures on individual clients also depends on the efficiency and fairness of the insolvency process, as Kathleen Tyson-Quah has pointed out to us in personal correspondence. In this respect there are grounds for concern. As noted, e.g. by J. Kelly (1977), there is a general perception that the insolvency experts, the accountants and lawyers absorb far too much of the available funds (and take far too long); that bank creditors get the next bite at what remains; and that investors/clients get only scrag-ends several years later.

Kathleen Tyson-Quah suggests that:

> A possible solution, in parallel with other countries, would be to give the Investors Compensation Scheme (ICS) authority to intervene in regulated firms' insolvencies. If the consequences of a default for investor protection and systemic integrity were improved, then the overall cost and complexity of regulation might be reduced without loss of protection overall. This might even lower costs for ICS, as ICS now bears losses which are not recoverable in the insolvency process and so indemnifies the high fees and dilatory practices of insolvency practitioners.

There is much more that could be written on the conduct and process of insolvencies, but it is both a specialist matter and somewhat peripheral to our main interests, so we do not pursue it further here.

9 Part 1 (January 1984); Part 2 was published in 1985.
10 See their 1996 *Economic Journal* article and the references therein.
11 For a review of some of these academic studies, see Flannery (1997).
12 As reported in Flannery (1997), in January 1997 the Federal Reserve Board's Governor Kelly explained that banks remain quite special in their susceptibility to runs and in the severe consequences that a large-scale banking panic would involve today. Balancing the need for a banking 'safety net' to defuse potential bank runs with the need to create the right incentives for banks in assessing and assuming risk is one of the most difficult challenges we face as central bankers (E. W. Kelly, 1997).
13 Alan Greenspan has summarised the implications of informationally opaque loans for bank valuation:

> bank loans are customized, privately negotiated agreements that, despite increases in availability of price information and in trading activity, still quite often lack transparency and liquidity. *This unquestionably makes the risks of many bank loans rather difficult to quantify and to manage.*
> (Greenspan, 1996a: 1–2, emphasis added)

14 This latter may now be changing through advances in credit risk management and accounting, as is described at greater length in Chapter 5. Also we are grateful to T. Shepheard-Walwyn for emphasising the relevance of this development in this context, in the course of personal correspondence. Thus he wrote:

> I was particularly struck by the emphasis which you place on the differential accounting treatment of banks' assets in the section on 'Why Banks are Special' as a justification for looking at banks on a going concern as opposed to a liquidation basis. I would argue somewhat the other way around. I think that the reason why banks have accounted on an accruals or going concern basis as opposed to a 'fair value' or mark-to-market basis is that this is consistent with the way they have traditionally seen credit risk. Put another way, credit risk has been defined simply as the risk of default, and this has only been provided for in accounting terms at the point at which a default happens, and this mindset has itself had a profound behavioural influence over bankers and banking supervisors.
>
> What has happened recently is that there has been a fundamental change in people's understanding of the nature of credit risk. Now, instead of assessing credit risk, as the exposure of the bank to the risk of actual default, we are coming to see credit risk as the exposure to a change in the net present value of the bank as a result of a change in the probability of default within the credit portfolio. But in order to measure this banks have to assess default probabilities on an ongoing basis, and to charge the change in the fair value of their portfolio to the P&L.
>
> This will, of course, result in a very different type of behaviour as well as of accounting within banks. It will also mean that we will need to rethink how we look at capital requirement for credit risk, given that much of what capital is currently there to protect against (i.e. a cyclical rise in ex post actual defaults) would already have been covered ex ante by the on-going provisioning for expected defaults. In addition, of course it would mean that the valuation of banks, at least within the developed markets, will become more of a science and less of an art, meaning that the liquidation of a bank through the sale of its portfolio could become much more straightforward than it is now.

You may think that this is still hypothetical and too far in the future to consider at this stage, but I believe that it's a much more immediate issue than many people think. In particular, the International Accounting Standards Committee on accounting for financial instruments, which forms part of the joint IASC/IOSCO 1998 project on agreed standards of accounts for international issuers, proposes to adopt, as an interim measure, a rather similar approach developed by the US Financial Accounting Standards Board. So it is not inconceivable that major banks with international equity listings will be required to account on this basis within the next four or five years. But equally important, even in the absence of a change in accounting standards, I think that the development of the credit derivatives market will itself force the regulators to move in this direction because otherwise there will be a real risk of regulatory arbitrage between the trading book and the banking book.

See also Chapter 5, Section (iii), and Swiss Bank Corporation (1996).

15 Even when securities firms form part of a bank group, this does not necessarily mean that they should be supervised by bank regulators. Alternative approaches, including *solo–plus*, may be more efficient. (This is where each part of an institution's business is regulated separately but an allowance is made for the aggregate business position; this is discussed in some detail in Chapter 8.) At the very least there is an evident need for co-operation, co-ordination and information sharing between bank and securities firms' regulators. As put by Howard Davies, the then Deputy Governor of the Bank of England (1996):

> It was agreed over ten years ago when setting up the current regulatory structure for securities firms that where securities business is carried on by a bank or by a securities firm in a group which contains a bank, the Bank of England would be the lead regulator for capital purposes while SFA took the lead on the rest. To make these arrangements work, increasingly close co-operation has been essential.

In the UK, this requirement for co-ordination was taken further in 1996 by the Deputy Governor of the Bank of England being appointed to the Securities and Investments Board and the Chairman of SIB being appointed to the Board of Banking Supervision.

16 The general position has again been put well by Davies:

> Systemic risk is still primarily transmitted through the banking system. But the world's banks are increasingly the dominant factor in the world's securities business. And in addition, the world's major non-bank securities houses have major positions in wholesale financial markets. If one of them were to become insolvent the effects would be widespread and that process would be magnified if several such houses were affected simultaneously. At the very least the ability of the wholesale markets to meet the needs of the corporate sector would be diminished. There could be serious repercussions for the banks whether through counterparty exposure in the OTC derivatives markets, a collapse in collateral values, gridlock in securities settlement systems or the downgrading of banks in groups which contain major securities firms.
>
> (Davies, 1996)

2 BARINGS AND THE NEED TO RECAST THE FORM OF EXTERNAL REGULATION IN DEVELOPED COUNTRIES

1 Also see Harris and Pigott (1977), especially Section III.

2 Bisignano (1997) has suggested that:

Arguably the two greatest changes that have occurred in the past decade in the structure of the financial industry are the relative decline in the proportion of total financial assets held by depository institutions, particularly in the United States, and the near or actual failure of major financial institutions around the globe following financial deregulation and the collapse of several asset price bubbles.

3 In the United States legal barriers still pose a dividing line between commercial and investment banking, despite the recent increase in the threshold of permissible corporate securities activities from 10 per cent to 25 per cent (through a more 'generous' interpretation of Section 20 of the Glass–Steagall Act).

4 As stated in the Executive Summary of the Group of Thirty Report (1997a):

The institutions active in international markets are becoming larger and more complex. A rapidly growing volume of transactions and an expanding array of new products are moving across borders at ever faster speeds. New entrants to the system, often from outside the Group of Ten (G-10) countries, are less well known to the international financial community and may be weakly supervised or not supervised at all. Indeed, the global operations of major financial institutions and markets have outgrown the national accounting, legal and supervisory systems on which the safety and soundness of individual institutions and the financial system rely.

Also see pp. 6 and 7 of the same Report.

5 Alan Greenspan spoke on 'Technological Change and the Design of Bank Supervisory Policies' at the FRB Chicago Conference on Bank Structure and Competition on 1 May 1997, and included the following statements in his remarks:

The second theme I want to explore is the large element of uncertainty underlying technological progress. Reflecting this uncertainty, it is inherently very difficult to predict the extent to which government policies may distort the private sector's incentives to innovate. This argues for supervisory and regulatory policies that are more "incentive-compatible," in the sense that they are reinforced by market discipline and the profit-maximizing incentives of bank owners and managers. To the extent this can be achieved, and I believe we have taken some innovative steps in this direction, supervisory and regulatory policies will be both less burdensome and more effective.

(p. 2)

I believe that in many cases, policymakers can reduce potential distortions by structuring policies to be more "incentive-compatible" – that is, by working with, rather than around, the profit-maximizing goals of investors and firm managers. In light of the underlying uncertainties illustrated in my earlier examples, I readily acknowledge this is often easier said than done. Nevertheless, I believe some useful guiding principles can be formulated.

The first guiding principle is that, where possible, we should attempt to strengthen market discipline, without compromising financial stability. As financial transactions become increasingly rapid and complex, I believe we have no choice but to harness market forces, as best we can, to reinforce our supervisory objectives. The appeal of market-led discipline lies not only in its cost-effectiveness and flexibility, but also in its limited intrusiveness and its greater adaptability to changing financial environments.

Measures to enhance market discipline involve providing private investors the incentives and the means to reward good bank performance and penalize poor performance. Expanded risk management disclosures by financial institutions is a significant step in this direction. In addition, Congress has undertaken important initiatives, including a national depositor preference statute and the least-cost resolution and prompt corrective action provisions of the FDIC Improvement Act. Of course, the value of these initiatives will depend on the credibility of regulators in implementing the legislative mandates consistently over time.

A second guiding principle is that, to the extent possible, our regulatory policies should attempt to simulate what would be the private market's response in the absence of the safety net. Such a principle suggests that supervisory and regulatory policies, like market responses, should be capable of evolving over time, along with changes in institutional practices and financial technologies. Almost certainly, such a principle implies that we avoid locking ourselves into formulaic, one-size-fits-all approaches to measuring and affecting bank safety and soundness. For example, as a bank's internal systems for measuring and managing market, credit, and operating risks improve with advances in technology and finance, our supervisory policies should become more tailored to that bank's specific needs and internal management processes.

(pp. 12, 13)

6 There have been many publications on the Barings débâcle, of rather varying quality. The two main official reports are by the Bank of England's Board of Banking Supervision (1995) and by the Inspectors appointed by the Minister of Finance in Singapore (1995); the Report of the Treasury Select Committee (1996) is also a useful reference.

7 Vicki Fitt from the UK Securities and Futures Authority gave us the following comments at a public conference at the London School of Economics:

One of the mistakes we have made, which acts as a big disincentive to self-control, is to have detailed, prescriptive rules. There are several reasons why this is the wrong approach:

- the focus should be on the risks, and not on the rules;
- rules cannot cover all circumstances, yet detail suggests that they do;
- they are never arbitrage free, so they influence in an artificial and unnecessary way how business is conducted;
- they only cover quantifiable risks, yet most accidents are caused as a direct consequence of the unquantifiable risks;
- they are resource intensive – a whole industry has grown up around regulator-set capital requirements;
- they give the impression of being reliable – but this is a false assumption.

The result of a rules-based approach is an expectation that capital requirements as dictated by detailed rules are in some sense both necessary and sufficient. This is not true, and not desirable. To be reliable they would need to cover each and every circumstance, which is too costly, *and* firms would have to abide by them, which is unlikely.

So we need to achieve some reasonable balance. And we need back-ups to guard against the limitations of capital requirements such as:

- more reliance on institutions to define their own capital requirements;
- greater regulatory emphasis on standards of internal control;
- industry self-control, and regulatory discretion to reward good behaviour and penalise bad.

8 The story of the attempts by the Securities and Futures Authority (SFA) to bring disciplinary charges against former Barings executives reveals what a complex

and difficult area this remains; see in particular the evidence of the SFA to the Treasury Select Committee (1996).

9 Thus its first recommendations, p. 27, were for the private sector financial industry to:

1 Create a standing committee to promulgate and review global principles for managing risk, covering the full range of management control functions; the full range of risks in a global firm; the efficacy of risk-reduction strategies; the type, format and location of information to be maintained by all institutions; etc.

2 Subject their worldwide operations to expanded review by a single, independent, external audit firm or firm group, and agree upon more consistent and meaningful disclosure of financial and risk information on a global, consolidated basis.

3 Support efforts to agree upon high quality, uniform accounting standards internationally.

10 In March 1997, NatWest announced that it had incurred a substantial loss on some derivatives trades undertaken by a single dealer. It appeared that many such trades had been systematically mispriced in a way that overstated the apparent profitability of the deals. This was a particularly significant case in that there was no fraud involved, all the derivatives the trader traded were on open view, and risk managers in the bank checked them all and approved their valuation. The *Financial Times* reported as follows (8 March 1997):

Managers at National Westminster Bank examined all the trades made by Mr. Kyriacos Papouis but failed to spot for up to a year that they were mispriced . . . . Risk managers did not have good enough computer models to value his positions accurately and independently.

This reinforces three central points which we are making: there is a strict limit to what can be achieved by regulation; there needs to be a shift towards internal risk analysis and control mechanisms; and, unless strict internal control mechanisms are in place and enforced, derivatives trading can generate very substantial losses within a relatively short period.

11 The question of the desirable extent of transparency in the supervisory process is difficult. For example, the publication of the supervisors' own risk ratings of the financial intermediaries which they supervise will increase the disciplinary effect, but may also add to risks of runs and of legal challenge (by those rated lowly). Not perhaps surprisingly, supervisors of intermediaries less prone to contagion are generally keener on publication and transparency than bank supervisors. A dispute between the Securities and Futures Authority (SFA), which wanted such publication, and the Securities and Investments Board (SIB), which was more cautious, became public knowledge and was reported in the *Financial Times* at the end of July 1997.

12 Sir Andrew Large, who retired from the position of Chairman of the SIB on 31 July 1997, has consistently promoted this risk-related approach. The Report to the Chancellor on *Reform of the Financial Regulatory System* (July 1997) clearly signalled that this would continue under the New Regulatory Organisation (or NewRO) (renamed the Financial Services Authority later in 1997). Thus, on page 2, in its discussion of 'Style and Process of Regulation', the Report states:

Risk-based approach. NewRO will adopt a flexible and differentiated risk-based approach to setting standards and to supervision, reflecting the nature of the business activities concerned, the extent of risk within particular firms and markets, the quality of firms' management controls and the relative sophistication of the consumers involved. NewRO will ensure that appropriate distinctions are made between the regulation of wholesale and retail business, reflecting the varying expertise of consumers and their relative need of protection.

3 INCENTIVE STRUCTURES FOR FINANCIAL REGULATION

1 A contract determines the actions to be taken by each party agreeing to it, and, possibly, the measures to be imposed on the parties who fail to undertake the agreed-upon actions. Economic contract theory, or the principal–agent model with asymmetric information, was originally developed for use in other areas, such as industrial organisation and utilities regulation. Many of the basic ideas are to be found in Williamson (1975, 1985). A rigorous application to utilities regulation is provided by Laffont and Tirole (1991). Another important contribution is Kydland and Prescott (1977). Early applications of the contract theoretical approach to issues of financial regulation are surveyed in Bhattacharya and Thakor (1993).

2 Our concept of 'social desirability' presumes that systemic risk, from the contagion effects of bank problems, constitutes a market failure. In order to achieve an 'optimal' overall risk allocation, excessive risk taking – the source of potential externalities – has to be 'taxed' in a monetary or, perhaps, non-monetary way. A 'Pigou tax' is the standard answer in economics to market failure through externalities (Pigou, 1920).

3 In Section B we show that the regulator is also an agent for society as a whole, and we discuss the importance of this second level of agency relationship for bank incentives.

4 The term 'screening' refers to actions undertaken by the *less informed* party in an asymmetric information problem. Because there are statistical difficulties in estimating the probability of large losses, however, the proposal, as incorporated in the recent market risk amendment of the Basle Committee (1996a), to apply capital add-ons on the basis of model back-tests, is somewhat problematical.

5 True, Barings' failure did not pose a systemic threat in the end, but it is easy to imagine examples where the external effects would be more serious.

6 Bisignano (1997) noted:

> Employees of some institutions have violated established codes of conduct as the changing employer–employee contracts of financial institutions changed employee incentives. The changes in the . . . types of constraints on financial intermediaries may in combination have increased "opportunism," requiring on the part of regulators, institutions and clients improved means of measuring compliance with operating and normative rules.

7 Particularly in the aftermath of Barings, there may now be increased awareness of the effect of the pay structure in general, and of bonuses in particular, on risk-taking behaviour in agents (Goodhart, 1996a; Davies, 1997). It is an issue that has exercised many bank boards and senior management. Some institutions are making more of their incentive payments on a deferred basis, and others are trying to apply some kind of risk weighting to agents' profit streams. But many obstacles to changes in customary habits remain.

8 The term 'signalling' refers to actions undertaken by the *informed* party in an asymmetric information problem, usually to create credibility *vis-à-vis* the uninformed party.

9 We assume that the new UK 'mega' regulator (see Chapter 8) will pursue this proposal after the transfer of banking supervision from the Bank.

10 See Banca Nazionale del Lavoro (1997).

11 However, a distinction should be drawn between general audit *procedures* and

specific internal audit *reports*. The former are a proper subject for discussion between the regulators and the regulated (e.g. Does institution X have an internal auditor? To whom does the auditor report? How are recommendations processed? How often are reports submitted? How are foreign subsidiaries/branches handled?), whereas the latter (specific, detailed reports) would be so changed by any formal requirement to submit to an external supervisor as to make the exercise valueless.

The Cadbury Report (1992) on corporate governance included a series of recommendations on the role and constitution of audit committees and their relationship with the internal audit function. These are now being adopted by UK listed companies and large unlisted companies and institutions. As these objective standards of good practice are developed (and reported on by external auditors) it might be possible to consider a less costly and less onerous regulatory approach for firms that meet the standard.

12 Boot and Thakor (1993) develop a formal theory of 'self-interested bank regulation'. They show that, if regulators face uncertainty about the healthiness of banks and care not only about general social welfare but also about their personal reputation, then they will sometimes close a bank later than is socially optimal.

Bruni and Paternò (1995) derive potential time-inconsistency problems in bank closures from a conflict between the stability and efficiency objectives of the regulators.

13 Forbearance is defined as allowing an insolvent financial institution to remain open. However, in practice it is not always clear where to draw the dividing line between an insolvency problem and an illiquidity problem. For example, whether total liabilities are larger than total assets may depend on how the assets are valued, and – in the case of banks – there is no 'objective' market price for most items in the loan book.

Forbearance is one possible feature of financial crisis management. In this section we focus mainly on the incentive issues involved *ex ante*, such as adverse market expectations and scope for regulatory pre-commitment. Chapter 7 discusses a whole range of *ex post* restructuring policies, based on practical experiences in several countries where financial crises have occurred in the past.

14 This *ratchet effect* is a common feature of hierarchical principal–agent problems, where strictly binding multi-period commitment technologies or contracts are unavailable. See Williamson (1985), Kreps (1990) and Laffont and Tirole (1991) for further discussions.

15 This happens in the case of capital market imperfections, which can be particularly severe in developing countries, where markets for bank equity or bank assets are thin or virtually non-existent (see Chapter 7).

16 An important part of bankruptcy costs can be the fees charged by the liquidators and other legal costs. For example, the *Financial Times* reported on 1 August 1997 (J. Kelly, 1997) that Deloitte & Touche, the BCCI liquidator, billed the fraudulent bank's creditors £2.9m after having recovered £4bn for them in the first six months after the collapse. (A Luxembourg judge ruled that this amount would have to be reduced by £1m.) The receivers to the personal estate of Robert Maxwell recovered £1.672m for creditors, but their fees, together with those of the solicitors, were £1.628m total, and almost consumed what they recovered.

The liquidation of large international financial institutions can be particularly slow and costly, because of the sometimes extreme difficulties in recovering funds from all types of national jurisdictions with different bankruptcy laws and procedures. (See the recent Group of Thirty (1996, 1997b) initiatives on international insolvencies in the financial sector on this issue.)

17 Several of these episodes are analysed further in Chapter 7.

18 This approach is roughly modelled on the Bank of England's Board of Banking Supervisors. It would be helpful to have some public discussion in the near future,

by insiders, on whether that model has been perceived as successful in practice. No doubt there are problems. Just as there is the question of how detailed a knowledge of the regulated do you want your supervisors to have, so, with a tendency towards infinite regress, there is the question of how detailed a knowledge of the supervisors do you want an independent board to have? Again, as with the question of how do you expect to get skilled regulators when they are offered a diet of low pay and public criticism, how do you expect to get a skilled and independent board (not subject to conflicts of interest)?

19 On the other hand, if there is enough political pressure, as there was with Barings, an independent body may be forced to investigate and publish immediately.

20 In this context, the effectiveness of penalties is important. Vicki Fitt (Executive Director at the UK Securities and Futures Authority (SFA)), one of our discussants at a public conference at the London School of Economics, told us what, in her practical experience, works best with firms:

> My experience suggests four key areas which will gain attention:
> 1 money (e.g. higher capital ratios or fines);
> 2 restrictions on business;
> 3 'accidents' (Barings, Orange County, NatWest, Sumitomo) raise awareness;
> 4 bad publicity (e.g. the SFA publishes disciplinary action, and any conditions imposed on a firm's authorisation).
> I believe we, as regulators, do not use them to their fullest extent.

21 Notice the close resemblance of the possible solutions to credibility problems in financial regulation – reputation, delegation and independence, incentive contract – to those raised in the discussion about central bank credibility in monetary policy! In this discussion, the central bank can be viewed as the agent of society charged with optimal monetary policy. Many papers discuss these issues; a summary can be found in Persson and Tabellini (1994). For a critical view, see Quinn (1996a). In particular, trying to impose binding rules *ex ante* might be beneficial to the parties involved in regulation as well (Kydland and Prescott, 1977). However, as pointed out most forcefully by Williamson (1985), on a very general basis, rules of governance or contracts can never anticipate *all* future contingencies and therefore always remain incomplete in some way. It might become mutually beneficial for the parties to renegotiate, although this might be at the expense of third parties not involved in the renegotiation (see Section B).

22 A third major provision was added later, making deposit insurance premiums dependent on capitalisation as well. According to a US Treasury report, quoted by Epps *et al.* (1996: 700, fn. 1), out of thirty countries with some form of explicit deposit insurance, the United States is the only one with (at least partially) risk-related premiums.

23 In this respect the reaction of our discussant at the LSE conference, Vicki Fitt, is instructive:

> I thought I would try and layer some practical experience on the theory . . . Firstly, I was delighted with the thrust of 'incentives'. It is reassuring to note that firms' behaviour is, in practice, close to that predicted by the theory. My own title would rather more suggestively be 'Discretion and Self-control'. That is *regulatory discretion* and industry self-control [italics our own]. We have been working on this for some months at the SFA with a view to
> * devising a more thoughtful range of sticks and carrots to promote good standards of behaviour and control in firms, and
> * reinforcing the fact that financial institutions are responsible for their own financial health (just because regulators set capital requirements does not mean that regulators are assuming this responsibility).

4 PROPORTIONALITY

1 See, for example, para 32, p. XV, vol. 1, as follows:

> The Barings case illustrated considerable weaknesses in the Bank's supervisory regime, in areas such as the evaluation of internal controls at banks, the internal communication at the Bank itself, and the application of existing Bank rules. To address these issues the Bank is now committing a significant increase in the resources devoted to supervision. Yet publicly the Bank is maintaining a strident defence of the existing supervisory stance which retains a non-rules based, judgmental approach. These apparently contradictory positions highlight the dilemma facing the Bank. If it fails to act in the face of the obvious shortcomings of its supervision of Barings it would be regarded as complacent, yet it is keen, and not without reason if the evidence from the Banking Associations is accurate, to retain the current discretionary stance of supervision. We recognise and welcome the Bank's current attempts to clarify the framework for its judgmental approach to supervision and urge the Bank to ensure that the type of laxity of management illustrated at Barings could not still go undetected under the new regime.

2 One of our discussants, Ian MacFarlane of the Reserve Bank of Australia, commented at the Central Bank Governors' Symposium, which discussed this monograph, that:

> In the UK [in contrast, for example, to Australia], there has been a huge amount of criticism from the public or more particularly the press and even more particularly Parliamentary committees. Why should the Bank of England be subject to all this criticism? In the UK three banks have failed, and each time a failure occurs the public identify this as a clear example of incompetence on the part of the supervisor. We all know differently. Economists and financial market experts know that in an optimal system of supervision the occasional failure should occur. But the public, despite an enormous amount of effort, have never accepted this.

3 But, as noted earlier, the role of compliance officer in a financial institution is usually neither well paid nor glamorous. It is not usually a role that young, ambitious personnel aspire to.

4 Of course, they will also try to capture the regulators/supervisors, to shift such procedures to their own advantage, e.g. by limiting entry and by other forms of possible anti-competitive pressures. The danger that the regulator may be captured by the regulated has been widely analysed, is generally well understood, and can be avoided by most regulators.

5 Especially p. 8, as follows:

> Because regulator–regulatee negotiations and contracts lack transparency, from a social-welfare point of view, regulatory discretion may be abused by seeking to impose costs on other parties that cannot quickly or costlessly defend themselves. Only if information flows freely and competition among regulators is strong, can abuses of regulatory discretion be reliably disciplined by private markets and the courts.
>
> What competition among alternative suppliers of regulation does reliably limit is the burdensomeness of the contract a particular government regulator may successfully impose on its regulated-institution counterparties. The equivalent of a regulator's price is the difference between the costs and benefits that the regulator's disciplinary activities generate for its regulatees. This difference may be described as a regulator's net regulatory benefit (if positive) or net regulatory burden (if negative).

As with any other valuable service, regulatory benefits can be produced governmentally or privately and can be sited nearby or far away. The existence of alternative regulators that offer different reporting and disciplinary protocols clarifies that even governmental regulatory relationships are not entirely coerced.

6 Vogel's (1996) study on deregulation in the UK and Japan makes the following comment (p. 13):

The deregulation movement poses a major challenge to the theory of regulation. The theory suggests that producer groups prevail over consumers and thus perpetuate inefficient regulation, yet the U.S. government deregulated in a wide range of sectors despite strong opposition by well-organized producer groups. Moreover, as Martha Derthick and Paul Quirk note, economic studies pointing to the costs of regulation played a major role in promoting the cause of deregulation.* Ironically, by successfully propagating their critique of regulation, these economists undermined their own theory of the politics of regulation. Stigler and his colleagues had in effect sought to explain why policymakers were not listening to them – only to find that these leaders had started listening.
* Derthick and Quirk (1985). Wilson (1979: 386–7) argues that American officials exposed as students in the 1960s to the critique of regulation went on to carry out the regulatory reforms of the 1970s: 'Intellectual descriptions (and criticisms) of institutional arrangements come to have practical consequences. Any generalization about how government works is vulnerable to the behavior of persons who have learned that generalization and wish to repeal it.'

7 We are grateful to Peter Andrews (SIB) for pointing out that, to a significant extent, regulation works through specific requirements. It may well be easier to assess the cost-effectiveness of individual measures, rather than of regulation 'as a whole'.

8 The same authors also have a forthcoming paper, 'Direct and Compliance Costs of Financial Regulation', to be published in the *Journal of Banking and Finance*.

9 As follows:

Accountability for regulatory mistakes requires making official actions and their consequences more transparent and imposing timely penalties on incompetent and corrupt behavior. Around the world, five time-wasting disinformational propensities are routinely exhibited by politicians and top bureaucrats. These dysfunctional propensities reflect perverse incentives created by inadequate accountability for poor performance in government office. The five propensities are:-

1 A propensity for top officials to keep themselves underinformed about threatening financial crises or scandals. We may call this the blindfold or ostrich reflex. The value of this propensity is that it creates deniability options that help to deflect blame once a long-standing problem transforms itself into a public scandal.

2 A propensity to use the weight of their high office as a weapon with which to denigrate critics in watchdog institutions and to calm the public even in the absence of reliable information. We may call this the denial or trust-me reflex.

3 A propensity to conceal past mistakes and to discredit critics in watchdog institutions by twisting facts and covering up unfavorable information. We may call this the cover-up reflex.

4 A propensity to misdirect public attention toward trivial issues or toward problems that lie in someone else's bailiwick. We may call this the distraction reflex.

5 A propensity to assign blame for errors rightly or (more frequently) wrongly to convenient, credible scapegoats. As a secondary form of cover-up,

selecting someone to take the fall for others is a weaseling effort to rewrite history. We may call this the guilt-shifting reflex.

10 Dr R. M. Lastra of Queen Mary and Westfield College provided the following comment:

> The *Bank of England's Board of Banking Supervisors* consists of three *ex officio* members, namely the Governor, Deputy Governor and the Executive Director in charge of banking supervision, and of six independent members with no executive responsibility in the Bank appointed jointly by the Chancellor of the Exchequer and the Governor (see Section 2 of the Banking Act 1987). The main duty of the independent members is to give [expert, practitioner-based] advice to the *ex officio* members in relation to general supervisory policy or to individual actions. However, the Board can take decisions against such advice, giving written notice to the Chancellor of the Exchequer. The Board provides a mechanism to stimulate efficiency and transparency in the supervisory process, albeit with deficiencies. Christos Hadjiemmanuil in a recent book, *Banking Regulation and the Bank of England* (1996, p. 141–143), points out some shortcomings: 'As the minutes of the Board's meeting are kept secret, its precise manner of operation and its true input to the Bank's decision-making cannot be ascertained easily'.

She recalls that although:

> The annual reports of the Board . . . duly report the number of meetings . . . no information is supplied on the actual discussions relating to particular regulatory issues and the substantive opinions expressed by members. The Board has reported on one occasion that advice given by the independent members was not followed by the Bank. No clarification, however, was provided other than that the advice concerned the application of the confidentiality requirements of the Banking Act. . . . The Bingham report noted that in the BCCI case the Board lacked important information which it needed to fulfil its role. This raises doubt as to the effectiveness of the Board as an internal control mechanism . . . [T]he fact that the Board relies entirely upon information provided by the supervisors sets important limits in the capacity of the Board's independent members to scrutinise regulatory performance. In addition, even though the Board is intended to bring the voice of the practitioners into the formal policy-making process, the partial control exercised by the Bank over the appointment of the independent members raises questions about their actual independence and reduces the Board's credibility.

11 As noted, this two-tier system is to be abolished, under the proposals announced by Gordon Brown, the Chancellor of the Exchequer in the incoming Labour government, on 21 May 1997.

12 In the UK, the structure of accountability has been complex. The Financial Services Act (1986) allowed for the creation of Designated Agencies, which are responsible to a relevant government department and hence to Parliament. At the same time, a Designated Agency (e.g. the SIB) is empowered, with the approval of the relevant Minister, to create front-line self-regulatory authorities who are responsible to the SIB itself. This creates a degree of ambiguity. In principle, the SRO is accountable directly to the SIB. On the other hand, the relevant Ministry (usually the Treasury) also has authority to deal directly with an SRO and to require it to regulate in a particular way. A good example of this is disclosure with respect to life assurance contracts, where the Treasury effectively overruled the judgement of the SIB and required disclosure to be made. There is also, therefore, ambiguity about the extent to which a Minister can be held responsible for the

activities of a front-line regulator. (When accountability involves several tiers of responsibility, ambiguity often arises.) How all this will change when the 1986 Act is revised, as has been announced by the Chancellor, has yet to be seen.

The United States provides another clear example of several public and private, federal and state, tiers of authorities who share responsibility for the supervision and regulation of financial markets. Some of the public agencies, such as the Fed (and to a lesser extent the FDIC), enjoy independence from the executive and are mainly accountable to Congress; other public agencies, such as OCC and OTS, are agencies under the Treasury and thus are politically motivated. Concerning the securities markets, the self-regulation of the NASD and the Exchanges is complemented by the (rather independent) public regulation of the SEC.

13 The Group of Thirty Study Group (1997a) did such a survey – see its Appendix B.
14 Tobin (1985) advocated 100 per cent reserve-backed funds for checkable deposits, following an early suggestion made by Friedman. Bryan (1988) advocated a model similar to Litan's narrow banking, although tied to the process of credit securitisation. See also Litan (1987), especially Chapter 5, pp. 144–89. A brief exposé and critique of Litan's narrow banking proposal is offered in Lastra (1996: 88–90).

5 THE NEW TECHNIQUES FOR RISK MANAGEMENT

1 For excellent descriptions of current market infrastructures, discussions of recent advances in their risk controls, and new proposals for further reform, see Summers (1994), Folkerts-Landau *et al.* (1996), European Monetary Institute (1996), Committee on Payment and Settlement Systems (1996a, 1996b; 1997a, 1997b), and Tyson-Quah (1997). The functioning of payments and settlements arrangements and their vulnerability to systemic risk, e.g. through the potential failures of clearing houses to execute transactions of (healthy) banks, are a broad and highly technical subject, which deserves much more detailed treatment than would be possible in the present monograph.
2 Hartmann (1997a) shows that any capital requirement implies an exposure limit.
3 In extreme cases, wrong risk weightings in capital adequacy regulations can cause portfolio reshufflings that even *increase* the likelihood of bank failures, rather than decrease it (Kim and Santomero, 1988; Rochet, 1992).
4 Ian Michael, Senior Manager in the Bank of England's Supervision and Surveillance Division, reacted to the criticism of the 1988 Basle Capital Accord as follows:

> I think the description of the Basle Accord risk-weightings as 'imprecise and partly incoherent' . . . needs to be set in the context of the difficulties of securing international agreements. An important issue concerns how strong are the arguments for 'level playing fields' (same minimum capital ratios, similar asset weighting schemes etc.). But assuming that is the right approach then, given the 'technology' of the time, the Basle Accord may have been about the most that could be hoped for. (Perhaps the difficulties of securing international agreements about rules, especially if highly detailed, is one reason to go as far as possible down the 'models' route. But a considerable part of bank assets in many (though not all) countries is accounted for by relatively small, unsophisticated institutions for which detailed rules presumably will be needed for some time to come.)

5 See Hartmann (1997a) for a description of the different proposals and the main arguments involved.
6 Since this decision, an increasing number of external trading and risk management software firms joined JP Morgan in providing solutions to financial institutions that do not develop their own internal models (among the products

are RiskWatch from Algorithmics, CARMA from CATS Software, and the Infinity Platform from Infinity Financial Technology).

7 JP Morgan 95 per cent, Citibank 95.4 per cent, Chase Manhattan 97.5 per cent, Bankers Trust 99 per cent (*Risk Magazine*, 1996).

8 However, as Barry Schachter (Chase Manhattan Bank, New York) pointed out to us, most trading banks that use variance–covariance analysis have some adjustments for non-linearities, although they are often imperfect compared with 'full valuation'. The Basle amendment requires non-linearities originating from option positions to be taken into account (Basle Committee, 1996a).

9 Bootstrapping refers to a methodology whereby random realisations of risk-factor returns are iteratively generated by drawing (with replacement) from the historical return distribution.

10 For a theoretical discussion of Monte Carlo simulations, see Jorion (1997: Chapter 12). New VaR approaches combining historical simulation with non- or semi-parametric kernel techniques are advanced by Butler and Schachter (1996) as well as Danielsson and de Vries (1997).

11 Model risk is not the only source of VaR heterogeneity. For example, Marshall and Siegel (1997) find differences in commercially provided VaR estimates even for the same model, data and choice of basic parameters ('system risk'). One source of system risk is differences in asset valuation approaches.

12 An alternative procedure is to compare the specific outcomes with those of a benchmark model. However, there is no agreement about such a risk management benchmark model.

13 For a comparison of various model evaluation techniques, see Lopez (1996).

14 If daily returns are drawn independently from the same distribution, the ten-day variance is equal to the sum of the ten daily portfolio variances. The standard deviation is then: $\sigma(10) = \sqrt{10\sigma(1)}$.

15 However, Danielsson and de Vries (1997) point out that extreme returns, as captured by the Basle 99 per cent confidence interval, do not appear to show any pattern of time-dependency. They therefore suggest that exponential weighting of the historical data – as is the case in many industry models – is not recommended. Indeed, Jackson *et al.* (1997) find that exponential weighting actually exacerbates the tail bias of variance–covariance VaR estimates, because it 'shortens' the historical data window.

16 Hendricks and Hirtle (1997) raise the question of the comparability of pre-commitment amounts announced by different firms. On the one hand, they would reflect the managements' *subjective* evaluations of their own risk management capacities. On the other hand, differences in the costs of capital (unrelated to portfolio risk) can lead to different pre-commitment amounts, even when the loss/penalty schedule is identical for firms. In the authors' view, this could have consequences for the usefulness of published pre-commitments to outside investors or rating agencies. However, the historical record comprising both pre-commitment amounts and subsequent trading outcomes should, in due course, be extremely valuable information for investors.

17 A similar point can also be made about the potential effect of the Basle internal models approach compared with the traditional market risk capital requirements.

18 However, as pointed out by Chairman Jim Moser at the Fed Chicago 'Bank Structure and Competition' Conference, this might not work *in practice*, because few regulators might actually impose large fines on institutions experiencing unusual losses. One reason is that large fines might drive an institution from a large trading loss into insolvency. Also, if the loss is perceived as due to residual risk ('bad luck'), and not adverse selection or moral hazard, sanctioning might be considered unfair. However, this distinction is difficult to make in practice. The lack of acceptability of monetary fines to the parties involved in particular

situations might well reduce their credibility. This should not apply to non-monetary sanctions.

An example of a regulatory authority's imposing a large fine on a major financial institution after considerable losses is provided by the UK Investment Management Regulatory Organisation (IMRO, in charge of UK fund business). It sentenced Morgan Grenfell International Funds Management and Morgan Grenfell Unit Trust Managers, two subsidiaries of Morgan Grenfell Asset Management (MGAM), to pay £3m (including £1m of costs) – the largest fine ever imposed by IMRO – after the investments in non-listed companies made by its manager Peter Young went wrong in 1996 (IMRO, 1997). Before IMRO's decision, MGAM's parent, Deutsche Bank, had already injected £400m to bail out its ailing investment business firm, which was facing withdrawing investors.

19 It has become increasingly unlikely, though, that these new EU market risk regulations can become effective in parallel with the Basle amendment, with the debate currently focused on the back-testing requirements for models and on fears that the capital adequacy requirements for commodity risks in the Basle standardised approach were too restrictive for non-bank commodity trading firms operating in the London market.

20 Notice that this 'pay-off' structure for credit risk losses is similar to that for options in the case of market risk.

21 There is also some slight left skew in many market risk returns (Duffie and Pan, 1997: Exhibit F), but it is generally presumed that this is less pronounced than in credit risk returns and may disappear in more diversified portfolios.

22 In the United States, recently relaxed regulatory restrictions on interstate banking may also have played a role.

23 An exact description of this technique, which has been developed by KMV Corporation, can be found in Peter Crosbie's chapter, 'Modelling Default Risk', in the British Bankers' Association (1997) publication, *Credit Derivatives*.

24 On the impact of how these techniques change bankers' view of credit risk and what are, or will be, their consequences for accounting procedures, see the remarks by Tim Shepheard-Walwyn quoted in Chapter 1, fn. 14.

25 Also, in the past, many banks did not store default experiences at all, or stored them in such a way that they cannot be usefully employed for quantitative modelling purposes.

26 For more comprehensive descriptions of 'plain vanilla' and more exotic credit derivative instruments, see Hattori (1996), Howard (1995) or Irving (1996).

27 We are grateful to Tim Shepheard-Walwyn for having drawn our attention to this point.

At present, both the Fed and the Bank of England indicate their willingness to make total return swaps and most credit default products eligible for the trading book (Bank of England, 1996, 1997; *Risk Magazine*, 1997). However, the Bank also points out that this eligibility mainly refers to credit default swaps referenced to listed securities (trading book items), not to those where the underlying asset is a loan (banking book items).

6 REGULATION IN DEVELOPING COUNTRIES

1 See 'the four to fear' (i.e. macroeconomic volatility, connected lending, government involvement, and financial liberalisation) in the recent survey in *The Economist* (1997a: 9–14), which can be usefully read in conjunction with this chapter.

As Dr J. Mwanza, Governor of the Central Bank of Zambia, one of our discussants at the Central Bank Governors' Symposium on 9 June 1997, remarked:

'In small and underdeveloped countries, influential political figures tend to interfere with the normal running of banks to the extent that instability results'.

2 Or CAMELS, since the issue of Sensitivity to interest rate variations has been added to Capital adequacy, Asset quality, Management ability, Earnings record and Liquidity in the standard checklist.

3 A somewhat similar story took place in Thailand in the spring and summer of 1997.

4 *The Economist* (1997a: 20) notes:

Derivatives. Again, few emerging-country regulators monitor banks' use of these adequately, or even understand how they work. This is all the more worrying because commercial banks in Asia, Latin America and Eastern Europe are becoming regular users, thanks in part to the advances of the international investment banks that offer complicated financial derivatives . . . David Folkerts-Landau, head of financial research at the IMF, reckons that commercial bankers' understanding of derivatives is "well ahead" of their central-bank overseers in several developing countries.

5 One of the commentators, Dr C. Stals, Governor of the Reserve Bank of South Africa, at the Central Bank Governors' Symposium on 9 June 1997 commented as follows:

One cannot make a large difference between financial regulation and prudential requirements in the emerging markets and in the more advanced economies. Emerging markets become advanced economies: we have our specific problems in our country, where we have to make special provision for community banks owned by their clients, for special small savings schemes, for micro lending. But basically the core requirements for bank regulation and supervision must be the same in a developing country and in a developed economy. Financial investors in the world make little distinction between emerging and industrial markets: they want you to apply the Basle Concordat.

6 The majority of the Central Bank Governors at the symposium held to discuss this monograph came from emerging and developing countries. They focused their critical comments on this chapter. While we have taken advantage of their helpful comments to extend the analysis at some points, we recognise that the problems of these countries ideally deserve much deeper study than has been possible for the purposes of this (more general) monograph.

7 The terms 'developing country' and 'emerging country' are often not well differentiated. A possible taxonomy is presented at the beginning of Chapter 1, particularly in the notes to Table A1.3.

8 A good source of analysis, and country case studies, on this subject can be found in European Commission (1997).

9 Two factors that tend to lead to an extended continuation of the situation are, first, concerns over the social consequences of 'shock therapy' privatisation and reform and, second, the lack of skilled political and economic entrepreneurs who are able to take the management of SEOs, TSBs and the central bank away from the officials of the earlier central-planning times.

10 We are grateful to discussants and members of the Central Bank Governors' Symposium for emphasising this point to us. One of them, Mr Q. Hermans, the Governor of the Central Bank of Botswana, referring to banks A and B, made the comment:

I will mention two or three of the sorts of things that I think need to be addressed. One is the question that in many small or emerging countries the banks are largely subsidiaries of large metropolitan banks. What are the special kinds of issues that that poses? One is that when you send in your own country banking supervisors, the top management of the bank say "Why do you bother? We are Bank A, and there is adequate supervision of Bank A in the UK, and this is paperwork that's a nuisance to us, and you are second-guessing management – we have a very powerful board in the UK that does that." That is in my experience totally incorrect. The management of the subsidiaries of large metropolitan banks in countries like Botswana is inadequate, and there are two or three sets of problems that we have experienced time and time again. One is that there are no internal auditors in the subsidiaries. They rely on a visit by an internal auditor from Head Office who comes out once a year for one week. That's wholly inadequate. A similar problem is that the external auditors go through the motions of saying that the statement of assets and liabilities reflects the true condition of the bank. They don't make subjective comments on the adequacy of the provisioning of bad debts, for example. If the internal and external auditors are not asking those questions, if you have a weak local board with very limited authority, that does mean that the domestic supervisors have got to play a different kind of role. They cannot simply rely on internal mechanisms.

A second set of issues (and I'm being quite critical here) is that typically in a country like Botswana the kind of person that Bank A or Bank B sends out to be the country Chief Executive is a young, relatively inexperienced banker on his way up. This is his chance to prove himself. They behave exactly the same way that we would. They take rather large risks because they want their three or four or five years in Botswana to look awfully good, and the way that you do that is to make the bank exceptionally profitable during that time. The way that you make it exceptionally profitable is to hide your bad loans or make high risk loans. That's a real problem we have to deal with. I've been through generations of these youngsters, all on their way up, and the mess they left behind the successor had to deal with, and had to shine by cleaning up the mess. Those are the sorts of problems that we face every day in Botswana – problems related to having a large part of your banking system run by subsidiaries of large metropolitan banks.

11 We are grateful to several of our discussants at the Central Bank Governors' Symposium for directing our attention to this issue. One of them specifically challenged us to answer the above question. We doubt whether we are competent to do so, in part because the problem is political, rather than economic, and in part because any answer may be country specific.

12 In the Bank for International Settlements Annual Report (1997: 114), it was stated that:

Effective market discipline, a potentially crucial mechanism for keeping banks prudent, depends on transparency. But because the very business of banking is built on the possession of confidential information about their customers, transparency has not always come easily to banks. Nevertheless, liberalisation, the proliferation of more sophisticated financial instruments and globalisation have given considerable impetus to fuller and more accurate disclosure by banks in the developing world as in the industrial world.

How the severity and persistence of recent banking crises in the emerging markets has affected the drive towards greater disclosure is somewhat unclear. On the one hand, heavy bank losses, often in the end borne by the taxpayer, have prompted many national authorities to strengthen disclosure requirements. In Latin America, Argentina and Mexico are striking recent examples. On the other hand, some supervisory authorities fear that full public knowledge of the true financial state of many banks would undermine confidence and that genuine progress towards greater disclosure – which they would support in principle – cannot be made while banks are very weak. In any event, some progress has been made in recent years in raising accounting accuracy, in increasing the frequency and detail of financial reports, in strengthening auditing procedures and in fostering the work of credit-rating agencies.

Several countries have taken steps to ensure that banks provide better information on the quality of their loans, combined in many cases with more rigorous rules on reserves to be set aside as loans are extended or as conditions change. Argentina, for instance, has used the interest rates on individual loans as a proxy for their perceived riskiness. India has recently tightened the rules for the prompt recognition of impaired loans.

13 This is a difficult area for regulators and supervisors in emerging countries. On the one hand, considering financial fragility and lack of (financial) information among the population at large, there is a desire among supervisors to maintain strict entry qualifications. One of the commentators Mr Q. Hermans, Governor of the Central Bank of Botswana, at our Central Bank Governors' Symposium said:

> There is a broader issue [which is not addressed in this paper], to which we attach particular importance, and that is setting high entry qualifications. In other words, in licensing a bank only license banks that are adequately capitalised, and have deep and experienced management skills. We have gone one step further [in our country], and we require something we call back-up capital. So if you meet the minimum capital requirements to get a banking licence, you've got to demonstrate that at all times you have exactly the equal amount of capital to bring in difficult times.

But at the same time there is a reverse pressure: to ease entry requirements in the interests of indigenous development, greater competition, and the provision of finance to disadvantaged sectors. Thus the same commentator also reported that:

> The other issue that has been touched on by other commentators, but certainly is very much on my mind, is the whole question of public perceptions. To generalise, in a country like my own they are exactly the reverse of what they are in a country like the UK or Australia. The public are totally indifferent to deposit risks. What they want the banking supervisors to do is to make sure that the banks perform a developmental role. The sorts of criticisms we get are not that we were too rigid in protecting their deposits by having high liquidity thresholds, or setting higher capital requirements, but why didn't you make the banks lend to small or medium-sized domestic borrowers? You find yourself playing exactly the reverse role – you become the apologist for financial institutions rather than a regulator. Just one example here – the most common criticism of the banks is exactly that: they do not make loans to small citizen firms and individuals. The fact of the matter is that 96% of all individual loans go to small citizens – about 68% of all loans to corporations go to citizen owned or controlled corporations. And incidentally over 30% go to female-run citizen firms. You try and tell that to the public, and they'll tell you you're absolutely wrong and that you aren't doing enough to get it higher. You get a kind of inversion of public perception, and one really has got to deal with it – the public is looking to you to perform a different kind of role from what I think it's looking to supervisors to do here.

As another commentator, Mr D. Venner, Governor of the Eastern Caribbean Monetary Authority, responded:

> In our countries we don't get the banks to do the developmental function that by convention they ought to do. This poses a question for your regulatory framework: how do you regulate these institutions without killing competition?

Do you let anyone enter, or do you set very high standards and make the licensing process so difficult that only those people who have this ability to do all these things can enter the system?

14 There is, of course, the argument that the attempt by the central bank to use its independence to seek to discipline a politically supported commercial bank could endanger that independence. Perhaps; but the international influence of the IMF and World Bank, and pressures from the central bank fraternity in other countries, might serve as a counterweight, inducing the politicians to hesitate before making, and then keeping, their own central bank excessively politically dependent.

15 The main determinant of the *real* value of such deposits is, of course, the rate of inflation. As outlined in Fry *et al.* (1996), such inflation will reflect the rate of monetary growth, and that, in turn, at a deeper level, will depend on the condition of the government's finances.

16 Indeed, one of our discussants at the Central Bank Governors' Symposium, Mr Dato Ahmad Don, Governor of the Central Bank of Malaysia, suggested that the need to rescue banks in difficulties would be even more widespread in emerging countries. He claimed that:

> Investors and depositors in emerging markets are generally not in a position to distinguish an institution-specific problem from a systemic one, tending to adopt the same adverse view, thereby threatening the overall stability of the system. In such markets, the case of rescuing only problem banks which are too big to fail could lead to a loss of confidence. Once a crisis of confidence sets in it would become difficult to restore.

Another commentator, Mr Q. Hermans, Governor of the Bank of Botswana, at the symposium noted that:

> In our experience, banking crises are of two kinds in the emerging markets context. One experience occurs when the parent bank has closed, or failed, Barings or BCCI, leaving the subsidiary solvent, but in desperate trouble, because nobody is going to bank with a subsidiary where a parent bank is closed, and when letters of comfort are no longer operable. Or secondly the circumstance when there is a locally operated bank, and it fails. In either of those two circumstances, if the government is not going to tolerate the closing of a bank, there is only one solution, and that is the regulatory authority, be it the central bank or anybody else, who has got to step in to manage that bank over a transitional period. So one of the lessons (and I hope you make this in your report) is that, whoever it is supervising the banks, has got to have the capacity – the banks' supervisors have got to be as good as management of the banks, who they will have to take over.

17 A concrete proposal from the report of the (G-10) Working Party on Financial Stability in Emerging Market Economies (1997: 56–60), which provides a useful survey of generally accepted wisdom in this field, is that the World Bank 'should take the lead in providing international advice to countries seeking to build strong financial systems', with the IMF only in a supporting role. Whether this diktat will resolve this particular 'turf war' between the two international bodies has yet to be seen.

However, at the Central Bank Governors' Symposium convened to discuss this monograph, it was the international role of the IMF that received most notice, albeit critically, in this respect. Thus, it was stated by our discussant Dr J. Mwanza, Governor of the Central Bank of Zambia, that:

> There is also the problem of the present arrangement of the IMF being an authority that provides general surveillance. I think that link with the African

market is very weak, because it is presumed that the problems can be treated from the financial market centres. I do think that the periphery has also been discovered and it is possible that we may face a situation where instability is triggered from even the smallest of the markets. So I would think that the IMF needs also to intensify its surveillance on the markets in the smaller economies. All in all, I think that we need a broader supervisory authority that will co-ordinate with individual countries' authorities, so that at least we respond to globalisation in a way that will protect the overall financial system.

In our view, this provides a useful (although fuzzy at the margin) dividing line between the two Bretton Woods institutions. IMF surveillance – as in other areas – should focus on international spillovers and contagion risk, while World Bank technical assistance concentrates on how improvements in domestic supervision can contribute to sustainable financial sector development and economic growth. Again, as in other areas, this will require some co-operation between both institutions.

18 Bank for International Settlements (1997: 114–15) states that:

Many countries continue to allow their banks to hide the full scale of losses on securities holdings and of non-performing loans. Only in relatively few countries are data publicly available on the unpaid debt servicing costs capitalised into bank loans.

19 One of the discussants Dr J. Mwanza, Governor of the Central Bank of Zambia, at the Central Bank Governors' Symposium asked:

What then needs to be done? I think that at a domestic level it is important to strengthen supervisory authorities; there is need for some international co-operation. The southern African region has already created the Southern African Bank Supervisors Association, which is intending to assist in training bank supervisors and also co-ordinating the activities of bank supervisors.

I would think that in the absence of a regional framework for managing problems that go beyond individual countries, such voluntary organisations should be encouraged and I would like to see similar organisations at a broader level.

20 Again, the European Commission (1997) gives further details on this topic. The survey in *The Economist* (1997a: 13–14) also emphasises the dangers attending liberalisation.

21 Harris and Pigott (1997: Section IV) discuss how liberalisation has also been associated with financial instability in developed countries:

Financial deregulation in many OECD countries has been accompanied by several economic developments that have either been problematic themselves or raised concerns about the potential risks or other drawbacks from financial deregulation. These developments include:

- wide swings in financial market prices that have given rise to concerns that markets have become more unstable and excessively volatile;
- credit market booms leading to build-up's in private sector debt to historically unprecedented levels in relation to income and, in some cases, boom and bust cycles in real estate and stock markets;
- widespread problems in banking and other credit institutions; and
- the international debt crises experienced by Mexico and several other countries that emerged in the mid-1990s in the wake of very large inflows of private capital over the previous several years.

However, . . . the problems do not seem to be an inherent feature of the liberalisation process, but more the result of its interactions with other economic problems and distortions present as liberalisation was occurring. The experiences do underscore the importance of key linkages between macroeconomic, financial and other policies for the relative success of the financial deregulation process.

22 At the Central Bank Governors' Symposium, one of our discussants (from an emerging country), Dr J. Mwanza, of the Central Bank of Zambia, commented:

We also have the other difficult area in bank supervision in our region, which really emanates from liberalisation and criminal activity, because countries have liberalised with a weak supervisory authority and money launderers seem to have discovered this. There are real potential dangers that these markets could get destabilised by money laundering.

23 For example, Lindgren *et al.* (1996: p. 100) note:

In recent years, many countries have implemented programmes of financial sector liberalization, often as part of a broader programme of stabilization and economic opening. While the long-term benefits of such programmes are clear, liberalization is a form of policy shock. Deregulation permits banks to enter into new and unfamiliar areas of business, where they may incur increased exposure to credit, foreign exchange, and interest rate risk . . . Some form of liberalization was under way in most instances of banking sector problems experienced by the sample countries. Although there is no direct connection between financial liberalization and financial crises, many banking systems have experienced significant problems following liberalization, particularly where adequate internal controls had not been developed and prudential regulation and supervision failed to contain the increased risk of new or expanded activities.

24 The European Commission (1997: 1) stated that:

Finance used to be of little concern to state enterprises in a centrally planned economy. As long as firms managed to have their activities included in the plan, and to fulfil their targets, funding was assured. State banks were functioning primarily as accounting agencies, recording the financial transactions corresponding with the allocations under the plan . . . . Since this was all planned centrally, banks were not supposed to run any risk. The system therefore did not require banking supervision or prudential regulations. In sharp contrast, finance is a vital concern for entrepreneurs in a market economy. They need to convince a commercial bank to lend to them if they do not have sufficient funds of their own. They cannot avoid bankruptcy when none of the banks is prepared to grant them a new loan. Moreover, commercial banks are in competition with each other, and thus require strict supervision and regulation to keep them sound. How have the transition economies tackled this radical change in their banking systems? Some countries initially adopted a very liberal attitude to the establishment of new banks. Among the central European countries, the Baltic states are the main examples of countries which have taken this free entry approach. They have by now all had a banking crisis, and they have seen many of the new banks disappear again. Other countries have taken a more gradualist approach, shielding the old banks from competition. By taking this route, they may generally have escaped a major banking crisis, but that is not to say that their banking systems are without problems. Many of the former state banks – if they have been privatized – have continued to lend to large state enterprises incapable of servicing previous loans. This obviously weakens those banks, and has held up the speed of bank restructuring. The large proportion of non-performing loans on their books also forces banks to maintain very large spreads between credit and deposit interest rates. This discourages both saving and investment.

25 Bank for International Settlements (1997: Chapter VI, 109) states that:

Asset price cycles funded by an excessive expansion of bank credit have been a central common feature in the financial crises in industrial countries as well as developing countries in recent years. Because the linkages between asset prices and changes in bank credit are self-reinforcing, at least in the short run, financial instability can be exacerbated as economies adjust to a more liberal financial environment. Before liberalisation, interest rate ceilings on deposits kept bank intermediation profitable. Moreover, bank credit was typically directed to government or industrial enterprises, with only a limited share typically channelled into equities or real estate. The removal of such restrictions not only gives banks greater latitude of action but also encourages them to search for new, profitable business as margins on their traditional business are squeezed.

A common development following liberalisation is that banks will extend loans for the purchase of equities and real estate. Banks themselves may acquire equities, and may even hold equity in other types of financial institution permitted to take more risks (e.g. heavy investment in property) than they are. Similarly, property-related loans may rise sharply for a number of years, fuelling an unprecedented property boom. Asset price booms will also "infect" lending for other purposes because both equities and property will appear to offer banks good collateral while prices are rising.

26 Bekaert and Harvey (1997: 70) report, however, that, whereas liberalisation increases emerging equity markets' covariance with major world markets, e.g. NYSE, it tends to reduce their (unconditional, overall) volatility.

27 Bank for International Settlements (1996: 109) stated:

The underlying causes of bank fragility in Asia are various. Among them are four principal common elements that typify the problems of adjustment to a more liberal and open environment – and are reminiscent of very similar difficulties seen in industrial countries not many years ago. First, a central cause of instability has been violent asset price cycles driven by an excessive expansion of bank and other credit. Banks that had developed under tight regulation often lacked the experience to evaluate credit risks properly in a new liberalised environment. Some took too many risks, with the tacit expectation of official support should they run into trouble. In many instances, the system of prudential oversight was not tightened sufficiently to cope with greater risks. Secondly, capital account liberalisation and greater freedom for domestic financial institutions to engage in international transactions have complicated the task of monetary policy. Exchange rate targets have often restricted the use of interest rates to maintain internal stability. A third cause is that the earlier policies of directed lending have left a legacy of bad debts. A final difficulty is that the intensification of competition among domestic institutions has not always led to the rationalisation of often very fragmented banking systems inherited from the past.

28 See Bank for International Settlements (1996: 110–11).

7 MANAGING FINANCIAL CRISES IN INDUSTRIAL AND DEVELOPING COUNTRIES

1 More examples of financial restructuring programmes are discussed in Sheng (1996).

2 Inevitably, some large holders of money market instruments, representing the liabilities of potentially failing banks, must be subsidised to some extent because the money markets must continue to work if the payments mechanism is to function successfully.

3 A loan charge-off is the process of removing an irrecoverable loan from the asset side of the balance sheet. The loan loss reserve account is the corresponding liability account that is reduced. (Often loan loss reserves are a contra asset item.) If loan loss reserves are inadequate, the charge-off forces a reduction in the capital account.

4 Press reports have described the difficulty that US real estate investors have faced in attempting to purchase properties in the Mexican market. For example, many of the properties used as collateral for loans in default have not been legally foreclosed; hence, they cannot be transferred to new owners.

5 Moreover, one of the most important arguments for government support in case of banking problems is the protection of small savers who keep their wealth in the form of bank deposits. Small savers also hold mutual funds. But here the mutual funds are required to hold their assets in certain specified and publicly disclosed marketable assets. So long as the investors are protected against fraud or misuse of client funds, there is no further need for specific protection.

6 On a number of occasions, banking problems have been exacerbated by sharp declines in the value of securities held by the banks. This does not call for government intervention to support the price of securities; instead, it calls for better designed regulations of bank holdings of such securities.

7 For descriptions of the S&L crisis, see Kane (1990) and White (1991).

8 For a description of banking crises in the Nordic countries and of the events leading up to these crises, see Drees and Pazarbasioglu (1995).

9 Colombia was also able to design a programme to rescue its banks in the mid-1980s without inflation. Colombia had maintained a tight fiscal policy that enabled it to use export earnings to resolve non-performing banks. A bank insurance fund was used to recapitalise impaired institutions, which were transferred to government ownership. By forcing stockholders of impaired banks to lose their investment, Colombian authorities strictly enforced the first principle for good crisis management.

10 This section draws heavily from Rojas-Suárez and Weisbrod (1996).

11 Chile's restructuring effort actually began in 1982, but, after proving inadequate for the task, was revised in 1984. The remainder of the section discusses only the revised programme, since it illustrates how regulators can successfully overcome funding constraints to execute a successful programme.

12 For a detailed description of events leading up to the Chilean crisis, see Velasco (1991). The case of Argentina is discussed in Baliño (1991).

13 Of course, Chile could have defaulted on its foreign debt as some borrowers did, but policy makers believed that the consequences of this action were too severe to make it a viable option.

14 In the case of Chile, loans include loans sold to, or placed with, the central bank. Gross borrowings from the central bank include these items as well since banks were required to buy them back.

15 A negative net position signifies banks are net borrowers.

16 Because of a lack of access to international credit markets, the foreign funding needed for the Chilean restructuring programme came from restructuring loans from foreign banks plus additional funding from multilateral organisations.

17 The ratio declined in 1986 and 1987, which were years of fiscal tightening. However, fiscal policy became highly expansionary again in 1988.

18 A short period of relatively low inflation (100 per cent per year) occurred in 1986 and 1987, and bank deposits as a percentage of GDP recovered to their pre-crisis

level (see Figure 7.4). However, in 1988 and 1989, the government again used the banks to fund a growing fiscal deficit, and the inflation rate rose to 3000 per cent. Deposits as a percentage of GDP fell precipitously to 8 per cent.

19 In that same year, all banks were net borrowers to the central bank in all currencies in the amount of $2 billion, including loans sold to the central bank.

20 There will always be people who save primarily through pensions and are therefore unable to reduce deposits. Additionally deposits are not perfect substitutes for pensions.

21 Analyses of the macroeconomic issues leading to the Mexican crisis are contained in Leiderman and Thorne (1996) and Sachs *et al.* (1996b).

22 Loan growth at individual banks varies considerably.

23 Although the loans are removed to a trust account, for reporting purposes the trust is consolidated into bank balance sheets.

24 A recent example of this can be found in the Japanese case, where, on 20 February 1997, the Vice Minister of Finance of Japan announced that the goverment may buy real estate held as collateral by banks against defaulted real estate loans.

25 For descriptions of these events, see Board of Banking Supervision (1995), Folkerts-Landau and Ito (1995), Inspectors appointed by the Minister of Finance (1995), Treasury Select Committee (1996).

8 THE INSTITUTIONAL STRUCTURE OF FINANCIAL REGULATION

1 Basle Committee on Banking Supervision, The supervision of financial conglomerates, text included in report number 8 on *International Developments in Banking Supervision*, September 1992.
Working Group of the Conference of Insurance Supervisors of the European Economic Community, *Financial Conglomerates*, 9 April 1992.
International Organisations of Securities Commissions, *Principles for the supervision of financial conglomerates*, October 1992.
Banking Advisory Committee of the Commission of the European Communities, *Financial Conglomerates*, XV/1008/92–EN–Rev.1, 21 October 1992.
The Insurance Committee of the Commission of the European Communities, *Financial Conglomerates*, XV/2009/93, 15 February 1994.

2 There is also a question of focus and specialisation. Few central bankers wish to become deeply involved in, or responsible for, contractual savings institutions, or for equity markets and their associated institutions (e.g. collective investment funds, brokers, etc.).

3 One important and unresolved question is how such linkages would work under European Monetary Union (EMU). Monetary policy is to be decided centrally, in the Governing Council of the ECB, but supervision and regulation will continue in a variety of national bodies. Will that separation, effectively enshrined in the Maastricht Treaty (Article 105.6 and chapter V of the Statute of the European System of Central Banks), cause problems? What co-ordinating mechanisms will be established?

4 This separation is often taken too far. For example, economists have much better techniques for predicting and assessing volatility and risk than for predicting the future direction of movement (around the trend) in efficient asset markets. Hence specialist economist advice is probably both more helpful and necessary in the supervisory wing. Yet, until recently at least, economists have been mostly excluded from the supervisory wing, which was the preserve of 'practitioners' – based indeed on concepts of 'best practice' – while the economists were segregated in a specialist group in the monetary policy department.

5 Any cumulative series of failures, even if the institutions are quite small, may

erode the reserves of the deposit insurance funds to the extent that they also need to be topped up again by injections of taxpayers' funds.

6 Thus, systemic stability need not be compromised if other countries have different conduct of business rules providing that those regulations which relate specifically to systemic stability are effective. Conversely, systemic stability is potentially compromised if, for instance, a country has capital adequacy rules for banks which are less than those necessary for prudential reasons as the lax regime may impose costs on other countries.

Bibliography

Altman, E. I. (1968), 'Financial Ratios, Discriminant Analysis, and the Prediction of Corporate Bankruptcy', *Journal of Finance*, 23, 589–609.

_____ (1983), *Corporate Financial Distress: A Complete Guide to Predicting, Avoiding, and Dealing with Bankruptcy* (New York: Wiley).

Alworth, J. S. and Bhattacharya, S. (1995), 'The Emerging Framework of Bank Regulation and Capital Control', *LSE Financial Markets Group Special Paper*, no. 78 (London: London School of Economics, December).

Baliño, T. J. T. (1991), 'The Argentine Banking Crisis of 1980', in *Banking Crises: Cases and Issues*, ed. V. Sundararajan and T. J. T. Baliño (Washington, DC: International Monetary Fund).

Baltensperger, E. and Dermine, J. (1987a), 'Banking Deregulation', *Economic Policy*, April.

_____ (1987b) 'The Role of Public Policy in Ensuring Financial Stability: A Cross-Country, Comparative Perspective', in *Threats to International Financial Stability*, ed. Richard Portes and Alexander Swoboda (Cambridge, MA: Cambridge University Press).

Banca Nazionale del Lavoro (1997), *Property, Control and the Corporate Governance of Banks*, Supplement to no. 200 of Banca Nazionale del Lavoro *Quarterly Review* (Rome: BNL, March).

Banco de México, *Indicadores Ecomómicos*, various issues (Mexico City: Banco de México).

Bank for International Settlements (1996), *Central Bank Survey of Foreign Exchange and Derivatives Market Activity* (Basle: BIS, Monetary and Economic Department).

_____ (1997), *67th Annual Report* (Basle: BIS, 9 June).

Bank of England (1996), *Developing a Supervisory Approach to Credit Derivatives* (London: Bank of England, Supervision and Surveillance, November).

_____ (1997), *Credit Derivatives: Amended Interim Capital Adequacy Treatment* (London: Bank of England, June).

Basle Committee on Banking Supervision (1988), *International Convergence of Capital Measurement and Capital Standards* (Basle: Bank for International Settlements, July).

_____ (1993), 'The Prudential Supervision of Netting, Market Risks and Interest Rate Risks', Consultative Paper.

_____ (1996a), *Amendment to the Capital Accord to Incorporate Market Risks* (Basle: Bank for International Settlements, January).

_____ (1996b), *Supervisory Framework for the Use of 'Backtesting' in Conjunction with the Internal Models Approach to Market Risk Capital Requirements* (Basle: Bank for International Settlements, January).

Beattie, V. A., Casson, P. D., Dale, R. S., McKenzie, G. W., Sutcliffe, C. M. and Turner, M. J. (1995), *Banks and Bad Debts* (Chichester: Wiley).

Beder, T. S. (1995), 'VAR: Seductive but Dangerous', *Financial Analysts Journal*, 51, 12–24.

Bekaert, G. and Harvey, C. R. (1997), 'Emerging Equity Market Volatility', *Journal of Financial Economics*, 43(1), 29–77.

Benink, H. and Llewellyn, D. T. (1995), 'Systemic Stability and Competitive Neutrality Issues in the International Regulation of Banking and Securities', *Journal of Financial Services Research*, 9(3/4), 393–407.

Benston, G. J. (1994), 'International Harmonisation of Banking Regulations and Co-operation among National Regulators: An Assessment', *Journal of Financial Services Research*, 8, 205–25.

Benston, G. J. and Carhill, M. (1992), 'FSLIC Forbearance and the Thrift Debacle', in *Proceedings of the 28th Annual Conference on Bank Structure and Competition* (Chicago, IL: Federal Reserve Bank of Chicago, May), 121–44.

Benston, G. J. and Kaufman, G. G. (1988), *Risk and Solvency Regulations of Depository Institutions: Past Policies and Future Options* (New York, NY: Graduate School of Business Administration, Monograph).

——— (1996), 'The Appropriate Role of Bank Regulation', *Economic Journal*, 106(436), May, 688–97.

Berger, A. N., Herring, R. J. and Szegö, G. P. (1995), 'The Role of Capital in Financial Institutions', *Journal of Banking and Finance*, 19(3–4), 393–430.

Bernanke, B. (1983), 'Non-Monetary Effects of the Financial Crisis in the Propagation of the Great Depression', *American Economic Review*, 73, 257–63.

Bhattacharya, S. and Jacklin, C. (1988), 'Distinguishing Panics and Information-Based Runs: Welfare and Policy Implications', *Journal of Political Economy*, 96, 568–92.

Bhattacharya, S. and Thakor, A. V. (1993), 'Contemporary Banking Theory', *Journal of Financial Intermediation*, 3(1), 2–50.

Bisignano, J. (1997), 'Towards an Understanding of the Changing Structure of Financial Intermediation: An Evolutionary Theory of Institutional Survival', *mimeo* (Basle: Bank for International Settlements, May).

Bliss, R. R. (1995), 'Risk-Based Capital: Issues and Solutions', *Economic Review*, Federal Reserve Bank of Atlanta, September/October, 32–9.

Board, J. and Sutcliffe, C. (1995), *The Effects of Trade Transparency in the London Stock Exchange* (London: London School of Economics, Financial Markets Group).

——— (1997), 'The Proof of the Pudding: The Effects of Increased Trade Transparency in the London Stock Exchange', *LSE Financial Markets Group Special Paper*, no. 95 (London: London School of Economics, March).

Board of Banking Supervision, Bank of England (1995), *The Report of the Board of Banking Supervision Inquiry into the Circumstances of the Collapse of Barings*, HC 673 (London: The Stationery Office, July).

Board of Governors of the Federal Reserve System (1996), *Supervisory Guidance for Credit Derivatives* (Washington, DC: Fed Board, Division of Banking Supervision and Regulation, 12 August).

Bollerslev, T., Chou, R. Y. and Kroner, K. F. (1992), 'ARCH Modelling in Finance – A Review of the Theory and Empirical Evidence', *Journal of Econometrics*, 52, 5–59.

Boot, A. W. A. and Thakor, A. V. (1993), 'Self-Interested Bank Regulation', *American Economic Review*, 83(2), 206–12.

Brimmer, A. F. (1989), 'Distinguished Lecture on Economics in Government: Central Banking and Systemic Risks in Capital Markets', *Journal of Economic Perspectives*, 3, 3–16.

British Bankers' Association (1996), *BBA Credit Derivatives Report 1996* (London: BBA).

_____ (1997), *Credit Derivatives: Key Issues* (London: BBA).

Brown, C. (1997), 'Legal, Documentation and Regulatory Issues of Credit Derivatives', *Butterworths Journal of International Banking and Financial Law*, 12(3), 119–27.

Bruni, F. and Paternò, F. (1995), 'Market Discipline of Banks' Riskiness: A Study of Selected Issues', *Journal of Financial Services Research*, 9, 303–25.

Bryan, L. (1988), *Breaking up the Bank: Rethinking an Industry under Siege* (Irwin, IL: Dow Jones).

Butler, J. S. and Schachter, B. (1996), 'Improving Value-at-Risk Estimates by Combining Kernel Estimation with Historical Simulation', in *Proceedings of the 32nd Annual Conference on Bank Structure and Competition* (Chicago: Federal Reserve Bank of Chicago), 363–80.

Cadbury Report (1992), 'The Financial Aspects of Corporate Governance', Report by the Committee on the Financial Aspects of Corporate Governance (London: Professional Publishing Ltd).

Cameron, R. (1967), *Banking in the Early Stages of Industrialization* (New York: Oxford University Press).

Capie, F., Goodhart, C., Fischer, S. and Schnadt, N. (1994), *The Future of Central Banking* (Cambridge: Cambridge University Press).

Caprio, G. and Klingebiel, D. (1996a), 'Bank Insolvencies: Cross-Country Experience', *Policy Research Working Paper*, no. 1620 (Washington, DC: The World Bank, July).

_____ (1996b), 'Bank Insolvency: Bad Luck, Bad Policy, or Bad Banking?', Paper presented at the Annual Bank Conference on Development Economics, 25–26 April (Washington, DC: The World Bank).

Chari, V. V. and Jagannathan, R. (1988), 'Banking Panics, Information, and Rational Expectations Equilibrium', *Journal of Finance*, 43, 749–61.

Chiappori, P. -A. and Hartmann, P. (1995), 'Le G 10 découvre le marché', *Le Figaro*, 28 Septembre, p. xi.

Coase, R. H. (1988), *The Firm, The Market and The Law* (Chicago: University of Chicago Press).

Comisión Nacional Bancaria y de Valores, *Boletín Estadístico de Banca Múltiple*, various issues (Mexico City: CNBV).

Commission Européenne (1997), *Projet de proposition de directive du Parlement Européenne et du Conseil portant modification de la directive 93/6/CEE du Conseil sur l'adéquation des fonds propres des entreprises d'investissement et des établissement de crédit* (Bruxelles: Commission des Communautés Européennes).

Committee on Payment and Settlement Systems of the Central Banks of the Group of Ten Countries (1996a), *Settlement Risk in Foreign Exchange Transactions* (Basle: Bank for International Settlements, March).

_____ (1996b), *Statistics on Payment Systems in the Group of Ten Countries* (Basle: Bank for International Settlements, December).

_____ (1997a), *Clearing Arrangements for Exchange-Traded Derivatives* (Basle: Bank for International Settlements, March).

_____ (1997b), *Real-Time Gross Settlement Systems* (Basle: Bank for International Settlements, March).

Conseil des Communautés Européennes (1993), 'Directive 93/6/CEE du 15 mars 1993 sur l'adéquation des fonds propres des entreprises d'investissements et des établissements de crédit', *Journal Officiel des Communautés Européennes*, no. L 141, 1–26.

Corrigan, G. (1992), 'Challenges Facing the International Community of Bank Supervisors', *Federal Reserve Bank of New York Quarterly Review*, Autumn.

Council of Financial Supervisors (1996), *Annual Report* (Sydney: Reserve Bank of Australia).

Cukierman, A. (1992), *Central Bank Strategy, Credibility and Independence* (Cambridge, MA: MIT Press).

Dale, R. (1984), *The Regulation of International Banking* (Cambridge, UK: Woodhead-Faulkner).

_____ (1996), 'Regulating the New Financial Markets', in *The Future of the Financial System*, ed. M. Edey (Sydney: Reserve Bank of Australia).

Danielsson, J. and de Vries, C. G. (1997), 'Extreme Returns, Tail Estimation and Value-at-Risk', *LSE Financial Markets Group Discussion Paper*, no. 273 (London: London School of Economics, September).

Das, S. R. (1995), 'Credit Risk Derivatives', *Journal of Derivatives*, 2(3), 7–23.

Davies, D. (1997), 'Remuneration and Risk', *Financial Stability Review*, issue 2, Spring, 18–22.

Davies, H. (1996), 'Financial Regulation: Why, How and By Whom?' Sixth Anthony Hewitt Lecture, December.

_____ (1997), 'Financial Regulation: Why, How and By Whom?', *Bank of England Quarterly Bulletin*, 37(1), 107–12.

Davis, E. P. (1992), *Debt, Financial Stability and Systemic Risk* (Oxford: Clarendon Press).

DeGennaro, R. P. and Thomson, J. B. (1996), 'Capital Forbearance and Thrifts: Examining the Costs of Regulatory Gambling', *Journal of Financial Services Research*, 10(3), 199–211.

Derthick, M. and Quirk, P. J. (1985), *The Politics of Deregulation* (Washington, DC: The Brookings Institution).

De Swaan, T. (1995), *The Supervision of Financial Conglomerates: A Report by the Tripartite Group of Banks, Securities and Insurance Regulators* (Basle: Bank for International Settlements).

Dewatripont, M. and Tirole, J. (1994), *The Prudential Regulation of Banks*, Walras-Pareto Lectures (Cambridge, MA: The MIT Press).

Diamond, D. V. and Dybvig, P. (1983), 'Bank Runs, Deposit Insurance, and Liquidity', *Journal of Political Economy*, 91, 401–19.

Dimson, E. and Marsh, P. (1994), 'The Debate on International Capital Requirements', The City Research Project, Subject Report VIII (London: London Business School, February).

_____ (1995), 'Capital Requirements for Securities Firms', *Journal of Finance*, 50(3), 821–51.

_____ (1996), 'Stress Tests of Capital Requirements', *The Wharton Financial Institutions Center Working Paper Series*, no. 96–50 (University of Pennsylvania, October).

Docking, D. S., Hirschey, M. and Jones, E. (1997), 'Information and Contagion Effects of Bank Loan-Loss Reserve Announcements', *Journal of Financial Economics*, 43(2), February, 219–40.

Dowd, K. (1996a), *Competition and Finance: A Reinterpretation of Financial and Monetary Economics* (London: Macmillan).

_____ (1996b), 'The Case for Financial *Laissez-Faire*', *Economic Journal*, 106(436), May, 679–87.

Drees, B. and Pazarbasioglu, C. (1995), 'The Nordic Banking Crisis: Pitfalls in Financial Liberalization?', *IMF Working Paper*, WP/95/65 (Washington, DC: International Monetary Fund, June).

Duffee, G. R. and Zhou, C. (1996), 'Banks and Credit Derivatives: Is it Always Good to Have More Risk Management Tools?', *The Wharton Financial Institutions Center Working Paper Series*, no. 96–42 (University of Pennsylvania, September).

Duffie, D. and Pan, J. (1997), 'An Overview of Value at Risk', *Journal of Derivatives*, 4(3), 7–49.

Dziobek, C., Frécaut, O. and Nieto, M. (1995), 'Non-G-10 Countries and Basle Capital Rules: How Tough a Challenge is it to Join the Basle Club?', *IMF Paper on Policy Analysis and Assessment*, PPAA/95/5 (Washington, DC: International Monetary Fund, March).

Economist (The), (1997a), 'Banking in Emerging Markets', 12 April, 48.

_____ (1997b), 'Can't Get Enough of that Zunk', 19 April, 99–101.

Edwards, F. R. and Patrick, H. T., eds (1992), *Regulating International Financial Markets: Issues and Policies* (Dordrecht: Kluwer Academic).

Eisenbeis, R. A. and Horvitz, P. M. (1994), 'The Role of Forbearance and its Costs in Handling Troubled and Failed Depository Institutions', in *Reforming Financial Institutions and Markets in the United States*, ed. George G. Kaufman (Boston, MA: Kluwer Academic Publishers), 49–68.

Epps, T. W., Pulley, Lawrence B. and Humphrey, D. B. (1996), 'Assessing the FDIC's Premium and Examination Policies Using "Soviet" Put Options', *Journal of Banking and Finance*, 20, 699–721.

European Commission (1997), 'Bank Restructuring in Central Europe', *European Economy*, no. 1, supplement C: Economic Reform Monitor (Brussels: European Commission, Directorate for Economic and Financial Affairs, February).

European Monetary Institute (1996), *Payment Systems in the European Union* (Frankfurt: EMI, April).

Fischer, S. (1994), 'Modern Central Banking', in *The Future of Central Banking*, ed. F. Capie, C. Goodhart, S. Fischer and N. Schnadt (Cambridge: Cambridge University Press), Chapter 2 .

Flannery, M. J. (1997), 'Using Market Information in Bank Supervision: A Review of the Empirical Evidence', 1997 JMCB Lecture (Ohio State University, Department of Economics, 12 May).

Folkerts-Landau, D. and Garber, P. (1997), 'Derivatives Markets and Financial System Soundness', Paper prepared for the MAE and IMF Institute Program on Banking Soundness and Monetary Policy in a World of Global Capital Markets (Washington, DC: International Monetary Fund, January).

Folkerts-Landau, D. and Ito, T. (1995), *International Capital Markets: Developments, Prospects and Policy Issues* (Washington, DC: International Monetary Fund, August).

Folkerts-Landau, D., Garber, P. and Schoenmaker, D. (1996), 'The Reform of Wholesale Payment Systems and its Impact on Financial Markets', *Group of Thirty Occasional Paper*, no. 21 (Washington, DC: Group of Thirty).

Franks, J. and Schaefer, S. (1993), 'The Costs and Effectiveness of the UK Financial Regulatory System', The City Research Project (London: London Business School, March).

_____ (forthcoming), 'Direct and Compliance Costs of Financial Regulation', *Journal of Banking and Finance*, forthcoming in December 1997.

Fry, M. J. (1997), *Emancipating the Banking System and Developing Markets for Government Debt* (London: Routledge).

Fry, M. J., Goodhart, C. A. E. and Almeida, A. (1996), *Central Banking in Developing Countries: Objectives, Activities and Independence* (London: Routledge).

Garcia, G. (1996), 'Deposit Insurance: Obtaining the Benefits and Avoiding the Pitfalls', *IMF Working Paper*, WP/96/83 (Washington, DC: International Monetary Fund, August).

George, E. A. J. (1996), 'Some Thoughts on Financial Regulation', *Bank of England Quarterly Bulletin*, May, 213–15.

Gerschenkron, A. (1962), *Economic Backwardness in Historical Perspective* (Cambridge, MA: The Belknap Press of Harvard University Press).

Goldstein, M. (1997), 'The Case for an International Banking Standard', *Policy*

Analyses in International Economics, no. 47 (Washington, DC: Institute for International Economics).

Goodhart, C. A. E. (1989a), *Money, Information and Uncertainty*, 2nd edn (London: Macmillan).

_____ (1989b), 'Structural Changes in the British Capital Market', in *The Operation and Regulation of Financial Markets*, ed. C. A. E. Goodhart *et al.* (London: Macmillan).

_____ (1996a), 'An Incentive Structure for Financial Regulation', *Swiss Journal of Economics and Statistics*, 132 (4/2), 637–48.

_____ (1996b), 'Some Regulatory Concerns', *Swiss Journal of Economics and Statistics*, 132(4/2), 613–35.

_____ (1996c), 'Expectations and Financial Regulation: What Are the Limits?', *The Financial Regulator*, 1(1), 18–21.

Goodhart, C. A. E. and Schoenmaker, D. (1995a), 'Institutional Separation between Supervisory and Monetary Agencies', in *The Central Bank and the Financial System*, ed. C. A. E. Goodhart (London: Macmillan), Chapter 16.

_____ (1995b), 'Should the Functions of Monetary Policy and Banking Supervision Be Separated?', *Oxford Economic Papers*, 40, 539–60.

Gower, L. C. B. (1984), *Review of Investor Protection*, Part 1, Command Paper, 9125 (London: Her Majesty's Stationery Office, January); (1985), Part 2.

Greenspan, A. (1996a), Remarks at the Financial Markets Conference of the Federal Reserve Bank of Atlanta (Coral Gables, FL: Fed Atlanta, 23 February).

_____ (1996b), Remarks at the VIIIth Frankfurt International Banking Evening (Frankfurt).

_____ (1997), 'Technological Change and the Design of Bank Supervisory Policies', Keynote speech at the 33rd Federal Reserve Bank of Chicago Conference on Bank Structure and Competition (Chicago: Fed Chicago, 1 May).

Grenadier, S. R. and Hall, B. J. (1996), 'Risk-Based Standards and the Riskiness of Bank Portfolios: Credit and Factor Risks', *Regional Science and Urban Economics*, 26, 433–64.

Group of Thirty (1993), *Derivatives: Practices and Principles* (New York, NY: Group of Thirty).

_____ (1996), 'International Insolvencies in the Financial Sector – Discussion Draft' (Washington, DC: Group of Thirty in co-operation with International Association of Insolvency Practitioners, August).

_____ (1997a), *Global Institutions, National Supervision and Systemic Risk – A Study Group Report* (Washington, DC: Group of Thirty).

_____ (1997b), *International Insolvencies in the Financial Sector – Summary of Comments from Respondent Countries* (Washington, DC: Group of Thirty in co-operation with International Association of Insolvency Practitioners, April).

Grundfest, J. (1990), 'Internationalisation of the World's Securities Markets', *Journal of Financial Services Research*, 4 (4), 349–78.

Hadjiemmanuil, C. (1996), *Banking Regulation and the Bank of England* (London: LLP Ltd).

Harris, S. L. and Pigott, C. A. (1997), 'Regulatory Reform in the Financial Services Industry: Where Have We Been? Where Do We Go?', *OECD Financial Market Trends*, no. 67 (Paris: Organisation for Economic Co-operation and Development, June), 31–96.

Hart, O. and Moore, J. (1995), 'The Governance of Exchanges: Members' Co-operatives *v.* Outside Ownership', *LSE Financial Markets Group Discussion Paper*, no. 229 (London: London School of Economics).

Hartmann, P. (1994), 'Foreign Exchange Risk Regulation: Issues for Industrial and Developing Countries', *IMF Working Paper*, WP/94/141 (Washington, DC: International Monetary Fund, December).

_____ (1996a), 'A Brief History of Value-at-Risk', *The Financial Regulator*, 1(3), 37–40.

_____ (1996b), 'The Future of the Euro as an International Currency: A Transactions Perspective', *LSE Financial Markets Group Special Paper*, no. 91 (London: London School of Economics, November).

_____ (1997a), 'Capital Adequacy and Foreign Exchange Risk Regulation – Theoretical Considerations and Recent Developments in Industrial Countries', *Kredit und Kapital*, 30(2), 186–218.

_____ (1997b), 'The Brown Plan', *Financial Regulation Report*, June, 3–5.

Hattori, P. K. (1996), *The Chase Guide to Credit Derivatives in Europe* (London: Chase Manhattan International).

Hedges, J. (1997), 'Profiling by Numbers', *Risk*, 10(4), 76–8.

Heller, H. R. (1991), 'Prudential Supervision and Monetary Policy', in *International Financial Policy: Essays in Honor of Jacques J. Polak*, ed. J. A. Frenkel and M. Goldstein (Washington, DC: International Monetary Fund), 269–81.

Hendricks, D. and Hirtle, B. (1997), 'Regulatory Minimum Standards for Banks: Current Status and Future Prospects', Paper presented at the 33rd Federal Reserve Bank of Chicago Conference on Bank Structure and Competition (Chicago: Fed Chicago, May).

Herring, R. J. (1997), 'Prospects for International Cooperation in the Regulation and Supervision of Financial Services', in *Developments in Supervision and Regulation*, ICMB Occasional Studies, no. 8 (Geneva: International Centre for Monetary and Banking Studies, June).

Herring, R. J. and Litan, R. E. (1995), *Financial Regulation in the Global Economy* (Washington, DC: The Brookings Institution).

Hoenig, T. M. (1996), 'Rethinking Financial Regulation', *The Financial Regulator*, 1(1), 22–9.

Honohan, P. (1997), 'Banking System Failures in Developing and Transition Countries: Diagnosis and Prediction', *BIS Working Paper*, no. 39 (Basle: Bank for International Settlements, January).

Howard, K. (1995), 'An Introduction to Credit Derivatives', *Derivatives Quarterly*, 2(2), 28–37.

Inquiry into the Supervision of the Bank of Credit and Commerce International (1992), *House of Commons Papers*, no. 198 (London: HMSO, October).

Inspectors appointed by the Minister of Finance, Singapore (1995), *The Report of the Inspectors appointed by the Minister of Finance* (concerning the collapse of Barings), (Singapore: Ministry of Finance).

International Monetary Fund, *International Financial Statistics*, various issues (Washington, DC: International Monetary Fund).

Investment Management Regulatory Organisation (1997), 'IMRO Fines Morgan Grenfell £2,000,000 for Mismanagement of European Funds', Press Release (London: IMRO, 16 April).

Irving, R. (1996), 'Credit Derivatives Come Good', *Risk*, 9(7), 22–6

Jackson, P., Maude, D. J. and Perraudin, W. (1997), 'Bank Capital and Value-at-Risk', Paper presented at the LSE Financial Markets Group Conference 'Internal Risk Models and Financial Regulation', published in *Journal of Derivatives*, 4(3), 73–89.

Jorion, P. (1996), 'Risk²: Measuring the Risk in Value at Risk', *Financial Analysts Journal*, November/December, 47–56.

_____ (1997), *Value at Risk: The New Benchmark for Controlling Market Risk* (Chicago: Irwin).

JP Morgan (1995), *RiskMetrics^{TM} – Technical Document*, 3rd edn (New York: JP Morgan Securities).

_____ (1997), *CreditMetrics^{TM} – Technical Document* (New York: JP Morgan Securities).

Kane, E. J. (1990), 'Principal–Agent Problems in S&L Salvage', *Journal of Finance*, 45(3), 755–64.

_____ (1995), 'Difficulties of Transferring Risk-Based Capital Requirements to Developing Countries', *Pacific-Basin Finance Journal*, 3, 193–216.

_____ (1997), 'Foundations of Financial Regulation', *mimeo* (Boston College, January).

Kaufman, G. G., ed. (1994), *Reforming Financial Institutions and Markets in the United States* (Boston, MA: Kluwer Academic).

Kelly, E. W. (1997), Remarks at the Seminar on Banking Soundness and Monetary Policy in a World of Global Capital Markets, Sponsored by the International Monetary Fund (Washington, DC: International Monetary Fund, 29 January).

Kelly, J. (1997), 'Insolvency Experts in Firing Line over Fees', *Financial Times*, 1 August, 9.

Kim, D. and Santomero, A. M. (1988), 'Risk in Banking and Capital Regulation', *Journal of Finance*, 43(5), 1219–33.

King, K. K. and O'Brien, J. M. (1991), 'Market-Based, Risk-Adjusted Examination Schedules for Depository Institutions', *Journal of Banking and Finance*, 15, 955–74.

Kreps, D. M. (1990), *A Course in Microeconomic Theory* (Princeton, NJ: Princeton University Press).

Kupiec, P. H. (1995), 'Techniques for Verifying the Accuracy of Risk Measurement Models', *Journal of Derivatives*, 3(2), 73–84.

Kupiec, P. H. and O'Brien, J. M. (1995a), 'A Pre-Commitment Approach to Capital Requirements for Market Risk', *Finance and Economics Discussion Series*, no. 95–34 (Washington, DC: Federal Reserve Board, July).

_____ (1995b), 'Internal Affairs', *Risk*, 8/5, 43–8.

_____ (1997a), 'Recent Developments in Bank Capital Regulation of Market Risks', in *Derivatives, Regulation and Banking*, ed. Barry Schachter (North-Holland: Elsevier Science).

_____ (1997b), 'The Pre-Commitment Approach: Using Incentives to Set Market Risk Capital Requirements', *Finance and Economics Discussion Series*, no. 1997–14 (Washington, DC: Federal Reserve Board, March).

Kydland, F. E. and Prescott, E. C. (1977), 'Rules Rather than Discretion: The Inconsistency of Optimal Plans', *Journal of Political Economy*, 85(3), 473–91.

Laffont, J. -J. and Tirole, J. (1991), *A Theory of Incentives in Procurement and Regulation* (Cambridge, MA: MIT Press).

Lamfalussy, A. (1992), 'The Restructuring of the Financial Industry: A Central Banking Perspective', *SUERF Papers on Monetary Policy and Financial Systems*, no. 12, March.

Large, A. (1996), 'Systemic Risk and the Securities Regulators', Speech to the Japanese Securities Dealers Association (Tokyo, March).

Lastra, R. M. (1996), *Central Banking and Banking Regulation* (London: LSE Financial Markets Group).

Lee, R. (1994), *The Ownership of Price and Quote Information: Law, Regulation, Economics and Business* (Oxford: Oxford Finance Group).

Leiderman, L. and Thorne, A. E. (1996), 'The 1994 Mexican Crisis and Its Aftermath: What Are the Lessons?', in *Private Capital Flows to Emerging Markets After the Mexican Crisis*, ed. Guillermo Calvo, Mario Goldestein and Eduard Hochreiter (Vienna: Institute for International Economics).

Lewis, M. and Davis, K. (1987), *Domestic and International Banking* (Oxford: Philip Alan).

Lindgren, C.-J., Garcia, G. and Saal, M. I. (1996), *Bank Soundness and Macroeconomic Policy* (Washington, DC: International Monetary Fund).

Litan, R. E. (1987), *What Should Banks Do?* (Washington, DC: The Brookings Institution).

Llewellyn, D. T. (1986), *The Regulation and Supervision of Financial Institutions* (London: Chartered Institute of Bankers).

_____ (1995a), 'Costs and Benefits of Regulation in Retail Investment Services', Paper presented at the AUTIF Annual Conference (London, November).

_____ (1995b), 'Regulation of Retail Investment Services', *Economic Affairs*, Spring, 1–6.

_____ (1996), 'Re-engineering the Regulator', *The Financial Regulator*, 1(3), December, 21–5.

Lomax, D. F. (1987), *London Markets after the Financial Services Act* (London: Butterworths).

Lopez, J. A. (1996), 'Regulatory Evaluation of Value-at-Risk Models', *The Wharton Financial Institutions Center Working Paper Series*, no. 96–51 (University of Pennsylvania, September).

Luce, E. (1997), 'European Banks to Draft Code for Selling on Loans', *Financial Times*, 28 July, 1.

Mann, J. and Ellis, B. (1993), *Development in Banking Law: 1992* (Boston, MA: Boston University Press).

Marshall, C. and Siegel, M. (1997), 'Value at Risk: Implementing a Risk Measurement Standard', *Journal of Derivatives*, 4(3), 91–111.

Marshall, D. and Venkataraman, S. (1997), 'Bank Capital Standards for Market Risk: A Welfare Analysis', Paper presented at the 33rd Federal Reserve Bank of Chicago Conference on Bank Structure and Competition (Chicago: Fed Chicago, May).

Mayer, C. (1993), 'The Regulation of Financial Services: Lessons from the UK', in *European Banking in the 1990s*, ed. Jean Dermine (Oxford: Blackwell).

McDonald, O. (1996), 'Financial Regulation in Germany and the UK: A Comparison', *LSE Financial Markets Group Special Paper*, no. 82 (London: London School of Economics, March).

Merton, R. C. (1977), 'An Analytic Derivation of the Cost of Deposit Insurance and Loan Guarantees', *Journal of Banking and Finance*, 1, 3–11.

Ministry of Finance Japan (1996), 'What is the Jusen Issue? MOF Answers', MOF Home Page (http://www. mof. go. jp/english/jusen/jusen1. htm), 26 July.

_____ (1997), 'About the Financial System Reform (The Japanese Version of the Big Bank)', MOF Home Page (http://www. mof. go. jp/english/big-bang/ebb1. htm), 18 August.

Murphy, D. (1996), 'Keeping Credit under Control', *Risk*, 9(9), 123–6.

Nagarajan, S. and Sealey, C. W. (1995), 'Forbearance, Deposit Insurance Pricing, and Incentive Compatible Bank Regulation', *Journal of Banking and Finance*, 19, 1109–30.

Nelson, L. (1997), 'Modelling and Pricing of Credit Risk', *Financial Stability Review*, issue 2, Spring, 11–17.

NERA (National Economic Research Associates) (1994), 'Costs and Benefits of Securities and Investment Board's Proposals to Improve and Commission Disclosure in Life Assurance', Report prepared for the SIB (London: NERA).

Oda, N. and Muranaga, J. (1997), 'A New Framework for Measuring the Credit Risk of a Portfolio – "ExVaR" Model', *IMES Discussion Paper Series*, no. 97–E-1 (Tokyo: Bank of Japan, February).

Organisation for Economic Co-operation and Development (1993), *Systemic Risks in Securities Markets* (Paris: OECD).

Padoa-Schioppa, T. (1996a), 'Address to the Conference', Speech given at the 9th International Conference of Banking Supervisors, Stockholm, 12–14 June.

_____ (1996b), 'Inter-Agency Co-operation in Financial Supervision', *Economic Bulletin*, no. 23 (Rome: Banca d'Italia, October).

Persson, T. and Tabellini, G. (1994), *Monetary and Fiscal Policy, Volume 1: Credibility* (Cambridge, MA: MIT Press).

Pigou, A. C. (1920), *The Economics of Welfare* (London: Macmillan).

Portes, R. and Swoboda, A. K., eds (1987), *Threats to International Financial Stability* (New York: Cambridge University Press).

Postlewaite, A. and Vives, X. (1987), 'Bank Runs as an Equilibrium Phenomenon', *Journal of Political Economy*, 95, 485–91.

Prescott, E. S. (1997), 'The Pre-Commitment Approach in a Model of Regulatory Banking Capital', *Federal Reserve Bank of Richmond Economic Quarterly*, Spring, 23–50.

Price Waterhouse (1991), *Bank Capital Adequacy and Capital Convergence* (London: PW).

Quinn, B. (1996a), 'Rules v Discretion in the Case of Banking Supervision in the Light of the Debate on Monetary Policy', *LSE Financial Markets Group Special Paper*, no. 85 (London: London School of Economics, July).

_____ (1996b), 'Interview', *The Financial Regulator,* 1(1), 30–3.

Reserve Bank of New Zealand (1995), *Disclosure Arrangements for Registered Banks: Reserve Bank's Conclusions* (Wellington: Reserve Bank of New Zealand, October).

_____ (1996), *New Disclosure Regime for Banks*, Press Release (Wellington: Reserve Bank of New Zealand, 22 May).

Risk Magazine (1996), *Value at Risk – A Risk Special Supplement* (London: Risk Publications, June).

_____ (1997), *Credit Risk – A Supplement to Risk Magazine* (London: Risk Publications, July).

Rochet, J.-C. (1992), 'Capital Requirements and the Behaviour of Commercial Banks', *European Economic Review*, 36, 1137–78.

Rojas-Suárez, L. and Weisbrod, S. R. (1996), 'The Do's and Don'ts of Banking Crisis Management', in *Banking Crisis in Latin America*, ed. Ricardo Hausmann and Liliana Rojas-Suárez (Washington, DC: Inter-American Development Bank).

Sachs, J., Tornell, A. and Velasco, A. (1996a), 'Financial Crises in Emerging Markets', *Brookings Papers on Economic Activity*, part 1, 147–98.

_____ (1996b), 'The Collapse of the Mexican Peso: What Have We Learned?', *Economic Policy*, 22, 13–56.

Schoenmaker, D. (1996), 'Contagion Risk in Banking', *LSE Financial Markets Group Discussion Paper*, no. 239 (London: London School of Economics, March).

Scott, H. S. (1992), 'Supervision of International Banking Post BCCI', *Georgia State University Law Review*, 8(3), 487–510.

Securities and Futures Authority (1996), 'Minutes of Evidence', in *Barings Bank and International Regulation*, Treasury Select Committee, II (London: The Stationery Office, 12 December), 103–20.

Securities and Investments Board (1997), *Reform of the Financial Regulatory System: A Report to the Chancellor* (London: SIB, July).

Sheng, A., ed. (1996), *Bank Restructuring: Lessons from the 1980s* (Washington, DC: The World Bank).

Smout, C. (1997), 'The Bank of England: What's on the Agenda?', Speech given at 'Basle/CAD2: The Changing Regulatory Environment' Conference (London: IBC Conferences, April).

Stahl, G. (1997), 'Three Cheers', *Risk*, 10(5), 67–9.

Steil, B. (1992), 'Regulatory Foundations for Global Capital Markets', in *Finance and the International Economy*, ed. R. O'Brien, no. 6 (Oxford: Oxford University Press).

Summers, B. J., ed. (1994), *The Payments System: Design, Management, and Supervision* (Washington, DC: International Monetary Fund).

Superintendencia de Bancos e Instituciones Financieras, *Información Financiera*, various issues (Santiago de Chile: SBIF).

Swiss Bank Corporation (1996), 'Change in Provisioning Methodology' (Basle: SBC, September).

Taylor, M. (1995), *Twin Peaks: A Regulatory Structure for the New Century* (London, Centre for the Study of Financial Innovation, December).

_____ (1996), *Peak Practice: How to Reform the UK's Regulatory System* (London: Centre for the Study of Financial Innovation, October).

Thompson, G. (1996), 'Regulatory Policy Issues in Australia', in *The Future of the Financial System*, ed. M. Edey (Sydney: Reserve Bank of Australia).

Tobin, J. (1985), 'Financial Innovation and Deregulation in Perspective', *Bank of Japan Monetary and Economic Studies*, 3(2), 1985,19–29.

Treasury Select Committee (1996), *Barings Bank and International Regulation*, 2 vols, HC 65–I/II (London: HMSO, 12 December).

Tyson-Quah, K. (1997), 'Clearing the Way', *Risk*, 10(8), 89–93.

Velasco, A. (1991), 'Liberalization, Crisis, Intervention: The Chilean Financial System', in *Banking Crises: Cases and Issues*, ed. V. Sundararajan and Tomas J. T. Baliño (Washington, DC: International Monetary Fund).

Vogel, S. K. (1996), *Freer Markets, More Rules* (Ithaca, NY: Cornell University Press).

Wallis Committee (1997), *Financial System Inquiry: Final Report* (Canberra: Australian Government Publishing Company).

White, L. J. (1991), *The S&L Debacle: Public Policy Lessons for Bank and Thrift Regulation* (Oxford: Oxford University Press).

White, W. R. (1996), 'International Agreements in the Area of Banking and Finance: Accomplishments and Outstanding Issues', *BIS Working Paper*, no. 38 (Basle: Bank for International Settlements, October).

Williamson, O. E. (1975), *Markets and Hierarchies: Analysis and Antitrust Implications* (New York: The Free Press).

_____ (1985), *The Economic Institutions of Capitalism: Firms, Markets, Relational Contracting* (New York, NY: The Free Press).

Wilson, J. Q. (1979), 'The Politics of Regulation', in *The Politics of Regulation*, ed. J. Q. Wilson (New York, NY: Basic Books).

Wolfe, S. (1997), 'MoF Interim Report on Prompt Corrective Action', *Financial Regulation Report*, February, 29–31.

Working Party on Financial Stability in Emerging Markets (1997), *Financial Stability in Emerging Market Economies* (Basle: Bank for International Settlements, Secretariat of the Group of Ten, April).

World Bank, *World Debt Tables*, various issues (Washington, DC: The World Bank).

Yellen, J. L. (1996), 'The "New" Science of Credit Risk Management at Financial Institutions', Speech given at 'Recent Developments in the Financial System' Conference (Annandale-on-Hudson, NY: Jerome Levy Economics Institute of Bard College, September).

Index

WITHDRAWN
from
STIRLING UNIVERSITY LIBRARY

33074305